THE DENT ATLAS OF AMERICAN HISTORY

THE DENT ATLAS OF
AMERICAN HISTORY

Third edition

Martin Gilbert

Fellow of Merton College, Oxford

JM Dent, London

First published 1968
Reprinted 1972
Revised edition 1985
Third edition 1993

Printed and bound in Great Britain by
Butler & Tanner Ltd, Frome and London

J M Dent Ltd
The Orion Publishing Group
Orion House
5 Upper St Martin's Lane
London WC2H 9EA

British Library Cataloguing-in-Publication Data

A catalogue record for this book is available from the British Library.

ISBN 0 460 861735 (hardcover)
ISBN 0 460 861743 (paperback)

Preface

The idea for this atlas came to me while I was teaching at the University of South Carolina. Its aim is to provide a short but informative visual guide to American history. I have tried to make use of maps in the widest possible way, designing each one individually, and seeking to transform statistics and facts into something easily seen and grasped. My material has been obtained from a wide range of historical works, encyclopaedias, and newspaper and Government reports.

More than twenty-five years have passed since the first publication of this atlas. It was a period marked first by the intensification and then by the ending of the Vietnam war, with more than 55,000 American dead. It was also a period marked by a substantial increase in the population of the United States, and continued immigration. This same period has seen the development of outer space as a region of defence policy. New maps cover these recent developments.

Since the revised edition was published in 1985, the pattern of events has led me to draw twenty-six new maps, to cover, among recent developments, the continuing growth of immigration, new ethnic and population changes, and the military and humanitarian actions of the United States overseas, culminating in the Gulf War (1991), aid to Somalia (1992), and air drops to Bosnia (1993). New domestic maps show the natural and accidental disasters of the past two decades, the continuing high death rate from motor accidents (more than a million dead in twenty years), murder (a quarter of a million dead in a single decade), and the new scourge of Aids (170,000 deaths in a decade).

The United States has also been the pioneer in exploring the solar system and in defence preparedness in space, for both of which I have drawn a special map. United States' arms sales, and economic help to poorer countries, as well as the ending of the Cold War confrontation, also required new maps, as did pollution. The continuing United States' presence in the Pacific, and her defence preparedness at home and abroad, are also mapped.

I have been helped considerably in the task of updating this atlas by Abe Eisenstat and Kay Thomson. Many individuals and institutions have provided extra material for the maps. I am particularly grateful to:

Martin Adams, Bureau of Political-Military Affairs, State Department, Washington DC
James T. Hackett, Member of the President's General Advisory Committee on Arms Control
Louan Hall, National Highway Traffic Safety Administration
Michael Hoeffer, Statistics Division, Immigration and Naturalisation Services
John Richter, Agency for International Development, State Department
Joshua Gilbert (for help on the space map)

For the first and second edition of this atlas, my draft maps were turned into clear and striking artwork by Arthur Banks and Terry Bicknell. For this new edition, I am grateful to the cartographic skills of Tim Aspden. At my publishers, JM Dent, David Swarbrick has made it possible to realise my ambition to re-issue all of my historical atlases updated. It is my hope that they will be of interest and service to teachers, students, and the general reader for whom the past is not a forbidden planet, but an integral part of today's world.

MARTIN GILBERT
Merton College, Oxford

14 June 1993

Maps

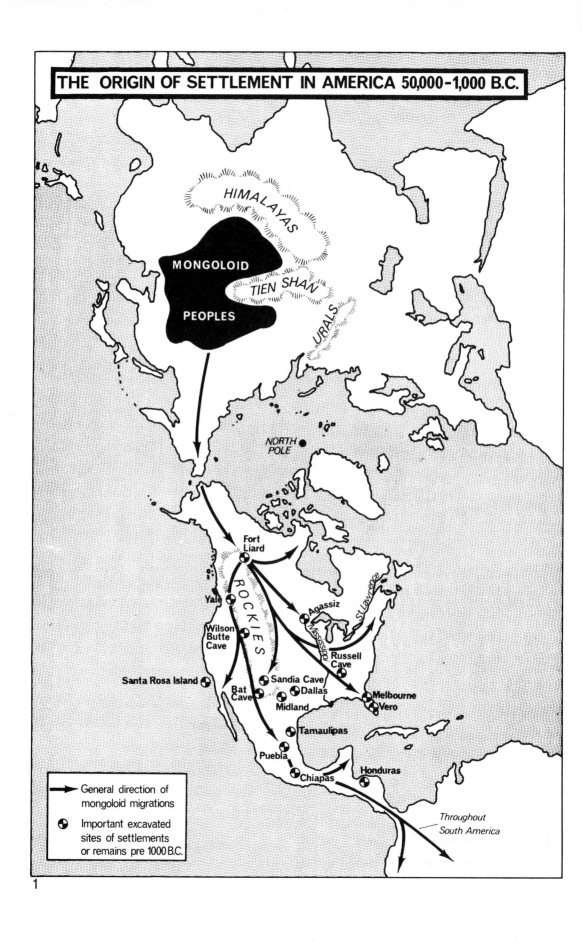

THE ORIGIN OF SETTLEMENT IN AMERICA 50,000–1,000 B.C.

HIMALAYAS

MONGOLOID

TIEN SHAN

PEOPLES

URALS

NORTH POLE

Fort Liard

ROCKIES

Yale

Agassiz

St. Lawrence

Wilson Butte Cave

Mississippi

Russell Cave

Santa Rosa Island

Sandia Cave

Bat Cave

Dallas

Melbourne

Midland

Vero

Tamaulipas

Puebla

Chiapas

Honduras

Throughout South America

→ General direction of mongoloid migrations

◑ Important excavated sites of settlements or remains pre 1000 B.C.

1

THE INDIAN TRIBES OF NORTH AMERICA BEFORE 1492

Eskimo
Koyukon
Ingalik
Kutchin
Tanaina
Han
Aleut
Tanana
Nabesna
Tuchone
Ahtena
Kaska
Tahltan
Tlingit
Hare
Bear Lake
Dogrib
Yellowknife
Slave
Sekani
Beaver
Chipewyan
Eskimo

Tsimshian
Bella Coola
Haida
Bella Bella
Kwakiutl
Nootka
Salish
Makah Puyallup
Nisqually
Chehalis
Chinook
Cowlitz
Tillamook
Yakima
Klikitat
Molala
Kalapuya
Coos
Umpqua
Takelma
Karok
Yurok
Wiyot
Shasta
Hupa
Yana
Mattole
Maidu
Yuki
Pomo
Wintun
Miwok
Costanoan
Yokuts
Salinan
Chumash

Cayuse

Carrier
Chilcotin
Shuswap
Lillooet
Thompson
Okanagan
Sanpoil
Colville
Spokane
Palouse
Walla Walla
Klamath
Modoc
Chomawi
Tsugewi
Kawaiisu
Mono
Panamint

Kaigani
Piegan
Kutenai
Kalispel
Atsina
Coeur D'Alene
Flathead
Crow
Nez Perce
Bannock
Shoshoni
Paviotso
Washo

Sarsi
Siksika (Blackfoot)
Cree

Ojibwa (Chippewa)
Ottawa
Plains Cree
Assiniboin

Hidatsa
Arikara
Teton
Yankton
Dakota
Pawnee
N.Cheyenne
Oto

Mandan

Santee Dakota

Dakota
Sauk
Ponca
Iowa
Fox
Omaha
Wea
Kansa
Peoria

Tobacco
Neutral
Winnebago

Menomini

Erie

Kickapoo
Miami

Naskapi Montagnais
Micmac
Malecite
Passamaquoddy
Penobscot
Abnaki
Huron

Beothuk

Pennacook

Mahican
Mohawk
Niomuc Oneida
Massachuset
Wampanoag
Narraganset
Pequot
Mohegan
Wappinger
Onondaga
Cayuga
Seneca
Delaware
Nanticoke
Powhatan
Chickahominy
Mattapony
Tutelo
Pamlico
Nottoway
Tuscarora
Catawba

Potawatomie
Susquehanna
Pamunkey
Piankashaw

Illinois
Shawnee
Cherokee
Yuchi
Chickasaw

Ute
Gosiute
S.Paiute
Navaho
Pueblo
Kiowa
Kiowa Apache
Mescalero Apache
Tawakoni
Comanche Wichita
Kichai
Waco
Tonkawa

Quapaw
Tuskegee
Choctaw Creek
Alabama

Natchez
Tunica

Seminole

Mohave
Serpano
Yavapai
Cahuilla
Yuma
Pima
Maricopa
Papago

Kavasupai
Chemehuevi
Walapai

Hopi
Zuni

W.Apache
Lipan Apache

Caddo
Opata
Seri

Cochiti
Concho
Tarahumara
Cahita
Acaxee

Karankawa
Coahuiltec
Tamaulipec
Huichol

Atakapa
Chitimacha
Biloxi
Mobile
Apalachee

Yamasee
Guale
Timucua
Hichiti

Calusa

Waicuri
Pericu
Yaqui

Huastec
Totonac
Tlaxcalan

Yucatan Maya

Taino

Ciboney

Toltec
Tarascan
Otomi

Aztec
Mixtec
Zapotec

Lacandon
Maya
Quiche
Maya

Mosquito

Chontal

N.Paiute S.Cheyenne Osage Missouri
Jicarilla Apache
Arapaho
Oto

There were approximately one million Indians
north of Mexico in 1492

0   600
Miles

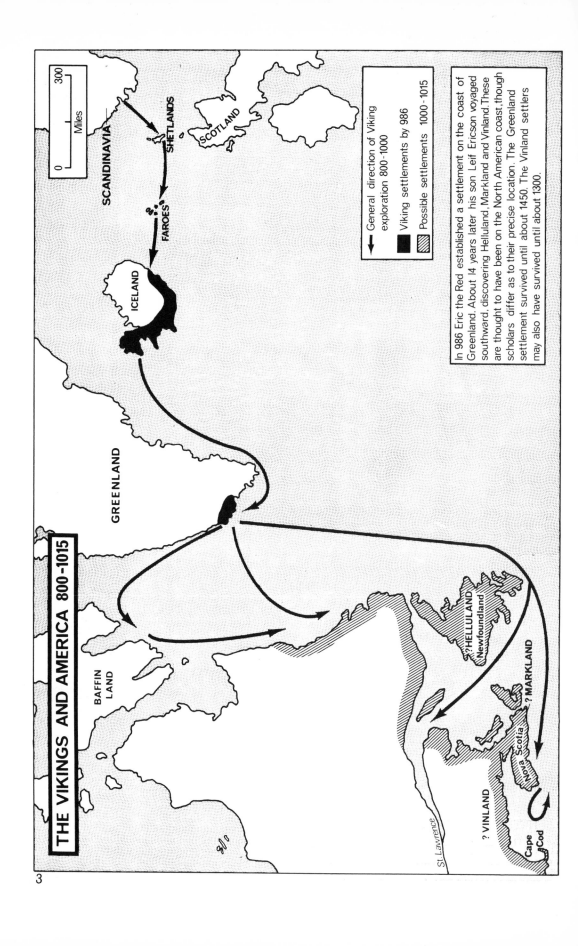

THE VIKINGS AND AMERICA 800-1015

SCANDINAVIA

SHETLANDS

SCOTLAND

FAROES

ICELAND

GREENLAND

BAFFIN LAND

? HELLULAND Newfoundland

? MARKLAND

Nova Scotia

? VINLAND

Cape Cod

St Lawrence

Miles

300

0

General direction of Viking exploration 800-1000

Viking settlements by 986

Possible settlements 1000-1015

In 986 Eric the Red established a settlement on the coast of Greenland. About 14 years later his son Leif Ericson voyaged southward, discovering Helluland, Markland and Vinland. These are thought to have been on the North American coast, though scholars differ as to their precise location. The Greenland settlement survived until about 1450. The Vinland settlers may also have survived until about 1300.

3

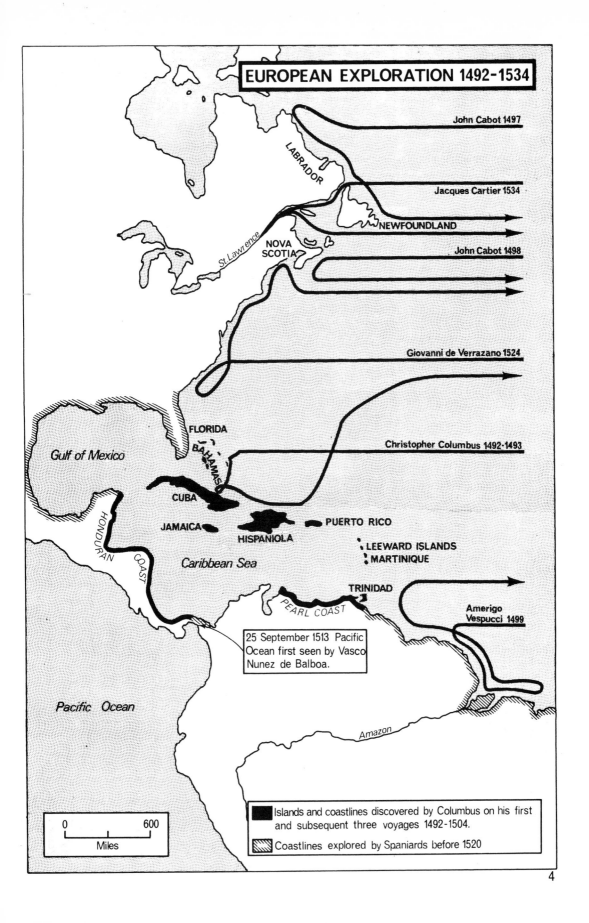

EUROPEAN EXPLORATION 1492-1534

John Cabot 1497

LABRADOR

Jacques Cartier 1534

NEWFOUNDLAND

John Cabot 1498

NOVA SCOTIA

St Lawrence

Giovanni de Verrazano 1524

FLORIDA

BAHAMAS

Christopher Columbus 1492-1493

Gulf of Mexico

CUBA

JAMAICA

HISPANIOLA

PUERTO RICO

HONDURAN COAST

Caribbean Sea

LEEWARD ISLANDS

MARTINIQUE

TRINIDAD

PEARL COAST

Amerigo Vespucci 1499

25 September 1513 Pacific Ocean first seen by Vasco Nunez de Balboa.

Pacific Ocean

Amazon

⬛ Islands and coastlines discovered by Columbus on his first and subsequent three voyages 1492-1504.

▨ Coastlines explored by Spaniards before 1520

0   600
        Miles

4

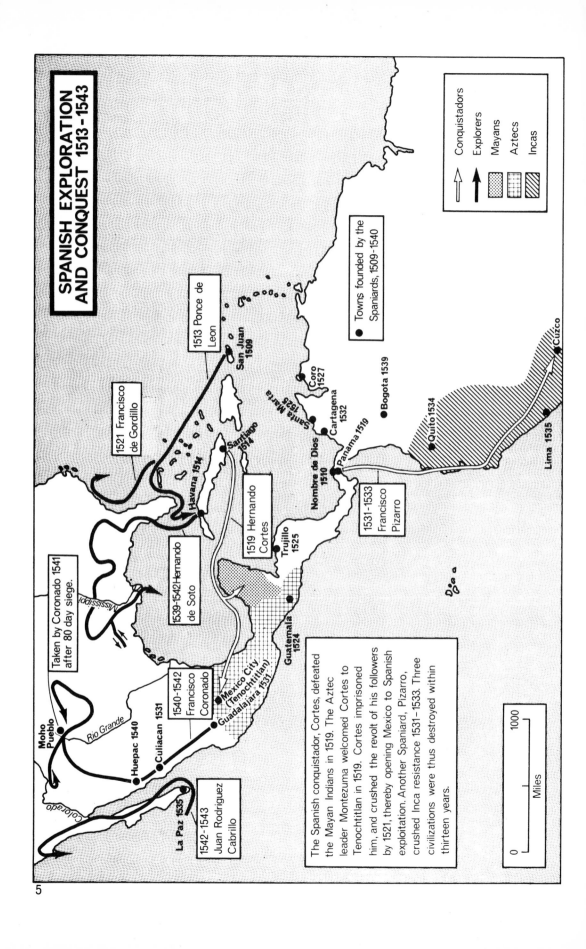

SPANISH EXPLORATION AND CONQUEST 1513-1543

Conquistadors
Explorers
Mayans
Aztecs
Incas

● Towns founded by the
Spaniards, 1509-1540

1513 Ponce de
Leon

San Juan
1509

Coro
1527

Santa María
1525

Cartagena
1532

● Bogota 1539

Panama 1519

Nombre de Dios
1510

Quito 1534

1521 Francisco
de Gordillo

Lima 1535

Cúzco

1531-1533
Francisco
Pizarro

Trujillo
1525

1519 Hernando
Cortes

Santiago
1514

Havana 1514

Mississippi

Taken by Coronado 1541
after 80 day siege.

1539-1542 Hernando
de Soto

Guatemala
1524

Moho
Pueblo

Rio Grande

Huepac 1540

Culiacan 1531

1540-1542
Francisco
Coronado

Mexico City
(Tenochtitlan)

Guadalajara 1531

Colorado

La Paz 1535

1542-1543
Juan Rodriguez
Cabrillo

The Spanish conquistador, Cortes, defeated
the Mayan Indians in 1519. The Aztec
leader Montezuma welcomed Cortes to
Tenochtitlan in 1519. Cortes imprisoned
him, and crushed the revolt of his followers
by 1521, thereby opening Mexico to Spanish
exploitation. Another Spaniard, Pizarro,
crushed Inca resistance 1531-1533. Three
civilizations were thus destroyed within
thirteen years.

0   Miles   1000

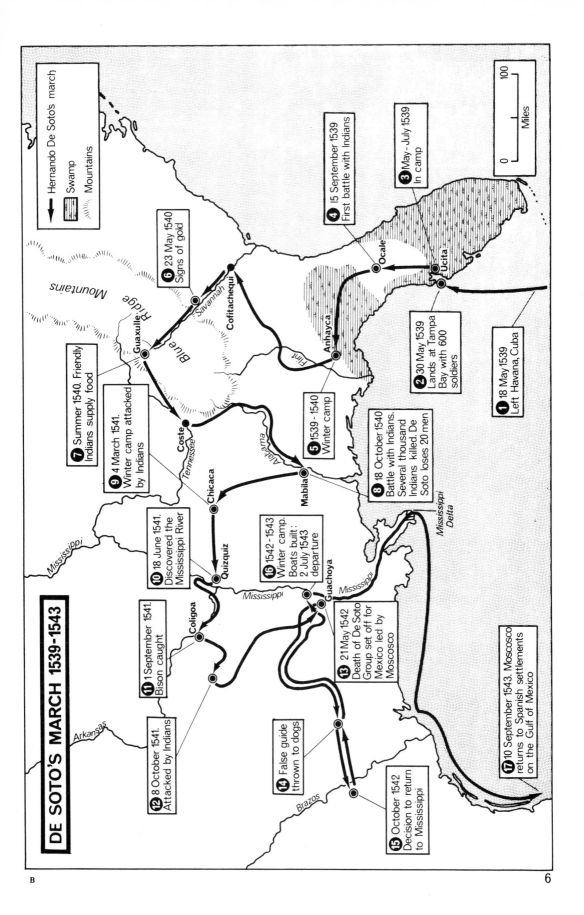

DE SOTO'S MARCH 1539-1543

Hernando De Soto's march
Swamp
Mountains

100
0
Miles

1 18 May 1539 Left Havana, Cuba

2 30 May 1539 Lands at Tampa Bay with 600 soldiers

3 May - July 1539 In camp

4 15 September 1539 First battle with Indians

5 1539 - 1540 Winter camp

6 23 May 1540 Signs of gold

7 Summer 1540. Friendly Indians supply food

8 18 October 1540 Battle with Indians. Several thousand Indians killed. De Soto loses 20 men

9 4 March 1541. Winter camp attacked by Indians

10 18 June 1541. Discovered the Mississippi River

11 1 September 1541. Bison caught

12 8 October 1541. Attacked by Indians

13 21 May 1542 Death of De Soto Group set off for Mexico led by Moscosco

14 False guide thrown to dogs

15 October 1542 Decision to return to Mississippi

16 1542 - 1543 Winter camp. Boats built: 2 July 1543 departure

17 10 September 1543. Moscosco returns to Spanish settlements on the Gulf of Mexico

Mountains
Blue Ridge
Guaxulle
Savannah
Cofitachequi
Flint
Ocale
Ucita
Anhayca
Coste
Tennessee
Alabama
Chicaca
Mabila
Quizquiz
Mississippi
Mississippi Delta
Coligoa
Mississippi
Guachoya
Mississippi
Arkansas
Brazos

B

6

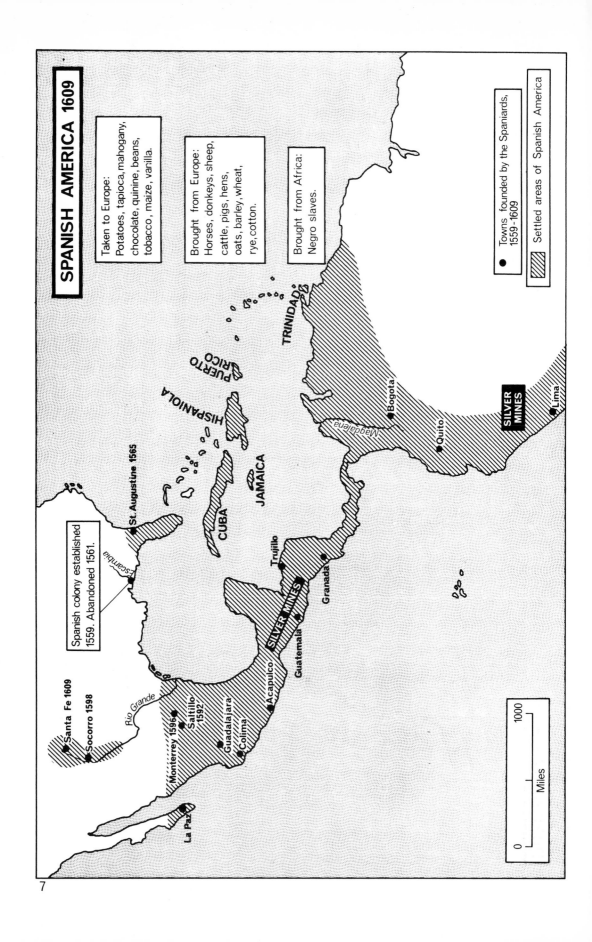

SPANISH AMERICA 1609

Taken to Europe:
Potatoes, tapioca, mahogany, chocolate, quinine, beans, tobacco, maize, vanilla.

Brought from Europe:
Horses, donkeys, sheep, cattle, pigs, hens, oats, barley, wheat, rye, cotton.

Brought from Africa: Negro slaves.

● Towns founded by the Spaniards, 1559-1609

▨ Settled areas of Spanish America

Santa Fe 1609
Socorro 1598
Rio Grande
Monterrey 1596
Saltillo 1592
Guadalajara
Colima
La Paz
Acapulco
Guatemala
SILVER MINES
Granada
Trujillo
CUBA
JAMAICA
HISPANIOLA
PUERTO RICO
TRINIDAD
St. Augustine 1565
Escambia

Spanish colony established 1559. Abandoned 1561.

Magdalena
Bogota
Quito
Lima
SILVER MINES

0   1000
Miles

7

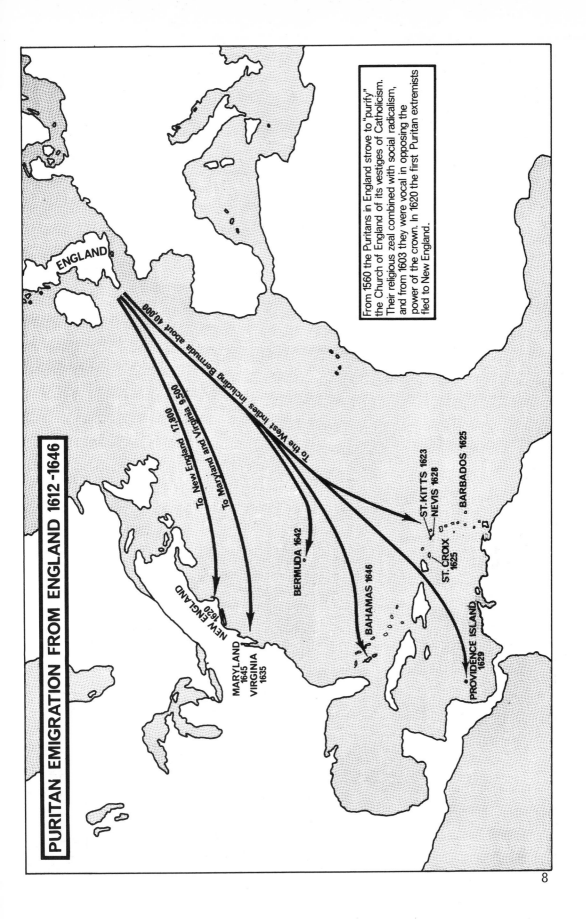

PURITAN EMIGRATION FROM ENGLAND 1612-1646

ENGLAND

From 1560 the Puritans in England strove to "purify" the Church of England of its vestiges of Catholicism. Their religious zeal combined with social radicalism, and from 1603 they were vocal in opposing the power of the crown. In 1620 the first Puritan extremists fled to New England.

To the West Indies including Bermuda about 40,000

To Maryland and Virginia 9,500

To New England 17,800

NEW ENGLAND 1620

MARYLAND 1645
VIRGINIA 1635

BERMUDA 1642

BAHAMAS 1646

ST. KITTS 1623
NEVIS 1628

ST. CROIX 1625

BARBADOS 1625

PROVIDENCE ISLAND 1629

8

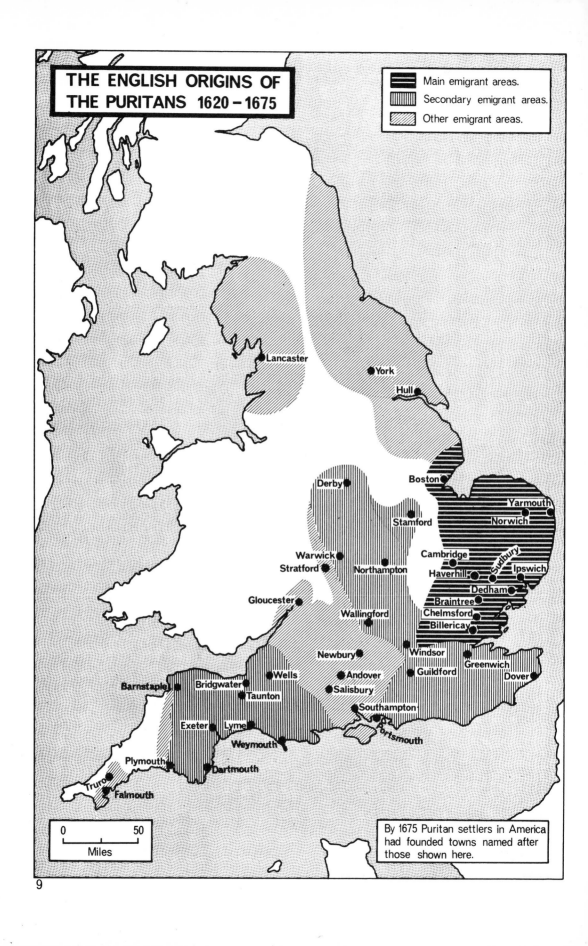

THE ENGLISH ORIGINS OF
THE PURITANS 1620–1675

Main emigrant areas.
Secondary emigrant areas.
Other emigrant areas.

Lancaster

York

Hull

Derby

Boston

Yarmouth

Stamford

Norwich

Warwick

Cambridge

Sudbury

Stratford

Northampton

Haverhill

Ipswich

Gloucester

Dedham

Braintree

Wallingford

Chelmsford

Billericay

Newbury

Windsor

Greenwich

Andover

Guildford

Dover

Barnstaple

Wells

Bridgwater

Salisbury

Taunton

Southampton

Exeter

Lyme

Portsmouth

Weymouth

Plymouth

Dartmouth

Truro

Falmouth

0   50
Miles

By 1675 Puritan settlers in America
had founded towns named after
those shown here.

9

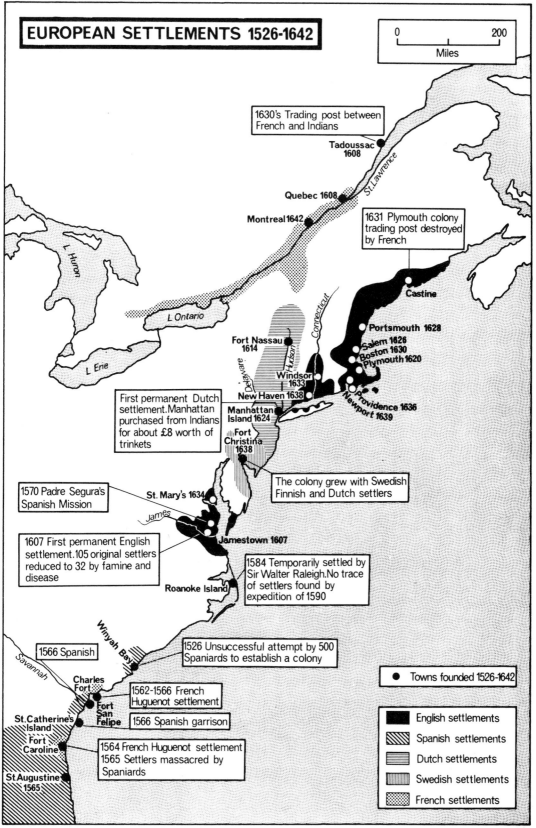

EUROPEAN SETTLEMENTS 1526-1642

0   200
Miles

1630's Trading post between French and Indians

Tadoussac 1608

Quebec 1608

Montreal 1642

St.Lawrence

L.Huron

L.Ontario

L.Erie

1631 Plymouth colony trading post destroyed by French

Castine

Portsmouth 1628

Salem 1626
Boston 1630
Plymouth 1620

Fort Nassau 1614

Connecticut

Windsor 1633

New Haven 1638

Delaware

Hudson

Providence 1636

Newport 1639

First permanent Dutch settlement. Manhattan purchased from Indians for about £8 worth of trinkets

Manhattan Island 1624

Fort Christina 1638

1570 Padre Segura's Spanish Mission

St. Mary's 1634

James

The colony grew with Swedish Finnish and Dutch settlers

1607 First permanent English settlement. 105 original settlers reduced to 32 by famine and disease

Jamestown 1607

1584 Temporarily settled by Sir Walter Raleigh. No trace of settlers found by expedition of 1590

Roanoke Island

Winyah Bay

1526 Unsuccessful attempt by 500 Spaniards to establish a colony

1566 Spanish

Savannah

Charles Fort

1562-1566 French Huguenot settlement

Fort San Felipe

1566 Spanish garrison

St.Catherine's Island

Fort Caroline

1564 French Huguenot settlement 1565 Settlers massacred by Spaniards

St.Augustine 1565

● Towns founded 1526-1642

■ English settlements
▨ Spanish settlements
▤ Dutch settlements
▥ Swedish settlements
▦ French settlements

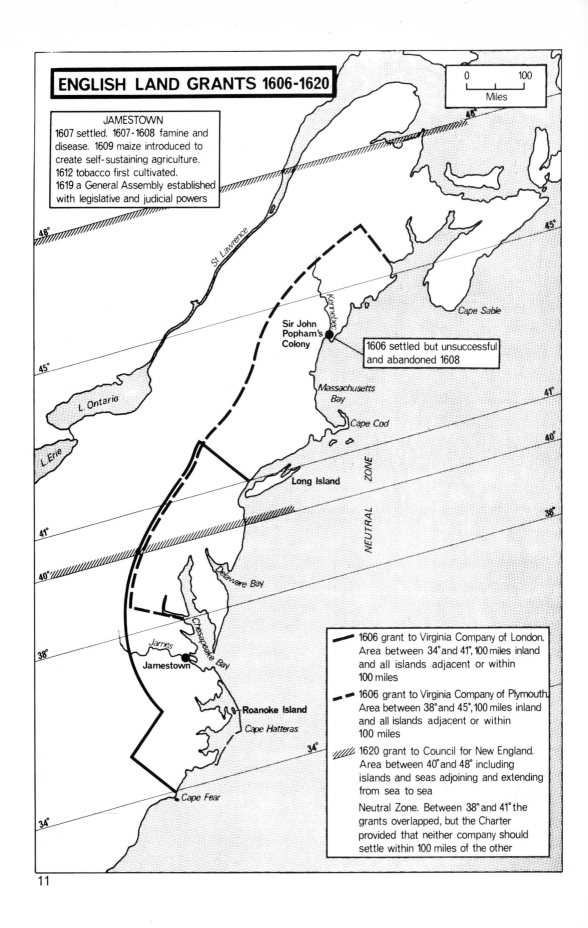

ENGLISH LAND GRANTS 1606-1620

0   100
Miles

JAMESTOWN
1607 settled. 1607-1608 famine and disease. 1609 maize introduced to create self-sustaining agriculture. 1612 tobacco first cultivated. 1619 a General Assembly established with legislative and judicial powers

48°

45°

St. Lawrence

Kennebec

Sir John Popham's Colony

1606 settled but unsuccessful and abandoned 1608

Cape Sable

45°

41°

Massachusetts Bay

Cape Cod

40°

L. Ontario

45°

L. Erie

Long Island

NEUTRAL ZONE

38°

41°

Delaware Bay

40°

James

Jamestown

Chesapeake Bay

38°

Roanoke Island

Cape Hatteras

34°

Cape Fear

34°

1606 grant to Virginia Company of London. Area between 34° and 41°, 100 miles inland and all islands adjacent or within 100 miles

1606 grant to Virginia Company of Plymouth. Area between 38° and 45°, 100 miles inland and all islands adjacent or within 100 miles

1620 grant to Council for New England. Area between 40° and 48° including islands and seas adjoining and extending from sea to sea

Neutral Zone. Between 38° and 41° the grants overlapped, but the Charter provided that neither company should settle within 100 miles of the other

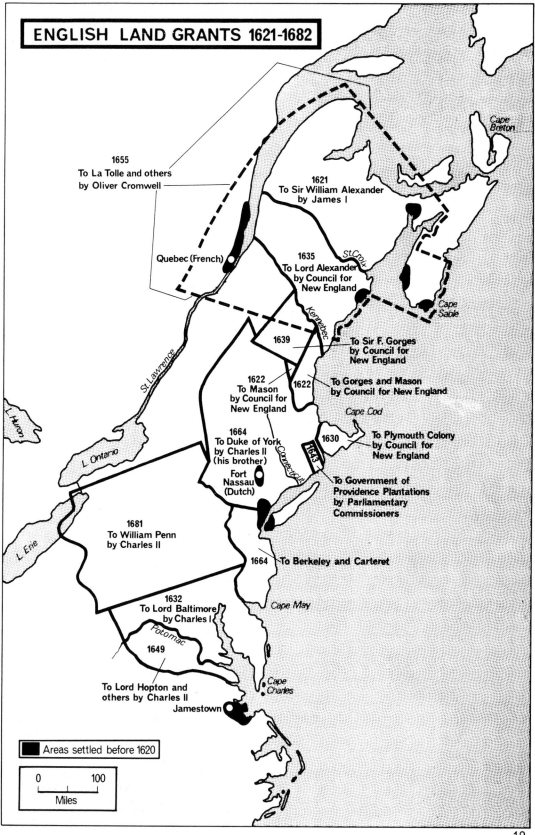

ENGLISH LAND GRANTS 1621-1682

1655
To La Tolle and others
by Oliver Cromwell

1621
To Sir William Alexander
by James I

Quebec (French)

St Croix

1635
To Lord Alexander
by Council for
New England

Kennebec

1639

To Sir F. Gorges
by Council for
New England

1622
To Mason
by Council for
New England

1622

To Gorges and Mason
by Council for New England

Cape Cod

L. Huron

L. Ontario

1664
To Duke of York
by Charles II
(his brother)

Fort
Nassau
(Dutch)

Connecticut

1630

To Plymouth Colony
by Council for
New England

1643

To Government of
Providence Plantations
by Parliamentary
Commissioners

1681
To William Penn
by Charles II

L. Erie

1664

To Berkeley and Carteret

Cape May

1632
To Lord Baltimore
by Charles I

Potomac

1649

To Lord Hopton and
others by Charles II

Jamestown

Cape
Charles

St. Lawrence

Cape
Breton

Cape
Sable

■ Areas settled before 1620

0   100

Miles

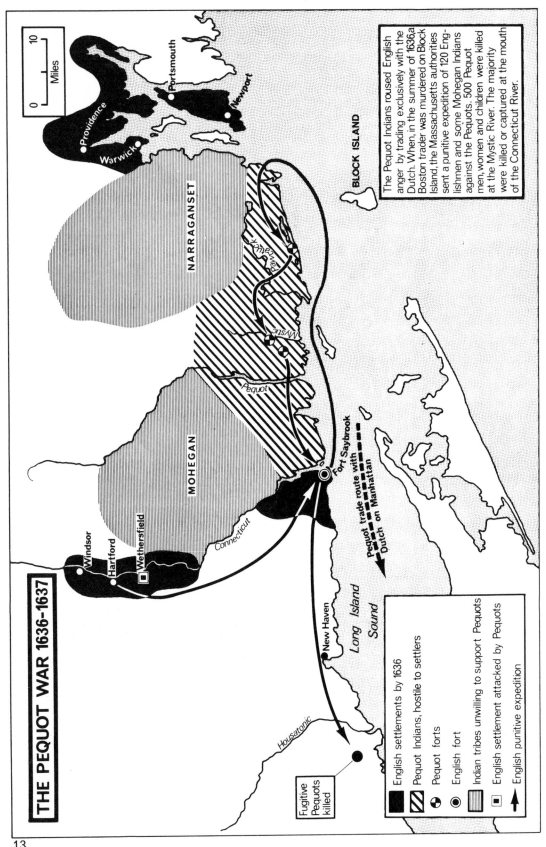

THE PEQUOT WAR 1636–1637

The Pequot Indians roused English anger by trading exclusively with the Dutch. When, in the summer of 1636 a Boston trader was murdered on Block Island, the Massachusetts authorities sent a punitive expedition of 120 Englishmen and some Mohegan Indians against the Pequots. 500 Pequot men, women and children were killed at the Mystic River. The majority were killed or captured at the mouth of the Connecticut River.

BLOCK ISLAND

NARRAGANSET

MOHEGAN

Providence
Warwick
Portsmouth
Newport

Pawcatuck

Mystic

Pequot

Windsor
Hartford
Wethersfield

Connecticut

Fort Saybrook

Pequot trade route with
Dutch on Manhattan

New Haven

Long Island
Sound

Housatonic

Fugitive
Pequots
killed

English settlements by 1636

Pequot Indians, hostile to settlers

Pequot forts

English fort

Indian tribes unwilling to support Pequots

English settlement attacked by Pequots

English punitive expedition

0   10
Miles

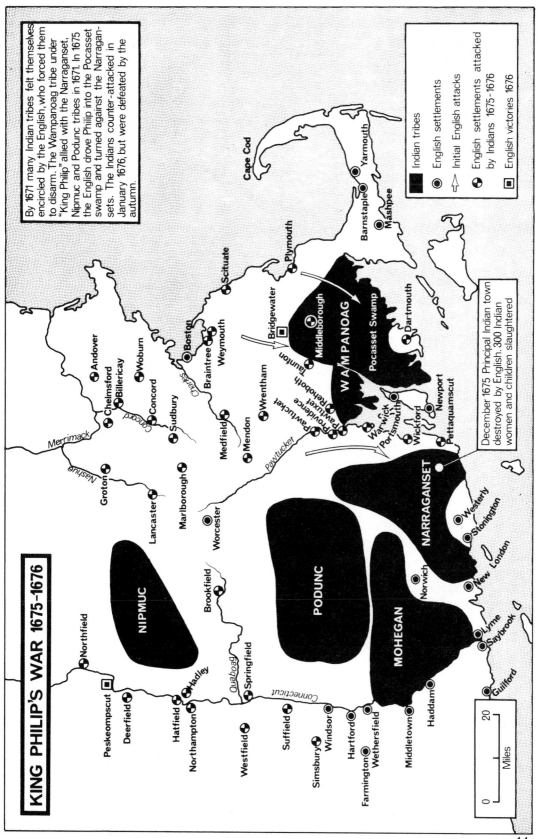

KING PHILIP'S WAR 1675–1676

By 1671 many Indian tribes felt themselves encircled by the English, who forced them to disarm. The Wampanoag tribe under "King Philip" allied with the Narraganset, Nipmuc and Podunc tribes in 1671. In 1675 the English drove Philip into the Pocasset swamp and turned against the Narragansets. The Indians counter-attacked in January 1676, but were defeated by the autumn.

December 1675 Principal Indian town destroyed by English. 300 Indian women and children slaughtered

Legend:
- Indian tribes
- ◉ English settlements
- ⟶ Initial English attacks
- ◓ English settlements attacked by Indians 1675–1676
- ▣ English victories 1676

Tribes: NIPMUC, PODUNC, MOHEGAN, NARRAGANSET, WAMPANOAG, Pocasset Swamp

Rivers: Merrimack, Nashua, Concord, Charles, Pawtucket, Quaboag, Connecticut

Places: Northfield, Peskeompscut, Deerfield, Hatfield, Northampton, Hadley, Westfield, Springfield, Suffield, Simsbury, Windsor, Hartford, Farmington, Wethersfield, Middletown, Haddam, Guilford, Saybrook, Lyme, New London, Stonington, Westerly, Norwich, Brookfield, Worcester, Lancaster, Groton, Marlborough, Sudbury, Concord, Billericay, Chelmsford, Andover, Woburn, Medfield, Mendon, Wrentham, Braintree, Weymouth, Boston, Scituate, Bridgewater, Taunton, Rehoboth, Pawtuxet, Providence, Pawtucket, Warwick, Portsmouth, Newport, Wickford, Pettaquamscut, Middleborough, Dartmouth, Plymouth, Barnstaple, Mashpee, Yarmouth, Cape Cod

Scale: 0 — 20 Miles

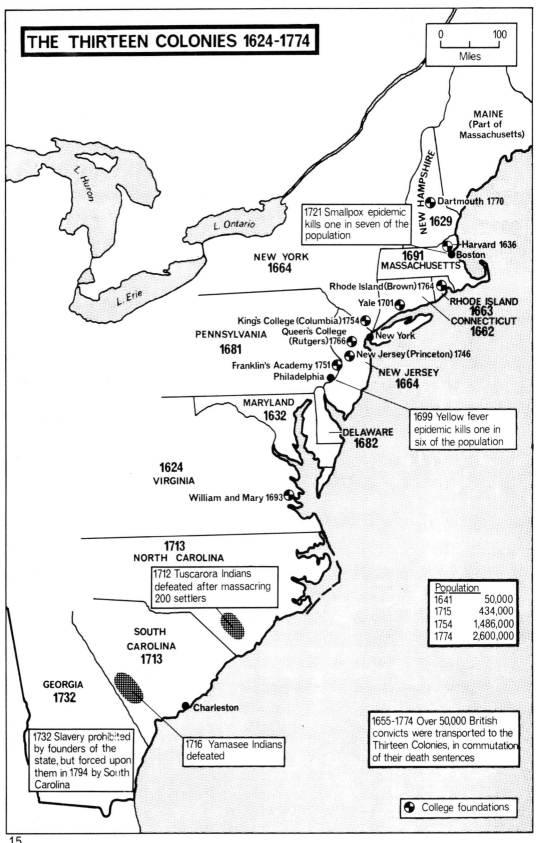

THE THIRTEEN COLONIES 1624-1774

0 ——— 100
Miles

MAINE
(Part of
Massachusetts)

NEW HAMPSHIRE
1629

Dartmouth 1770

Harvard 1636
Boston

1691
MASSACHUSETTS

1721 Smallpox epidemic kills one in seven of the population

NEW YORK
1664

L. Huron

L. Ontario

L. Erie

Rhode Island(Brown)1764

Yale 1701

RHODE ISLAND
1663
CONNECTICUT
1662

King's College (Columbia)1754

PENNSYLVANIA
1681

Queen's College (Rutgers)1766

New York

New Jersey (Princeton) 1746

Franklin's Academy 1751

Philadelphia

NEW JERSEY
1664

MARYLAND
1632

DELAWARE
1682

1699 Yellow fever epidemic kills one in six of the population

1624
VIRGINIA

William and Mary 1693

1713
NORTH CAROLINA

1712 Tuscarora Indians defeated after massacring 200 settlers

SOUTH
CAROLINA
1713

Population	
1641	50,000
1715	434,000
1754	1,486,000
1774	2,600,000

GEORGIA
1732

Charleston

1732 Slavery prohibited by founders of the state, but forced upon them in 1794 by South Carolina

1716 Yamasee Indians defeated

1655-1774 Over 50,000 British convicts were transported to the Thirteen Colonies, in commutation of their death sentences

College foundations

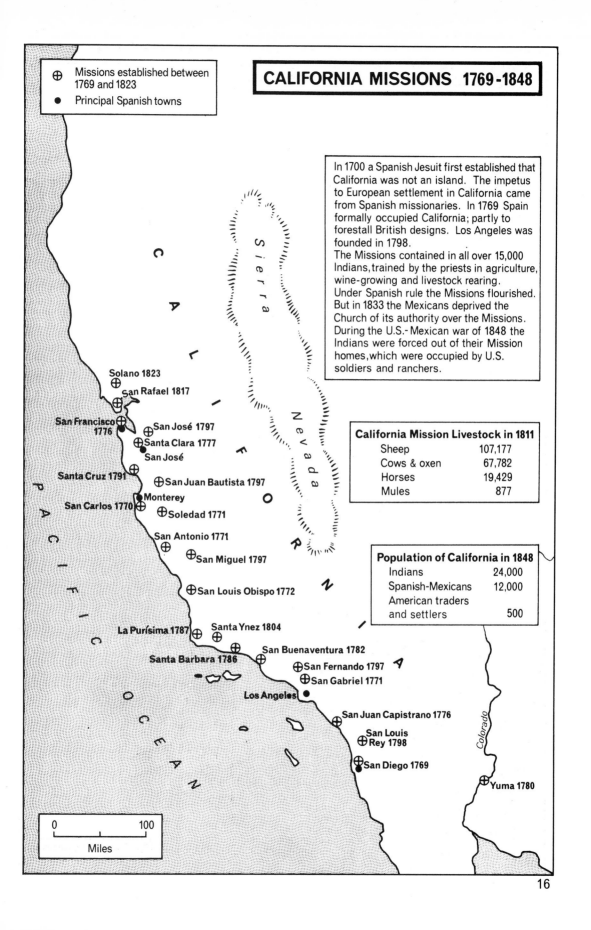

CALIFORNIA MISSIONS 1769-1848

⊕ Missions established between 1769 and 1823
● Principal Spanish towns

In 1700 a Spanish Jesuit first established that California was not an island. The impetus to European settlement in California came from Spanish missionaries. In 1769 Spain formally occupied California; partly to forestall British designs. Los Angeles was founded in 1798.

The Missions contained in all over 15,000 Indians, trained by the priests in agriculture, wine-growing and livestock rearing.

Under Spanish rule the Missions flourished. But in 1833 the Mexicans deprived the Church of its authority over the Missions. During the U.S.-Mexican war of 1848 the Indians were forced out of their Mission homes, which were occupied by U.S. soldiers and ranchers.

California Mission Livestock in 1811	
Sheep	107,177
Cows & oxen	67,782
Horses	19,429
Mules	877

Population of California in 1848	
Indians	24,000
Spanish-Mexicans	12,000
American traders and settlers	500

Sierra Nevada

CALIFORNIA

PACIFIC OCEAN

Solano 1823
San Rafael 1817
San Francisco 1776
San José 1797
Santa Clara 1777
San José
Santa Cruz 1791
San Juan Bautista 1797
Monterey
San Carlos 1770
Soledad 1771
San Antonio 1771
San Miguel 1797
San Louis Obispo 1772
La Purísima 1787
Santa Ynez 1804
San Buenaventura 1782
Santa Barbara 1786
San Fernando 1797
San Gabriel 1771
Los Angeles
San Juan Capistrano 1776
San Louis Rey 1798
San Diego 1769
Yuma 1780

Colorado

0   100
Miles

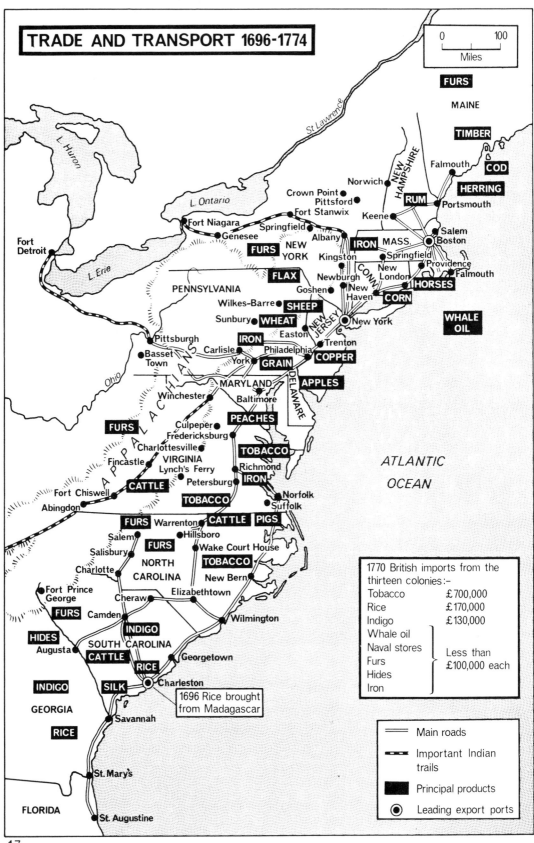

TRADE AND TRANSPORT 1696-1774

0   100
Miles

FURS

MAINE

TIMBER

St Lawrence

Falmouth

COD

Norwich

NEW HAMPSHIRE

RUM

HERRING

L. Huron

Crown Point

Pittsford

Portsmouth

Keene

L. Ontario

Fort Stanwix

Salem

Fort Niagara

Springfield

Albany

IRON

MASS.

Boston

Genesee

FURS

NEW YORK

Kingston

Springfield

Providence

Fort Detroit

L. Erie

Newburgh

New London

Falmouth

FLAX

Goshen

New Haven

HORSES

PENNSYLVANIA

Wilkes-Barre

SHEEP

CORN

Sunbury

WHEAT

NEW JERSEY

New York

WHALE OIL

Ohio

Pittsburgh

Easton

Trenton

Carlisle

IRON

Philadelphia

COPPER

Basset Town

York

GRAIN

APPALACHIAN

APPLES

MARYLAND

DELAWARE

Winchester

Baltimore

FURS

Culpeper

Fredericksburg

PEACHES

Charlottesville

Fincastle

VIRGINIA

Lynch's Ferry

TOBACCO

Richmond

CATTLE

Petersburg

IRON

Fort Chiswell

Norfolk

Abingdon

TOBACCO

Suffolk

FURS

Warrenton

CATTLE

PIGS

Salem

Hillsboro

Salisbury

FURS

Wake Court House

Charlotte

NORTH CAROLINA

TOBACCO

Fort Prince George

New Bern

FURS

Cheraw

Elizabethtown

Camden

Wilmington

INDIGO

HIDES

SOUTH CAROLINA

Augusta

CATTLE

Georgetown

INDIGO

RICE

SILK

Charleston

GEORGIA

Savannah

RICE

1696 Rice brought from Madagascar

ATLANTIC OCEAN

St Mary's

FLORIDA

St. Augustine

1770 British imports from the thirteen colonies:-
Tobacco   £700,000
Rice   £170,000
Indigo   £130,000
Whale oil
Naval stores
Furs   Less than
Hides   £100,000 each
Iron

—— Main roads

■–■ Important Indian trails

■ Principal products

◉ Leading export ports

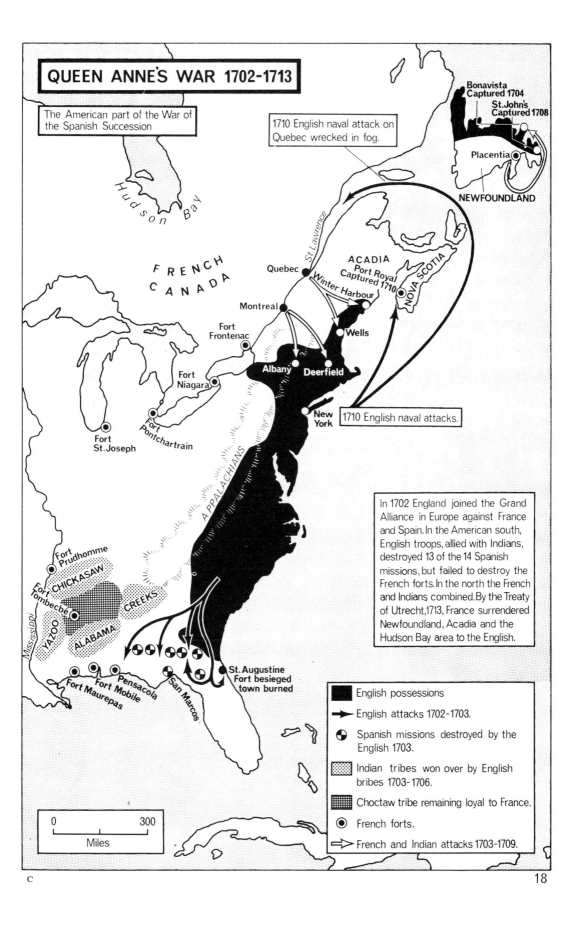

QUEEN ANNE'S WAR 1702-1713

The American part of the War of the Spanish Succession

1710 English naval attack on Quebec wrecked in fog.

Bonavista Captured 1704
St.John's Captured 1708
Placentia
NEWFOUNDLAND

Hudson Bay

FRENCH CANADA

St Lawrence

Quebec

ACADIA
Port Royal Captured 1710

NOVA SCOTIA

Winter Harbour

Montreal

Fort Frontenac

Wells

Fort Niagara

Albany   Deerfield

Fort Pontchartrain

New York

1710 English naval attacks.

Fort St.Joseph

APPALACHIANS

In 1702 England joined the Grand Alliance in Europe against France and Spain. In the American south, English troops, allied with Indians, destroyed 13 of the 14 Spanish missions, but failed to destroy the French forts. In the north the French and Indians combined. By the Treaty of Utrecht, 1713, France surrendered Newfoundland, Acadia and the Hudson Bay area to the English.

Fort Prudhomme

CHICKASAW

Fort Tombecbe

CREEKS

Mississippi

YAZOO

ALABAMA

St. Augustine Fort besieged town burned

Fort Maurepas   Fort Mobile   Pensacola   San Marcos

■ English possessions

➤ English attacks 1702-1703.

◕ Spanish missions destroyed by the English 1703.

▨ Indian tribes won over by English bribes 1703-1706.

▦ Choctaw tribe remaining loyal to France.

◉ French forts.

⇨ French and Indian attacks 1703-1709.

C

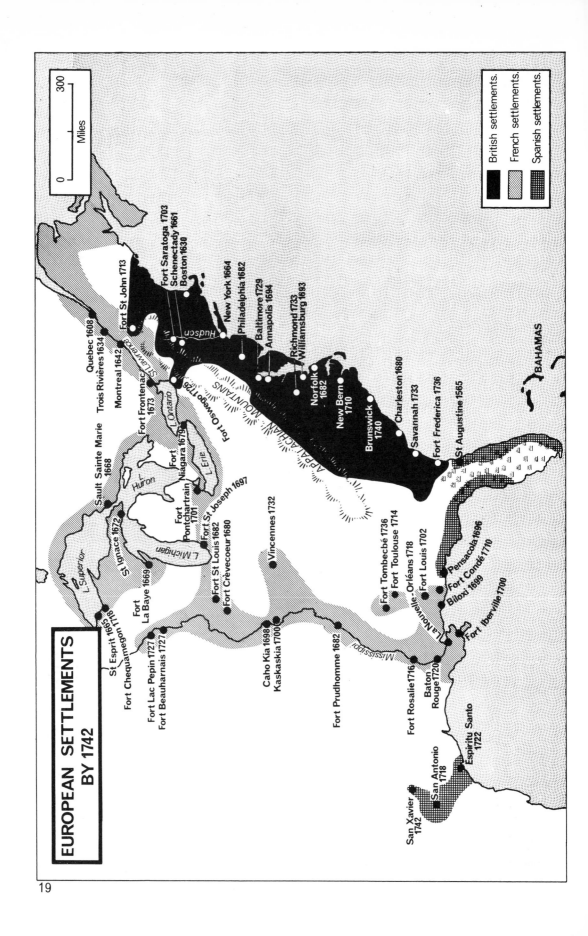

EUROPEAN SETTLEMENTS BY 1742

300

Miles

0

British settlements.
French settlements.
Spanish settlements.

Quebec 1608
Trois Rivières 1634
Montreal 1642
Fort Frontenac 1673
L. Ontario
Fort Oswego 1726
St Lawrence
Fort St John 1713
Fort Saratoga 1703
Schenectady 1661
Boston 1630
New York 1664
Philadelphia 1682
Baltimore 1729
Annapolis 1694
Richmond 1733
Williamsburg 1683
Hudson
Norfolk 1682
New Bern 1710
Brunswick 1740
Charleston 1680
Savannah 1733
Fort Frederica 1736
St Augustine 1565
APPALACHIAN MOUNTAINS
BAHAMAS

Sault Sainte Marie 1668
St Ignace 1672
Huron
L. Michigan
Fort Pontchartrain 1701
Fort Niagara 1679
L. Erie
Fort St Joseph 1697
Vincennes 1732
Fort St Louis 1682
Fort Crèvecoeur 1680

St Esprit 1665
Fort Chequamegon 1718
L. Superior
Fort La Baye 1669
Fort Lac Pepin 1727
Fort Beauharnais 1727
Caho Kia 1698
Kaskaskia 1700
Fort Prudhomme 1682
Mississippi
Fort Tombecbé 1736
Fort Toulouse 1714
La Nouvelle-Orléans 1718
Fort Louis 1702
Pensacola 1696
Fort Condé 1710
Biloxi 1699
Fort Iberville 1700
Fort Rosalie 1716
Baton Rouge 1720
Espiritu Santo 1722
San Antonio 1718
San Xavier 1742

19

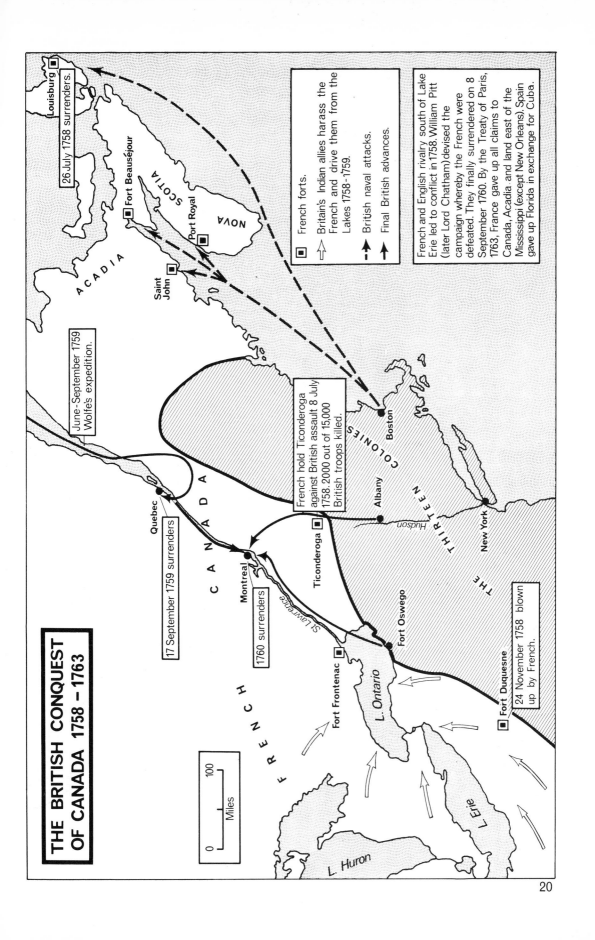

THE BRITISH CONQUEST OF CANADA 1758 – 1763

Louisburg
26 July 1758 surrenders.

Fort Beauséjour

NOVA SCOTIA

Port Royal

ACADIA

Saint John

June – September 1759 Wolfe's expedition.

□ French forts.

⇨ Britain's Indian allies harass the French and drive them from the Lakes 1758 – 1759.

➤ British naval attacks.

➤ Final British advances.

French and English rivalry south of Lake Erie led to conflict in 1758. William Pitt (later Lord Chatham) devised the campaign whereby the French were defeated. They finally surrendered on 8 September 1760. By the Treaty of Paris, 1763, France gave up all claims to Canada, Acadia, and land east of the Mississippi (except New Orleans). Spain gave up Florida in exchange for Cuba.

Boston

THE THIRTEEN COLONIES

Albany

Hudson

New York

French hold Ticonderoga against British assault 8 July 1758. 2000 out of 15,000 British troops killed.

Quebec
17 September 1759 surrenders

Montreal
1760 surrenders

□ Ticonderoga

CANADA

St Lawrence

FRENCH

□ Fort Frontenac

Fort Oswego

L. Ontario

□ Fort Duquesne
24 November 1758 blown up by French.

L. Erie

L. Huron

0   100
Miles

20

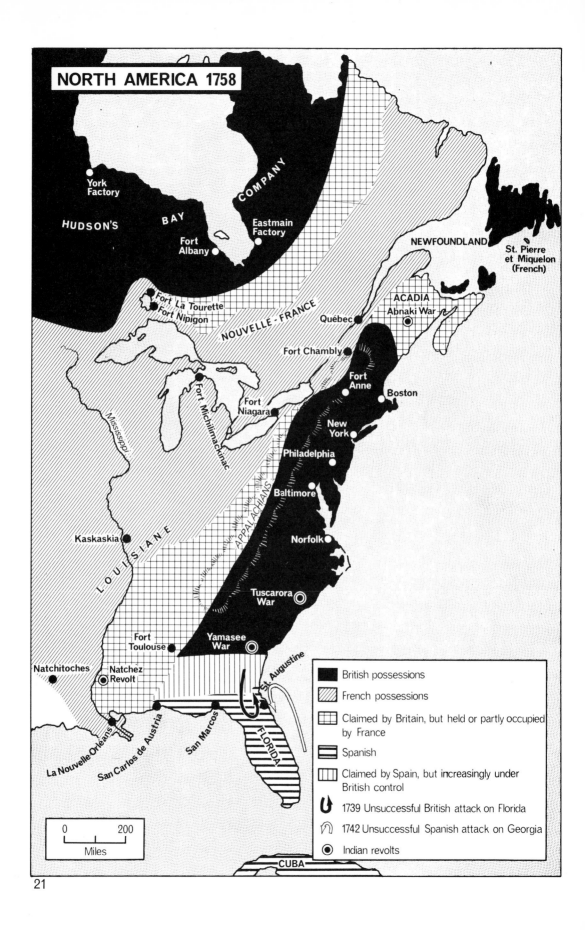

NORTH AMERICA 1758

York Factory

HUDSON'S BAY COMPANY

Eastmain Factory

Fort Albany

NEWFOUNDLAND

St. Pierre et Miquelon (French)

Fort La Tourette

Fort Nipigon

NOUVELLE - FRANCE

ACADIA

Abnaki War

Québec

Fort Chambly

Fort Anne

Boston

Fort Michilimackinac

Fort Niagara

New York

Fort Niagara

Mississippi

Philadelphia

Baltimore

Kaskaskia

APPALACHIANS

Norfolk

L O U I S I A N E

Tuscarora War

Fort Toulouse

Yamasee War

Natchitoches

Natchez Revolt

St. Augustine

La Nouvelle-Orléans

San Carlos de Austria

San Marcos

FLORIDA

CUBA

■ British possessions

▨ French possessions

⊞ Claimed by Britain, but held or partly occupied by France

⊟ Spanish

⊞ Claimed by Spain, but increasingly under British control

↻ 1739 Unsuccessful British attack on Florida

⌒ 1742 Unsuccessful Spanish attack on Georgia

◉ Indian revolts

0   200
Miles

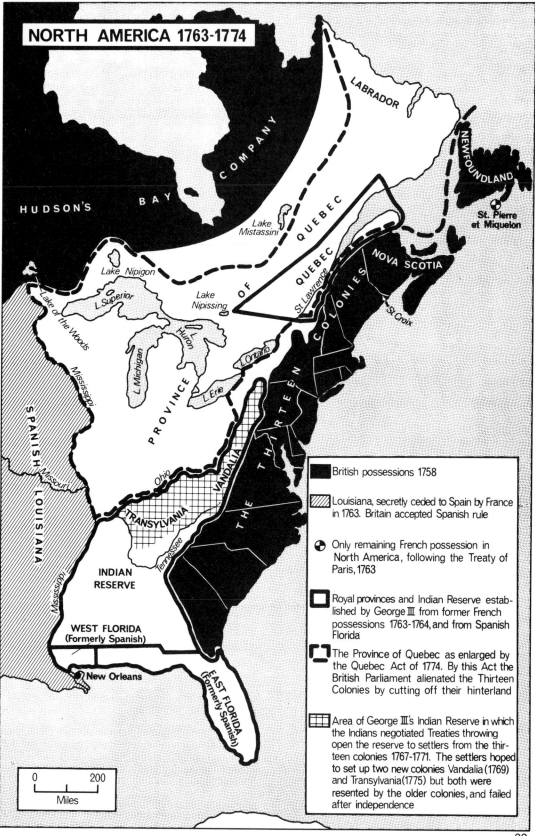

NORTH AMERICA 1763-1774

HUDSON'S BAY COMPANY

LABRADOR

NEWFOUNDLAND

St. Pierre et Miquelon

Lake Mistassini

QUEBEC

PROVINCE OF QUEBEC

Lake Nipigon

Lake Nipissing

Lake of the Woods

L. Superior

L. Michigan

L. Huron

L. Ontario

L. Erie

St. Lawrence

NOVA SCOTIA

St. Croix

COLONIES

THE THIRTEEN

SPANISH LOUISIANA

Mississippi

Missouri

Ohio

Tennessee

VANDALIA

TRANSYLVANIA

INDIAN RESERVE

WEST FLORIDA
(Formerly Spanish)

EAST FLORIDA
(Formerly Spanish)

New Orleans

Mississippi

0   200
Miles

British possessions 1758

Louisiana, secretly ceded to Spain by France in 1763. Britain accepted Spanish rule

Only remaining French possession in North America, following the Treaty of Paris, 1763

Royal provinces and Indian Reserve established by George III from former French possessions 1763-1764, and from Spanish Florida

The Province of Quebec as enlarged by the Quebec Act of 1774. By this Act the British Parliament alienated the Thirteen Colonies by cutting off their hinterland

Area of George III's Indian Reserve in which the Indians negotiated Treaties throwing open the reserve to settlers from the thirteen colonies 1767-1771. The settlers hoped to set up two new colonies Vandalia (1769) and Transylvania (1775) but both were resented by the older colonies, and failed after independence

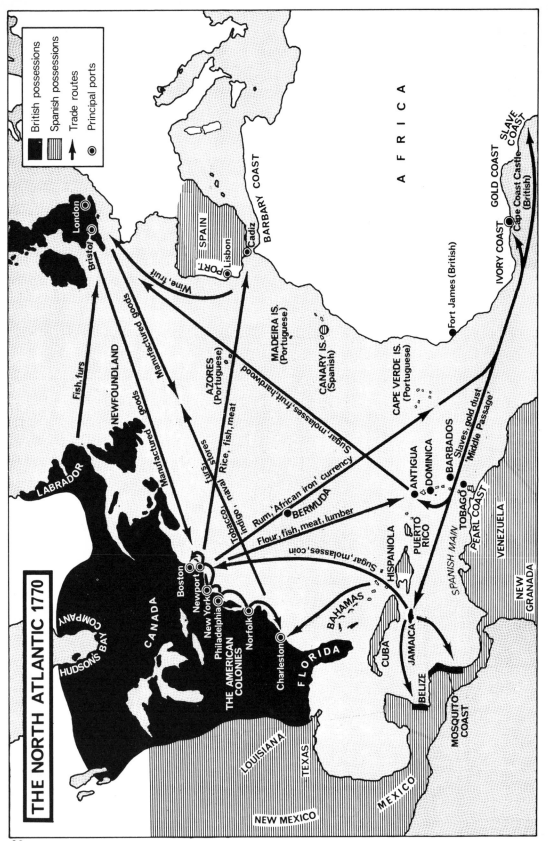

THE NORTH ATLANTIC 1770

British possessions
Spanish possessions
Trade routes
Principal ports

HUDSON'S BAY COMPANY

LABRADOR

CANADA

NEWFOUNDLAND

THE AMERICAN COLONIES

Boston
Newport
New York
Philadelphia
Norfolk
Charleston

FLORIDA

LOUISIANA

TEXAS

NEW MEXICO

MEXICO

BAHAMAS

CUBA

HISPANIOLA

JAMAICA

BELIZE

MOSQUITO COAST

SPANISH MAIN

PUERTO RICO

VENEZUELA

NEW GRANADA

BERMUDA

ANTIGUA
DOMINICA
BARBADOS
TOBAGO

PEARL COAST

London
Bristol

PORT.
Lisbon
Cadiz

SPAIN

BARBARY COAST

AZORES (Portuguese)

MADEIRA IS. (Portuguese)

CANARY IS. (Spanish)

CAPE VERDE IS. (Portuguese)

A F R I C A

GOLD COAST

IVORY COAST

SLAVE COAST

Cape Coast Castle (British)

Fort James (British)

Fish, furs

Manufactured goods

Manufactured goods

Wine, fruit

Sugar, molasses, fruit, hardwood

Furs, stores

Rice, fish, meat

Tobacco, naval stores

Indigo, 'African iron' currency

Rum, 'African iron' currency

Flour, fish, meat, lumber

Sugar, molasses, coin

Slaves, gold dust

'Middle Passage'

23

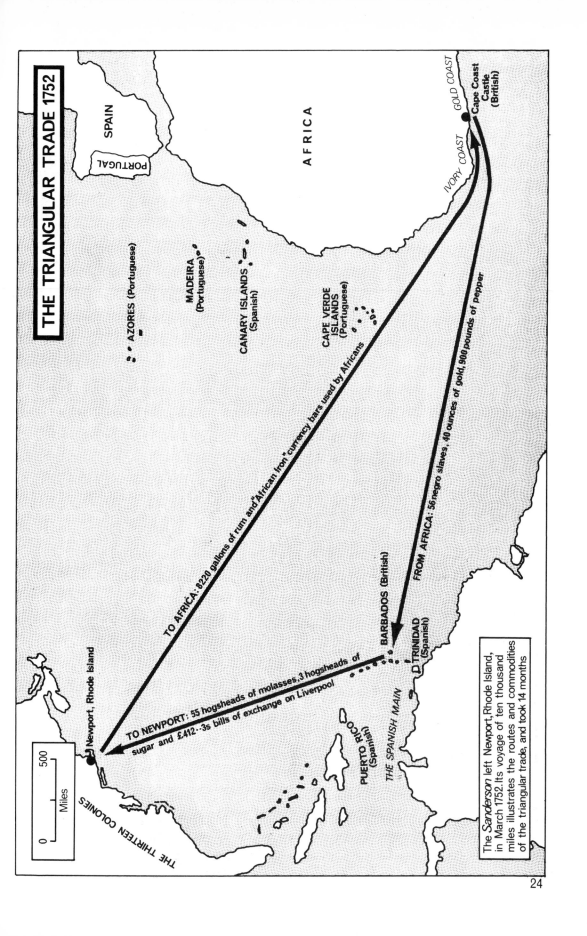

THE TRIANGULAR TRADE 1752

SPAIN

PORTUGAL

AFRICA

GOLD COAST

Cape Coast Castle (British)

IVORY COAST

AZORES (Portuguese)

MADEIRA (Portuguese)

CANARY ISLANDS (Spanish)

CAPE VERDE ISLANDS (Portuguese)

TO AFRICA: 8220 gallons of rum and "African Iron" currency bars used by Africans

FROM AFRICA: 56 negro slaves, 40 ounces of gold, 900 pounds of pepper

BARBADOS (British)

TRINIDAD (Spanish)

Newport, Rhode Island

TO NEWPORT: 55 hogsheads of molasses, 3 hogsheads of sugar and £412 · ·3s bills of exchange on Liverpool

PUERTO RICO (Spanish)

THE SPANISH MAIN

500

Miles

0

THE THIRTEEN COLONIES

The *Sanderson* left Newport, Rhode Island, in March 1752. Its voyage of ten thousand miles illustrates the routes and commodities of the triangular trade, and took 14 months

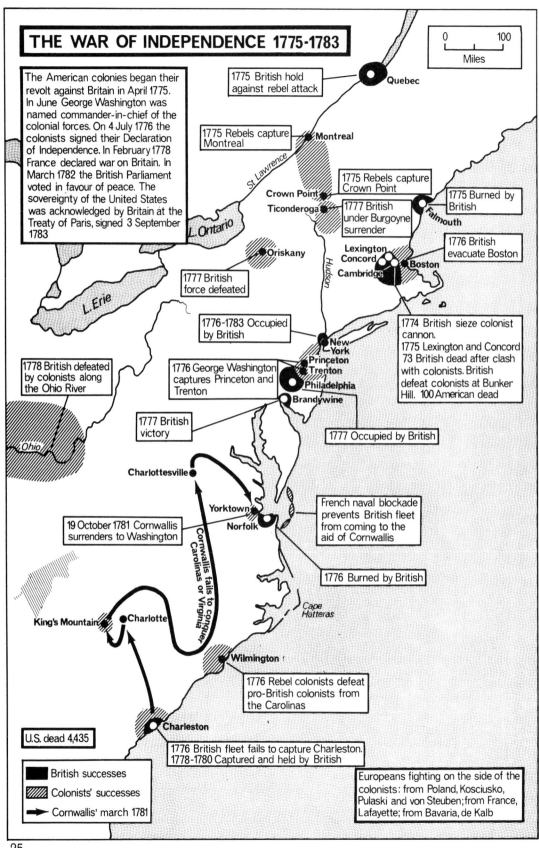

THE WAR OF INDEPENDENCE 1775-1783

0   100
Miles

The American colonies began their revolt against Britain in April 1775. In June George Washington was named commander-in-chief of the colonial forces. On 4 July 1776 the colonists signed their Declaration of Independence. In February 1778 France declared war on Britain. In March 1782 the British Parliament voted in favour of peace. The sovereignty of the United States was acknowledged by Britain at the Treaty of Paris, signed 3 September 1783

1775 British hold against rebel attack

Quebec

1775 Rebels capture Montreal

Montreal

St Lawrence

1775 Rebels capture Crown Point

Crown Point
Ticonderoga

1777 British under Burgoyne surrender

1775 Burned by British

Falmouth

L. Ontario

Oriskany

Lexington
Concord
Cambridge

Boston

1776 British evacuate Boston

1777 British force defeated

L. Erie

Hudson

1776-1783 Occupied by British

1774 British sieze colonist cannon.
1775 Lexington and Concord 73 British dead after clash with colonists. British defeat colonists at Bunker Hill. 100 American dead

New York
Princeton
Trenton
Philadelphia
Brandywine

1778 British defeated by colonists along the Ohio River

1776 George Washington captures Princeton and Trenton

Ohio

1777 British victory

1777 Occupied by British

Charlottesville

Yorktown
Norfolk

French naval blockade prevents British fleet from coming to the aid of Cornwallis

19 October 1781 Cornwallis surrenders to Washington

Cornwallis fails to conquer Carolinas or Virginia

1776 Burned by British

Cape Hatteras

King's Mountain
Charlotte

Wilmington

1776 Rebel colonists defeat pro-British colonists from the Carolinas

U.S. dead 4,435

Charleston

1776 British fleet fails to capture Charleston.
1778-1780 Captured and held by British

■ British successes
▨ Colonists' successes
➤ Cornwallis' march 1781

Europeans fighting on the side of the colonists: from Poland, Kosciusko, Pulaski and von Steuben; from France, Lafayette; from Bavaria, de Kalb

25

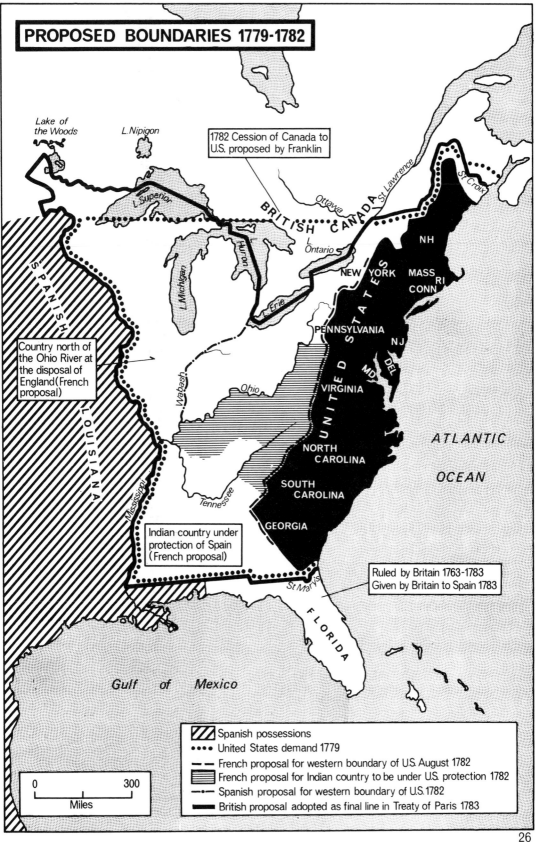

PROPOSED BOUNDARIES 1779-1782

Lake of the Woods

L.Nipigon

1782 Cession of Canada to U.S. proposed by Franklin

Ottava

St Lawrence

St Croix

BRITISH CANADA

L.Superior

L. Ontario

Erie

L. Michigan

L Huron

NH

NEW YORK

MASS

RI

CONN

PENNSYLVANIA

NJ

Country north of the Ohio River at the disposal of England(French proposal)

Wabash

MD

DEL

UNITED STATES

VIRGINIA

Ohio

ATLANTIC

OCEAN

NORTH CAROLINA

Tennessee

SOUTH CAROLINA

Indian country under protection of Spain (French proposal)

GEORGIA

Ruled by Britain 1763-1783
Given by Britain to Spain 1783

St Marys

Mississippi

S
P
A
N
I
S
H

L
O
U
I
S
I
A
N
A

F
L
O
R
I
D
A

Gulf   of   Mexico

0   300
Miles

//// Spanish possessions
•••• United States demand 1779
– – French proposal for western boundary of U.S. August 1782
≡ French proposal for Indian country to be under U.S. protection 1782
–•– Spanish proposal for western boundary of U.S. 1782
▬▬ British proposal adopted as final line in Treaty of Paris 1783

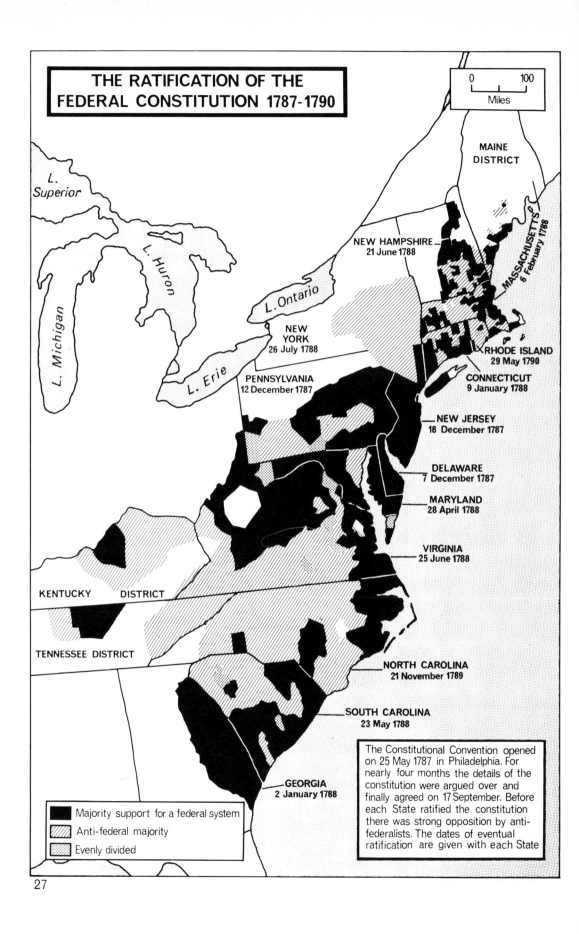

THE RATIFICATION OF THE FEDERAL CONSTITUTION 1787-1790

0   100
Miles

MAINE DISTRICT

L. Superior

L. Huron

L. Michigan

L. Ontario

L. Erie

NEW HAMPSHIRE
21 June 1788

MASSACHUSETTS
6 February 1788

NEW YORK
26 July 1788

RHODE ISLAND
29 May 1790

CONNECTICUT
9 January 1788

PENNSYLVANIA
12 December 1787

NEW JERSEY
18 December 1787

DELAWARE
7 December 1787

MARYLAND
28 April 1788

VIRGINIA
25 June 1788

KENTUCKY   DISTRICT

TENNESSEE DISTRICT

NORTH CAROLINA
21 November 1789

SOUTH CAROLINA
23 May 1788

GEORGIA
2 January 1788

■ Majority support for a federal system
▨ Anti-federal majority
▦ Evenly divided

The Constitutional Convention opened
on 25 May 1787 in Philadelphia. For
nearly four months the details of the
constitution were argued over and
finally agreed on 17 September. Before
each State ratified the constitution
there was strong opposition by anti-
federalists. The dates of eventual
ratification are given with each State

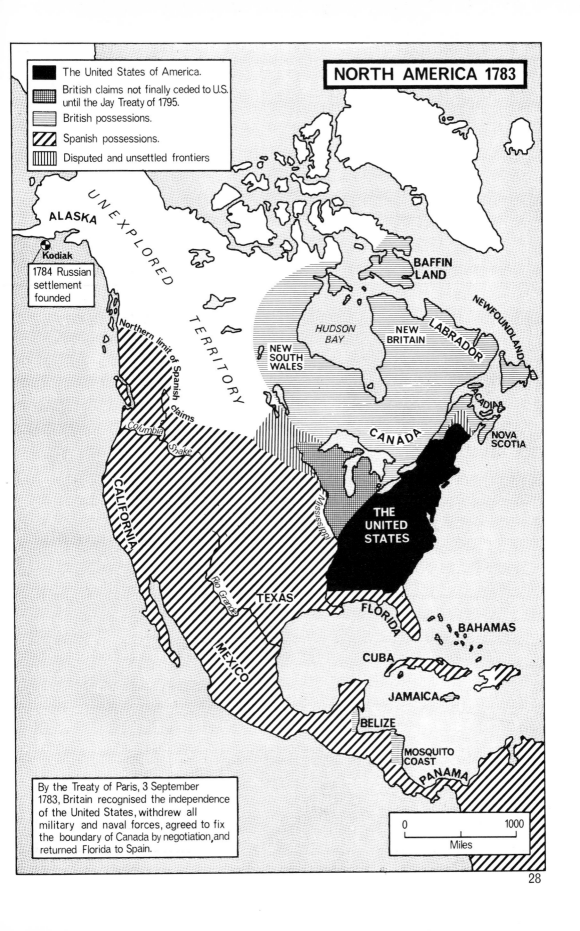

The United States of America.

British claims not finally ceded to U.S. until the Jay Treaty of 1795.

British possessions.

Spanish possessions.

Disputed and unsettled frontiers

NORTH AMERICA 1783

ALASKA

Kodiak

1784 Russian settlement founded

UNEXPLORED TERRITORY

BAFFIN LAND

NEWFOUNDLAND

HUDSON BAY

NEW BRITAIN

LABRADOR

NEW SOUTH WALES

Northern limit of Spanish claims

Columbia

Snake

CANADA

ACADIA

NOVA SCOTIA

CALIFORNIA

Mississippi

THE UNITED STATES

Rio Grande

TEXAS

FLORIDA

BAHAMAS

MEXICO

CUBA

JAMAICA

BELIZE

MOSQUITO COAST

PANAMA

By the Treaty of Paris, 3 September 1783, Britain recognised the independence of the United States, withdrew all military and naval forces, agreed to fix the boundary of Canada by negotiation, and returned Florida to Spain.

0   1000
Miles

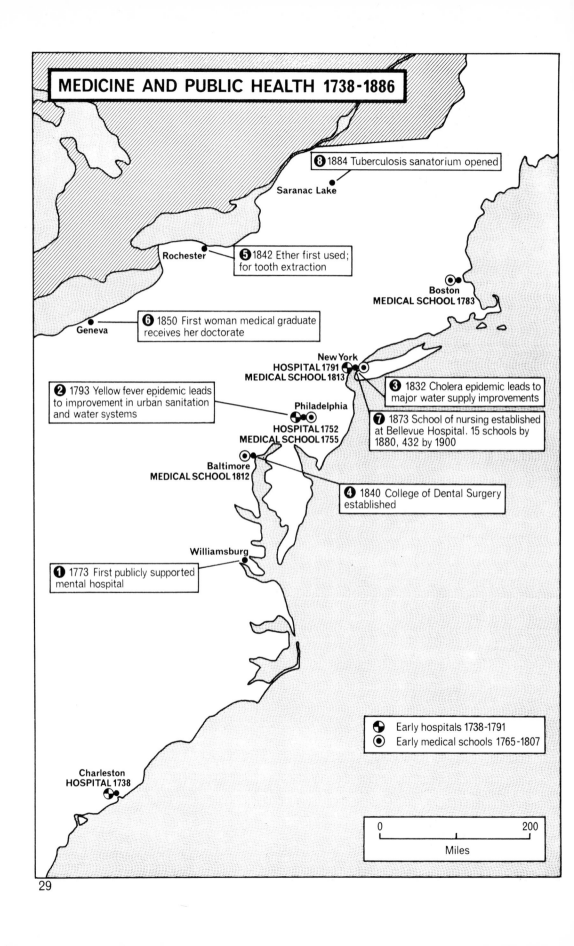

MEDICINE AND PUBLIC HEALTH 1738-1886

8 1884 Tuberculosis sanatorium opened

Saranac Lake

5 1842 Ether first used; for tooth extraction

Rochester

Boston
MEDICAL SCHOOL 1783

6 1850 First woman medical graduate receives her doctorate

Geneva

New York
HOSPITAL 1791
MEDICAL SCHOOL 1813

2 1793 Yellow fever epidemic leads to improvement in urban sanitation and water systems

3 1832 Cholera epidemic leads to major water supply improvements

Philadelphia
HOSPITAL 1752
MEDICAL SCHOOL 1755

7 1873 School of nursing established at Bellevue Hospital. 15 schools by 1880, 432 by 1900

Baltimore
MEDICAL SCHOOL 1812

4 1840 College of Dental Surgery established

Williamsburg

1 1773 First publicly supported mental hospital

Early hospitals 1738-1791
Early medical schools 1765-1807

Charleston
HOSPITAL 1738

0   200

Miles

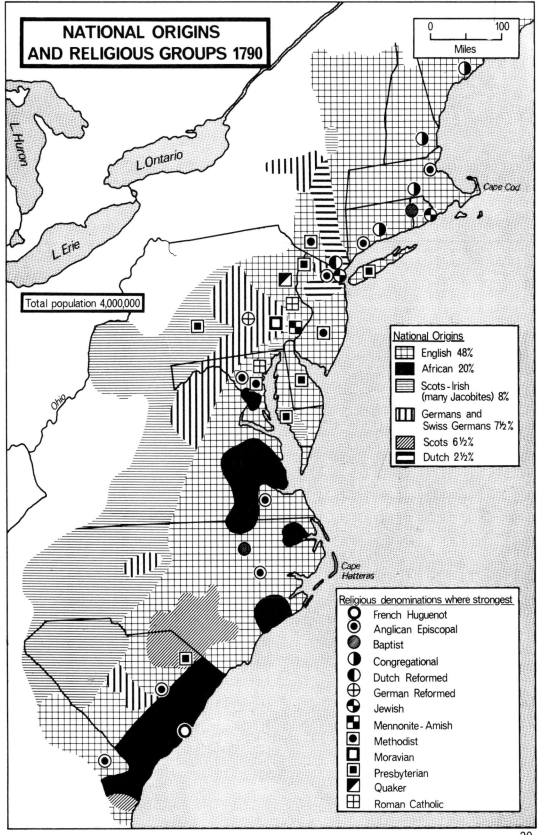

NATIONAL ORIGINS AND RELIGIOUS GROUPS 1790

0   100
Miles

L. Huron

L. Ontario

L. Erie

Cape Cod

Ohio

Total population 4,000,000

Cape Hatteras

National Origins
English	48%
African	20%
Scots-Irish (many Jacobites)	8%
Germans and Swiss Germans	7½%
Scots	6½%
Dutch	2½%

Religious denominations where strongest
◐	French Huguenot
◉	Anglican Episcopal
◕	Baptist
◑	Congregational
◑	Dutch Reformed
⊕	German Reformed
⊕	Jewish
▦	Mennonite-Amish
▣	Methodist
□	Moravian
■	Presbyterian
◪	Quaker
⊞	Roman Catholic

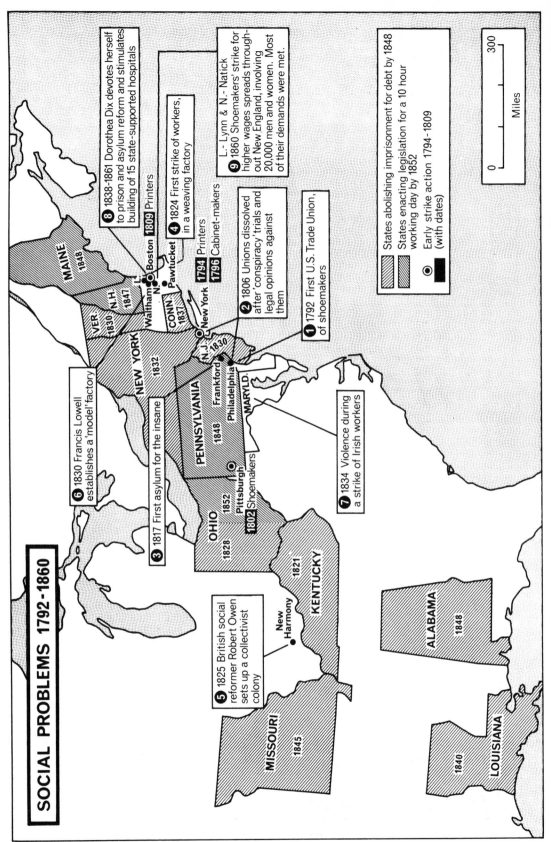

SOCIAL PROBLEMS 1792-1860

8 1838-1861 Dorothea Dix devotes herself to prison and asylum reform and stimulates building of 15 state-supported hospitals

1809 Printers

4 1824 First strike of workers, in a weaving factory

L.- Lynn & N.- Natick
9 1860 Shoemakers' strike for higher wages spreads through-out New England, involving 20,000 men and women. Most of their demands were met.

1794 Printers
1796 Cabinet-makers

2 1806 Unions dissolved after 'conspiracy' trials and legal opinions against them

1 1792 First U.S. Trade Union, of shoemakers

6 1830 Francis Lowell establishes a 'model' factory

3 1817 First asylum for the insane

7 1834 Violence during a strike of Irish workers

5 1825 British social reformer Robert Owen sets up a collectivist colony

MAINE 1848

VER. 1830

N.H. 1847

CONN. 1831

Boston
Waltham
Pawtucket
New York

NEW YORK 1832

N.J. 1830

Frankford
Philadelphia

PENNSYLVANIA 1848

MARYLD.

OHIO 1828   1852

Pittsburgh
1802 Shoemakers

New Harmony

KENTUCKY 1821

MISSOURI 1845

ALABAMA 1848

LOUISIANA 1840

States abolishing imprisonment for debt by 1848

States enacting legislation for a 10 hour working day by 1852

Early strike action 1794-1809 (with dates)

0   300
Miles

31

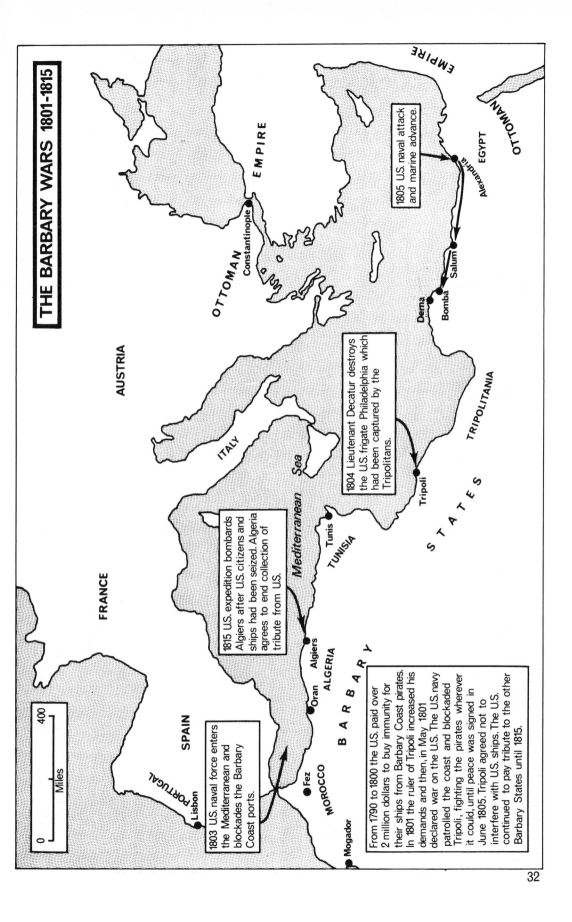

THE BARBARY WARS 1801-1815

OTTOMAN EMPIRE

AUSTRIA

FRANCE

SPAIN

PORTUGAL

Lisbon

ITALY

Mediterranean Sea

Constantinople

OTTOMAN EMPIRE

Alexandria

EGYPT

OTTOMAN

1805 U.S. naval attack and marine advance.

Salum

Bomba

Derna

TRIPOLITANIA

1804 Lieutenant Decatur destroys the U.S. frigate Philadelphia which had been captured by the Tripolitans.

Tripoli

S T A T E S

Tunis

TUNISIA

Algiers

ALGERIA

Oran

1815 U.S. expedition bombards Algiers after U.S. citizens and ships had been seized. Algeria agrees to end collection of tribute from U.S.

Fez

MOROCCO

B A R B A R Y

Mogador

1803 U.S. naval force enters the Mediterranean and blockades the Barbary Coast ports.

0   400

Miles

From 1790 to 1800 the U.S. paid over 2 million dollars to buy immunity for their ships from Barbary Coast pirates. In 1801 the ruler of Tripoli increased his demands and then, in May 1801 declared war on the U.S. The U.S. navy patrolled the coast and blockaded Tripoli, fighting the pirates wherever it could, until peace was signed in June 1805. Tripoli agreed not to interfere with U.S. ships. The U.S. continued to pay tribute to the other Barbary States until 1815.

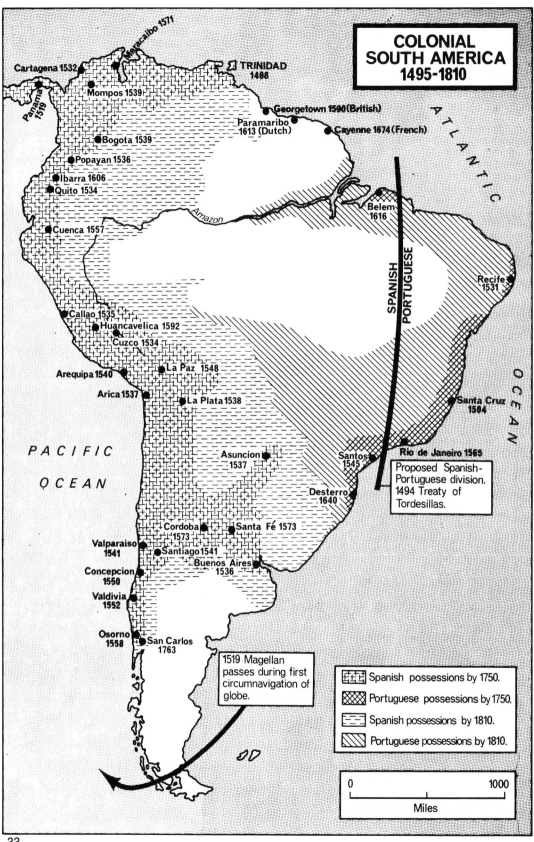

COLONIAL SOUTH AMERICA 1495-1810

Maracaibo 1571

Cartagena 1532

TRINIDAD 1498

Panama 1519

Mompos 1539

Georgetown 1590 (British)

Paramaribo 1613 (Dutch)

Cayenne 1674 (French)

Bogota 1539

Popayan 1536

Ibarra 1606

Quito 1534

Amazon

Belem 1616

SPANISH

PORTUGUESE

Cuenca 1557

Recife 1531

Callao 1535

Huancavelica 1592

Cuzco 1534

Arequipa 1540

La Paz 1548

Arica 1537

La Plata 1538

Santa Cruz 1504

PACIFIC

OCEAN

Asuncion 1537

Santos 1545

Rio de Janeiro 1565

ATLANTIC

OCEAN

Desterro 1640

Proposed Spanish-Portuguese division. 1494 Treaty of Tordesillas.

Cordoba 1573

Santa Fé 1573

Valparaiso 1541

Santiago 1541

Buenos Aires 1536

Concepcion 1550

Valdivia 1552

Osorno 1558

San Carlos 1763

1519 Magellan passes during first circumnavigation of globe.

Spanish possessions by 1750.

Portuguese possessions by 1750.

Spanish possessions by 1810.

Portuguese possessions by 1810.

0   1000
Miles

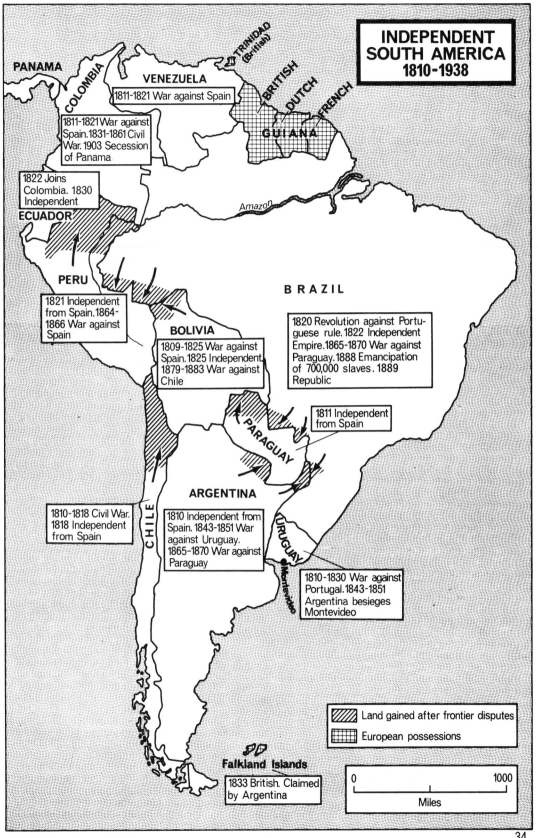

INDEPENDENT
SOUTH AMERICA
1810-1938

PANAMA

COLOMBIA

VENEZUELA

1811-1821 War against Spain

TRINIDAD (British)

BRITISH DUTCH FRENCH

GUIANA

1811-1821 War against Spain. 1831-1861 Civil War. 1903 Secession of Panama

1822 Joins Colombia. 1830 Independent

ECUADOR

Amazon

PERU

1821 Independent from Spain. 1864-1866 War against Spain

BRAZIL

BOLIVIA

1809-1825 War against Spain. 1825 Independent. 1879-1883 War against Chile

1820 Revolution against Portuguese rule. 1822 Independent Empire. 1865-1870 War against Paraguay. 1888 Emancipation of 700,000 slaves. 1889 Republic

1811 Independent from Spain

PARAGUAY

ARGENTINA

1810-1818 Civil War. 1818 Independent from Spain

CHILE

1810 Independent from Spain. 1843-1851 War against Uruguay. 1865-1870 War against Paraguay

URUGUAY

Montevideo

1810-1830 War against Portugal. 1843-1851 Argentina besieges Montevideo

Land gained after frontier disputes

European possessions

Falkland Islands

1833 British. Claimed by Argentina

0   1000

Miles

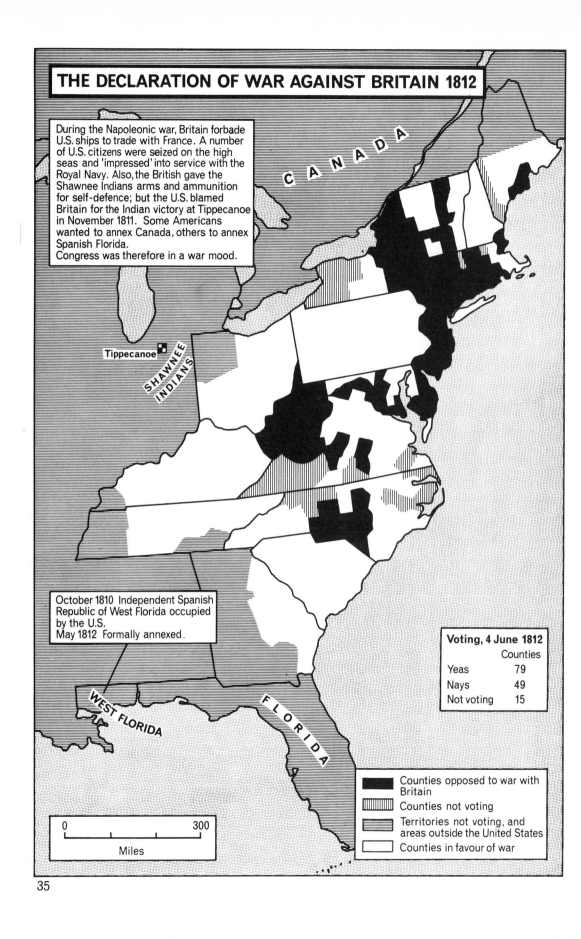

THE DECLARATION OF WAR AGAINST BRITAIN 1812

During the Napoleonic war, Britain forbade U.S. ships to trade with France. A number of U.S. citizens were seized on the high seas and 'impressed' into service with the Royal Navy. Also, the British gave the Shawnee Indians arms and ammunition for self-defence; but the U.S. blamed Britain for the Indian victory at Tippecanoe in November 1811. Some Americans wanted to annex Canada, others to annex Spanish Florida.
Congress was therefore in a war mood.

C A N A D A

Tippecanoe

SHAWNEE INDIANS

October 1810 Independent Spanish Republic of West Florida occupied by the U.S.
May 1812 Formally annexed.

WEST FLORIDA

FLORIDA

Voting, 4 June 1812

	Counties
Yeas	79
Nays	49
Not voting	15

■ Counties opposed to war with Britain

▥ Counties not voting

▤ Territories not voting, and areas outside the United States

☐ Counties in favour of war

0   300

Miles

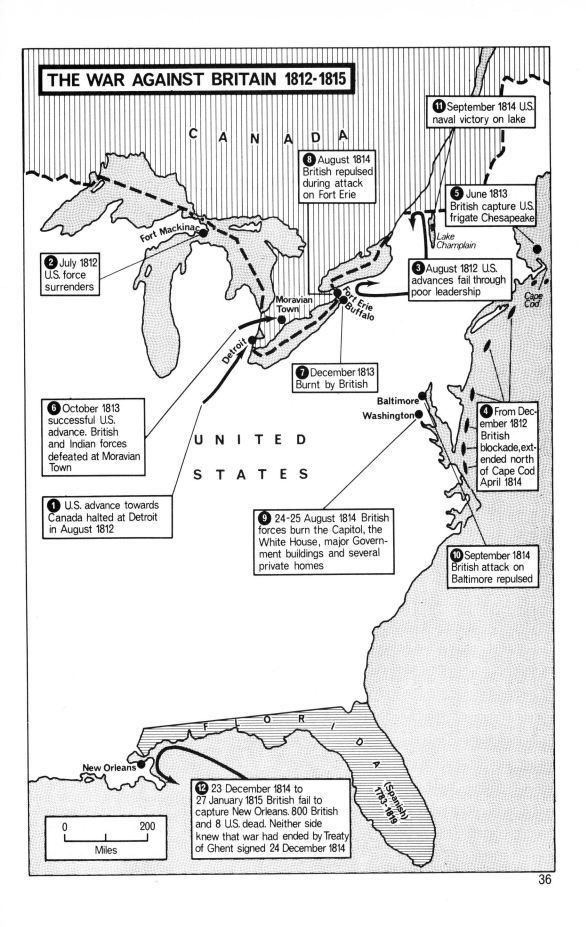

THE WAR AGAINST BRITAIN 1812-1815

C A N A D A

11 September 1814 U.S. naval victory on lake

8 August 1814 British repulsed during attack on Fort Erie

5 June 1813 British capture U.S. frigate Chesapeake

Fort Mackinac

2 July 1812 U.S. force surrenders

Lake Champlain

Cape Cod

3 August 1812 U.S. advances fail through poor leadership

Moravian Town

Fort Erie
Buffalo

Detroit

7 December 1813 Burnt by British

6 October 1813 successful U.S. advance. British and Indian forces defeated at Moravian Town

Baltimore
Washington

4 From December 1812 British blockade, extended north of Cape Cod April 1814

U N I T E D

S T A T E S

1 U.S. advance towards Canada halted at Detroit in August 1812

9 24-25 August 1814 British forces burn the Capitol, the White House, major Government buildings and several private homes

10 September 1814 British attack on Baltimore repulsed

F   L   O   R   I   D   A

(Spanish) 1783-1819

New Orleans

12 23 December 1814 to 27 January 1815 British fail to capture New Orleans. 800 British and 8 U.S. dead. Neither side knew that war had ended by Treaty of Ghent signed 24 December 1814

0   200
Miles

36

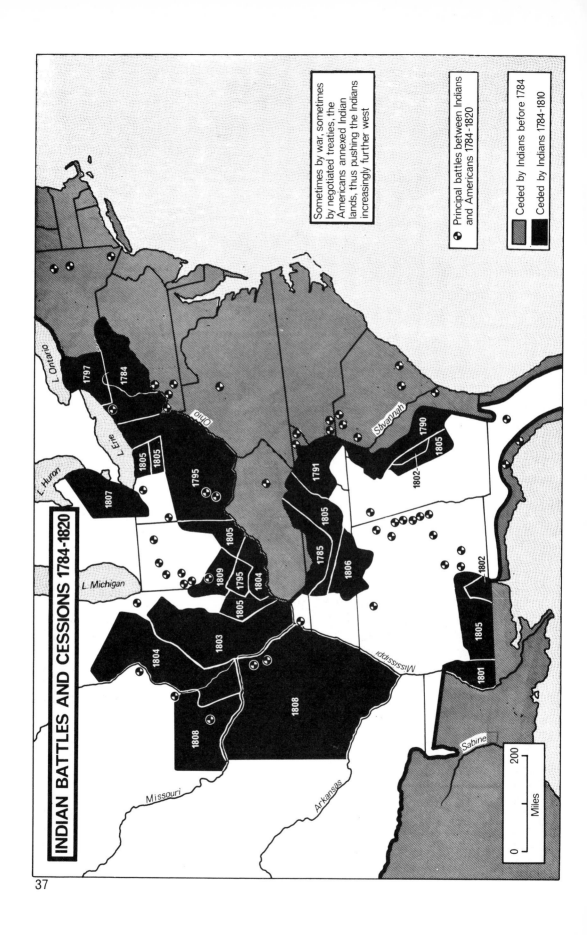

INDIAN BATTLES AND CESSIONS 1784-1820

Sometimes by war, sometimes by negotiated treaties, the Americans annexed Indian lands, thus pushing the Indians increasingly further west

⊕ Principal battles between Indians and Americans 1784-1820

Ceded by Indians before 1784

Ceded by Indians 1784-1810

L. Ontario

1797

1784

L. Erie

Ohio

1805

1805

L. Huron

1807

1795

L. Michigan

1805

1809

1795

1804

1805

1803

1804

1808

1808

Missouri

Arkansas

1791

1805

1785

1806

Savannah

1790

1805

1802

1802

1805

1801

Mississippi

Sabine

0   200

Miles

37

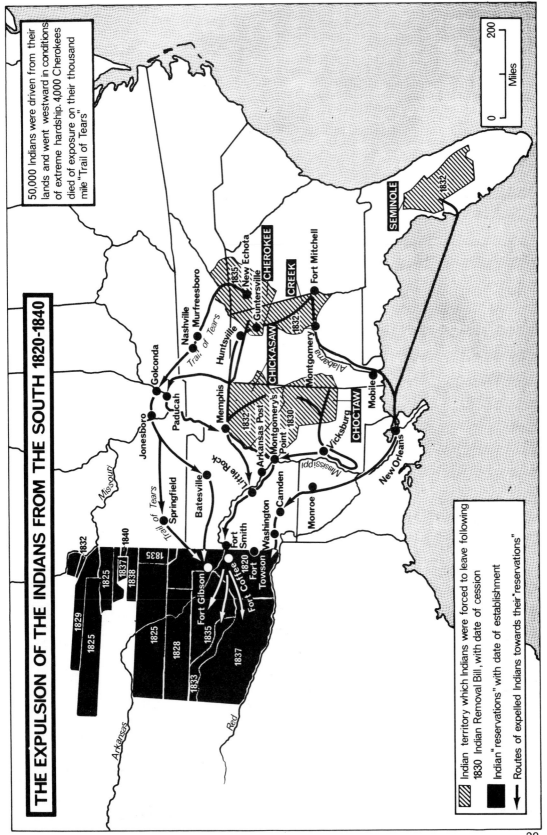

THE EXPULSION OF THE INDIANS FROM THE SOUTH 1820-1840

50,000 Indians were driven from their lands and went westward in conditions of extreme hardship. 4,000 Cherokees died of exposure on their thousand mile "Trail of Tears"

SEMINOLE
1832

CHEROKEE
New Echota
Guntersville
1835
CREEK
Fort Mitchell
1832

CHICKASAW
Montgomery
Alabama

CHOCTAW
Mobile

Murfreesboro
Nashville
Huntsville
Trail of Tears
Golconda
Paducah
Memphis
1832
Arkansas Post
Montgomery's
Point
1830
Vicksburg
Mississippi
New Orleans

Jonesboro
Springfield
Trail of Tears
Batesville
Little Rock
Camden
Monroe
Washington
Fort Smith

Missouri

1832
1829
1825
1825
1840
1837
1838
1835
1828
1825
1833
1835
Fort Gibson
Fort Coffee
Fort Towson
1820
Fort
1837

Arkansas
Red

Indian territory which Indians were forced to leave following 1830 Indian Removal Bill, with date of cession

Indian "reservations" with date of establishment

Routes of expelled Indians towards their "reservations"

0   200
Miles

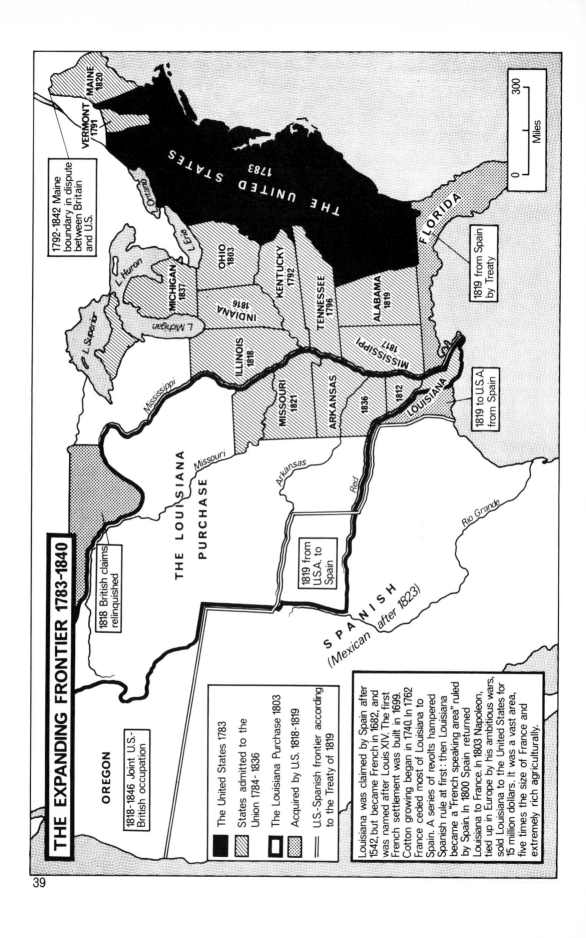

THE EXPANDING FRONTIER 1783-1840

0 ——— 300
Miles

1792-1842 Maine boundary in dispute between Britain and U.S.

MAINE 1820

VERMONT 1791

THE UNITED STATES 1783

L. Ontario

L. Erie

L. Huron

MICHIGAN 1837

L. Michigan

OHIO 1803

KENTUCKY 1792

TENNESSEE 1796

INDIANA 1816

ILLINOIS 1818

MISSOURI 1821

ARKANSAS 1836

ALABAMA 1819

MISSISSIPPI 1817

LOUISIANA 1812

FLORIDA

1819 from Spain by Treaty

1819 to U.S.A. from Spain

Mississippi

Missouri

Arkansas

Red

Rio Grande

THE LOUISIANA PURCHASE

1818 British claims relinquished

1819 from U.S.A. to Spain

SPANISH
(Mexican after 1823)

OREGON

1818-1846 Joint U.S.-British occupation

The United States 1783

States admitted to the Union 1784-1836

The Louisiana Purchase 1803

Acquired by U.S. 1818-1819

U.S.-Spanish frontier according to the Treaty of 1819

Louisiana was claimed by Spain after 1542, but became French in 1682, and was named after Louis XIV. The first French settlement was built in 1699. Cotton growing began in 1740. In 1762 France ceded most of Louisiana to Spain. A series of revolts hampered Spanish rule at first: then Louisiana became a "French speaking area" ruled by Spain. In 1800 Spain returned Louisiana to France. In 1803 Napoleon, tied up in Europe by his ambitious wars, sold Louisiana to the United States for 15 million dollars. It was a vast area, five times the size of France and extremely rich agriculturally.

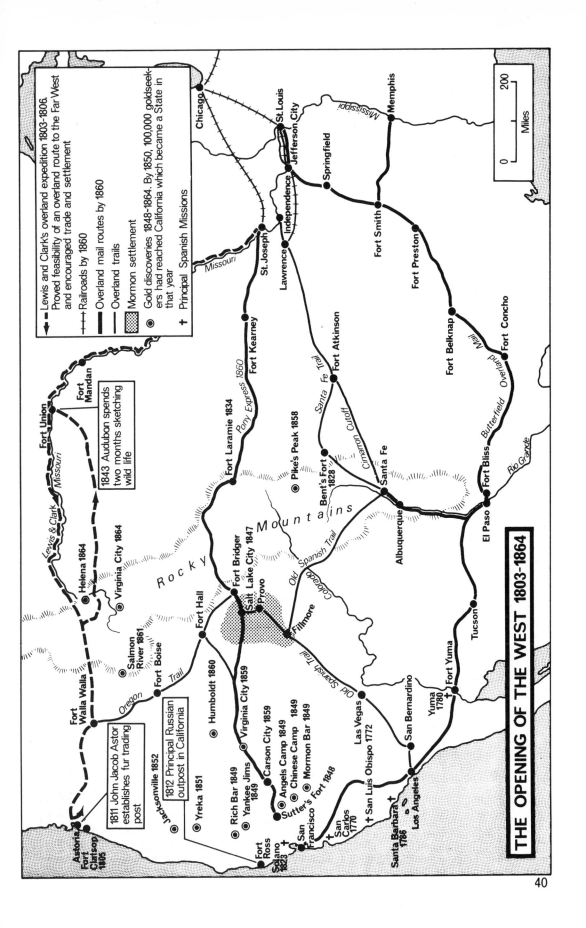

THE OPENING OF THE WEST 1803-1864

Legend:
- Lewis and Clark's overland expedition 1803-1806. Proved feasibility of an overland route to the Far West and encouraged trade and settlement
- Railroads by 1860
- Overland mail routes by 1860
- Overland trails
- Mormon settlement
- Gold discoveries 1848-1864. By 1850, 100,000 goldseekers had reached California which became a State in that year
- Principal Spanish Missions

Boxed annotations:
- 1843 Audubon spends two months sketching wild life
- 1811 John Jacob Astor establishes fur trading post
- 1812 Principal Russian outpost in California

Scale: 0 — 200 Miles

Labels (selection):
Chicago, St. Louis, Jefferson City, Springfield, Memphis, Independence, Lawrence, St. Joseph, Fort Smith, Fort Preston, Missouri, Mississippi, Fort Kearney, Fort Atkinson, Fort Belknap, Fort Concho, Pony Express 1860, Santa Fe Trail, Cimarron Cutoff, Santa Fe, Bent's Fort 1828, Pike's Peak 1858, Fort Laramie 1834, Fort Mandan, Fort Union, Lewis & Clark, Missouri, Helena 1864, Virginia City 1864, Rocky Mountains, Fort Bridger, Salt Lake City 1847, Provo, Fort Hall, Fort Boise, Salmon River 1861, Fort Walla Walla, Oregon Trail, Astoria Fort Clatsop 1805, Jacksonville 1852, Yreka 1851, Rich Bar 1849, Yankee Jims 1849, Carson City 1859, Virginia City 1859, Humboldt 1860, Angels Camp 1849, Chinese Camp 1849, Mormon Bar 1849, Sutter's Fort 1848, San Francisco, Solano 1823, San Carlos 1770, Santa Barbara 1786, Los Angeles, San Luis Obispo 1772, San Bernardino, Las Vegas, Yuma 1780, Fort Yuma, Tucson, San Diego, Fillmore, Fort Bliss, El Paso, Albuquerque, Rio Grande, Colorado, Old Spanish Trail, Butterfield Overland Mail

40

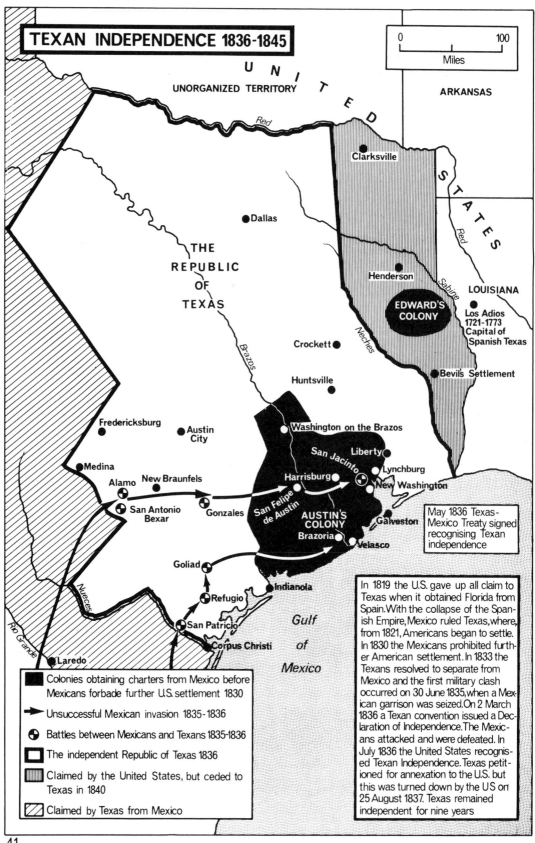

TEXAN INDEPENDENCE 1836-1845

0   100
Miles

U N I T E D
UNORGANIZED TERRITORY   ARKANSAS

S T A T E S

Red

●Clarksville

Red

LOUISIANA

●Dallas

THE
REPUBLIC
OF
TEXAS

Henderson
●

EDWARD'S
COLONY

Los Adios
1721-1773
Capital of
Spanish Texas

Crockett●

Huntsville
●

Bevils Settlement
●

Neches

Brazos

Fredericksburg
●

Austin
City
●

Washington on the Brazos
●

San Jacinto

Liberty●
Lynchburg
●

●Medina
New Braunfels
Harrisburg●
●New Washington

Alamo
⊕

San Felipe
de Austin

⊕
Gonzales

AUSTIN'S
COLONY

Galveston
●

San Antonio
Bexar
⊕

Brazoria
●

Velasco
●

May 1836 Texas-
Mexico Treaty signed
recognising Texan
independence

Goliad
⊕

Indianola
●

Gulf
of
Mexico

Refugio
⊕

San Patricio
⊕
Corpus Christi
●

Nueces

Rio Grande

●Laredo

In 1819 the U.S. gave up all claim to
Texas when it obtained Florida from
Spain. With the collapse of the Spanish Empire, Mexico ruled Texas, where,
from 1821, Americans began to settle.
In 1830 the Mexicans prohibited further American settlement. In 1833 the
Texans resolved to separate from
Mexico and the first military clash
occurred on 30 June 1835, when a Mexican garrison was seized. On 2 March
1836 a Texan convention issued a Declaration of Independence. The Mexicans attacked and were defeated. In
July 1836 the United States recognised Texan Independence. Texas petit-
ioned for annexation to the U.S. but
this was turned down by the US on
25 August 1837. Texas remained
independent for nine years

■ Colonies obtaining charters from Mexico before
Mexicans forbade further U.S. settlement 1830

→ Unsuccessful Mexican invasion 1835-1836

⊕ Battles between Mexicans and Texans 1835-1836

□ The independent Republic of Texas 1836

▥ Claimed by the United States, but ceded to
Texas in 1840

▨ Claimed by Texas from Mexico

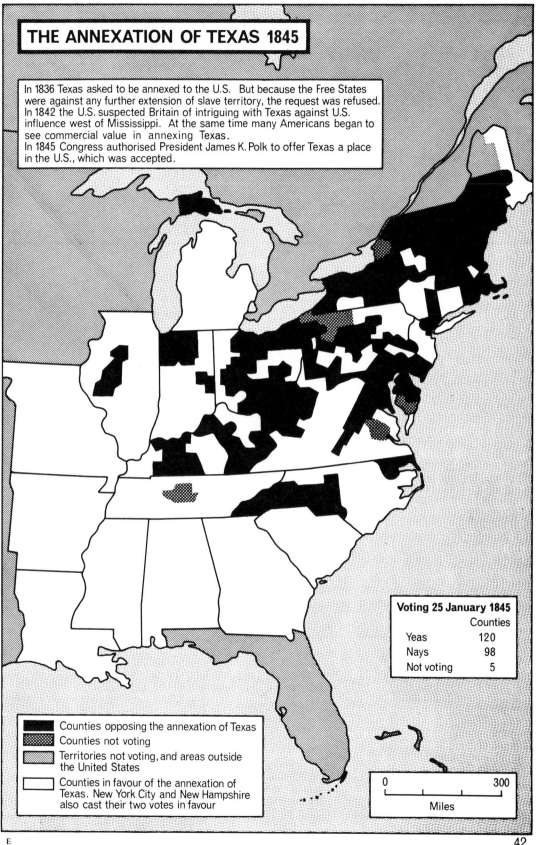

THE ANNEXATION OF TEXAS 1845

In 1836 Texas asked to be annexed to the U.S. But because the Free States were against any further extension of slave territory, the request was refused. In 1842 the U.S. suspected Britain of intriguing with Texas against U.S. influence west of Mississippi. At the same time many Americans began to see commercial value in annexing Texas.
In 1845 Congress authorised President James K. Polk to offer Texas a place in the U.S., which was accepted.

Voting 25 January 1845

	Counties
Yeas	120
Nays	98
Not voting	5

■ Counties opposing the annexation of Texas
▓ Counties not voting
▨ Territories not voting, and areas outside the United States
□ Counties in favour of the annexation of Texas. New York City and New Hampshire also cast their two votes in favour

0 ⊢—————⊣ 300
Miles

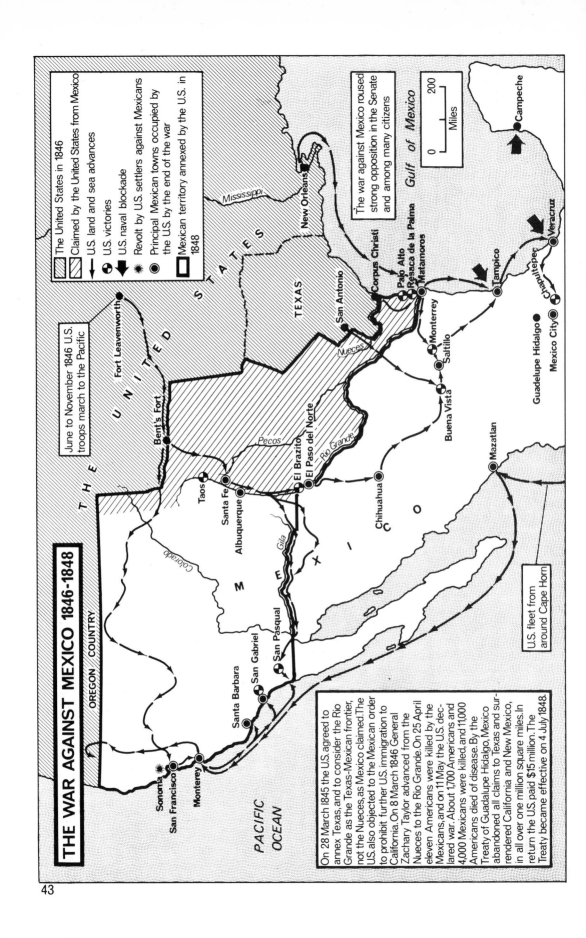

THE WAR AGAINST MEXICO 1846-1848

OREGON COUNTRY

THE UNITED STATES

TEXAS

PACIFIC OCEAN

M E X I C O

Gulf of Mexico

Legend:
- The United States in 1846
- Claimed by the United States from Mexico
- → U.S. land and sea advances
- ⚫ U.S. victories
- ⬇ U.S. naval blockade
- ✳ Revolt by U.S. settlers against Mexicans
- ⦿ Principal Mexican towns occupied by the U.S. by the end of the war
- ▢ Mexican territory annexed by the U.S. in 1848

June to November 1846 U.S. troops march to the Pacific

The war against Mexico roused strong opposition in the Senate and among many citizens

0   200
Miles

U.S. fleet from around Cape Horn

Places labelled:
Fort Leavenworth, Bent's Fort, Taos, Santa Fe, Albuquerque, El Brazito, El Paso del Norte, Chihuahua, Mazatlan, San Pasqual, San Gabriel, Santa Barbara, Monterey, San Francisco, Sonoma, San Antonio, New Orleans, Corpus Christi, Palo Alto, Resaca de la Palma, Matamoros, Monterrey, Saltillo, Buena Vista, Guadelupe Hidalgo, Mexico City, Chapultepec, Tampico, Veracruz, Campeche

Mississippi, Nueces, Pecos, Rio Grande, Gila, Colorado

On 28 March 1845 the U.S. agreed to annex Texas, and to consider the Rio Grande as the Texas-Mexican frontier, not the Nueces, as Mexico claimed. The U.S. also objected to the Mexican order to prohibit further U.S. immigration to California. On 8 March 1846 General Zachary Taylor advanced from the Nueces to the Rio Grande. On 25 April eleven Americans were killed by the Mexicans, and on 11 May the U.S. declared war. About 1,700 Americans and 4,000 Mexicans were killed, and 11,000 Americans died of disease. By the Treaty of Guadalupe Hidalgo, Mexico abandoned all claims to Texas and surrendered California and New Mexico, in all over one million square miles. In return the U.S. paid $15 million. The Treaty became effective on 4 July 1848.

43

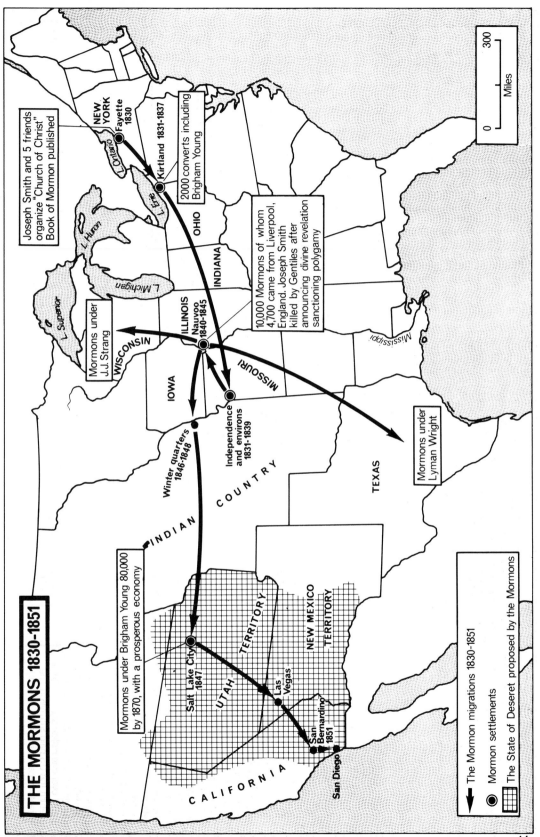

THE MORMONS 1830-1851

Joseph Smith and 5 friends organize "Church of Christ" Book of Mormon published

NEW YORK
Fayette 1830

Kirtland 1831-1837

2000 converts including Brigham Young

OHIO

INDIANA

10,000 Mormons of whom 4,700 came from Liverpool, England. Joseph Smith killed by Gentiles after announcing divine revelation sanctioning polygamy

L. Huron

L. Michigan

L. Superior

ILLINOIS
Nauvoo 1840-1845

WISCONSIN

Mormons under J.J. Strang

IOWA

MISSOURI

Mississippi

Winter quarters 1846-1848

Independence and environs 1831-1839

INDIAN COUNTRY

TEXAS

Mormons under Lyman Wright

Mormons under Brigham Young 80,000 by 1870, with a prosperous economy

Salt Lake City 1847

UTAH TERRITORY

NEW MEXICO TERRITORY

Las Vegas

San Bernardino 1851

San Diego

CALIFORNIA

300
0
Miles

The Mormon migrations 1830-1851
Mormon settlements
The State of Deseret proposed by the Mormons

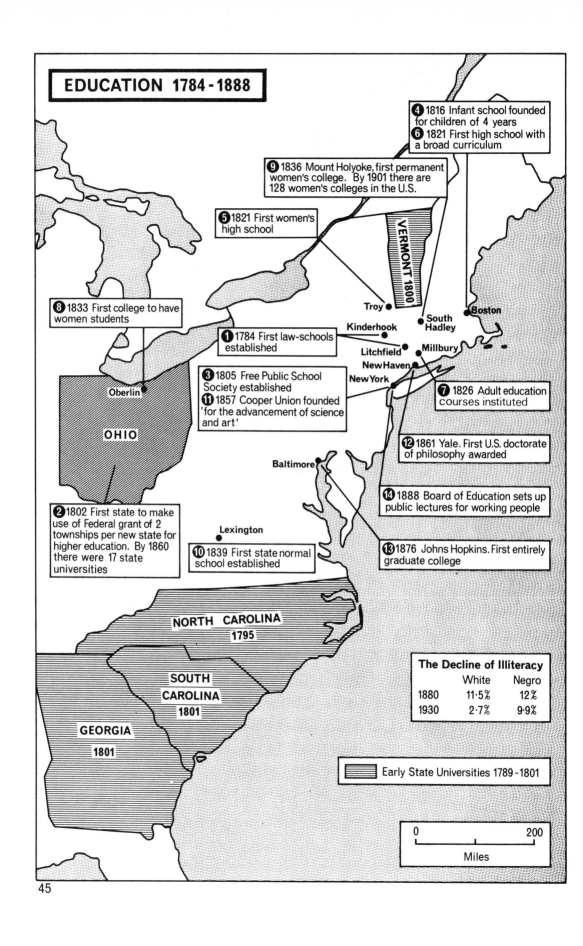

EDUCATION 1784-1888

4 1816 Infant school founded for children of 4 years

6 1821 First high school with a broad curriculum

9 1836 Mount Holyoke, first permanent women's college. By 1901 there are 128 women's colleges in the U.S.

5 1821 First women's high school

VERMONT 1800

8 1833 First college to have women students

1 1784 First law-schools established

3 1805 Free Public School Society established

11 1857 Cooper Union founded 'for the advancement of science and art'

OHIO

Oberlin

Troy

Kinderhook

South Hadley

Boston

Litchfield

Millbury

New Haven

New York

7 1826 Adult education courses instituted

12 1861 Yale. First U.S. doctorate of philosophy awarded

Baltimore

14 1888 Board of Education sets up public lectures for working people

2 1802 First state to make use of Federal grant of 2 townships per new state for higher education. By 1860 there were 17 state universities

Lexington

10 1839 First state normal school established

13 1876 Johns Hopkins. First entirely graduate college

NORTH CAROLINA
1795

SOUTH CAROLINA
1801

GEORGIA
1801

The Decline of Illiteracy		
	White	Negro
1880	11·5%	12%
1930	2·7%	9·9%

Early State Universities 1789-1801

0   200
Miles

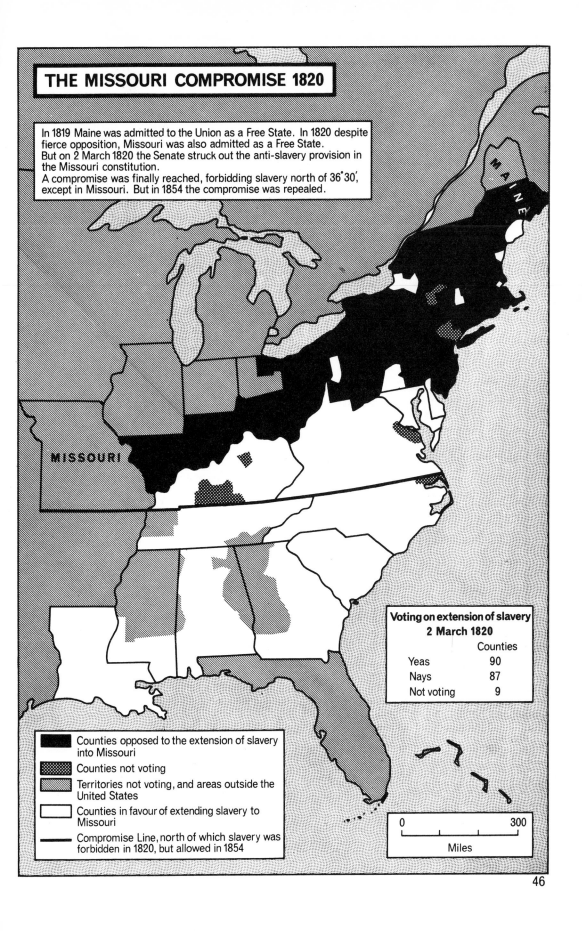

THE MISSOURI COMPROMISE 1820

In 1819 Maine was admitted to the Union as a Free State. In 1820 despite fierce opposition, Missouri was also admitted as a Free State.
But on 2 March 1820 the Senate struck out the anti-slavery provision in the Missouri constitution.
A compromise was finally reached, forbidding slavery north of 36°30′, except in Missouri. But in 1854 the compromise was repealed.

MAINE

MISSOURI

**Voting on extension of slavery
2 March 1820**

	Counties
Yeas	90
Nays	87
Not voting	9

Counties opposed to the extension of slavery into Missouri

Counties not voting

Territories not voting, and areas outside the United States

Counties in favour of extending slavery to Missouri

Compromise Line, north of which slavery was forbidden in 1820, but allowed in 1854

0   300

Miles

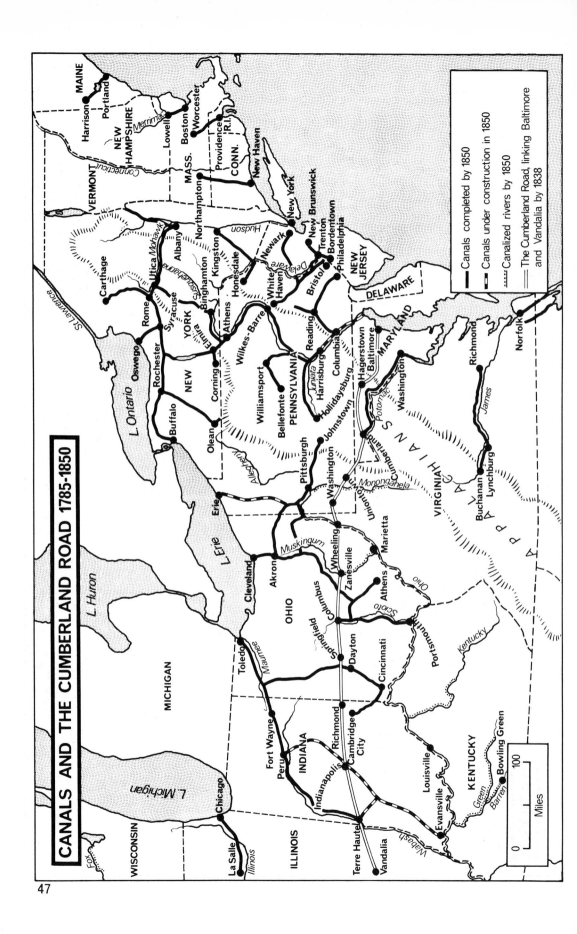

CANALS AND THE CUMBERLAND ROAD 1785-1850

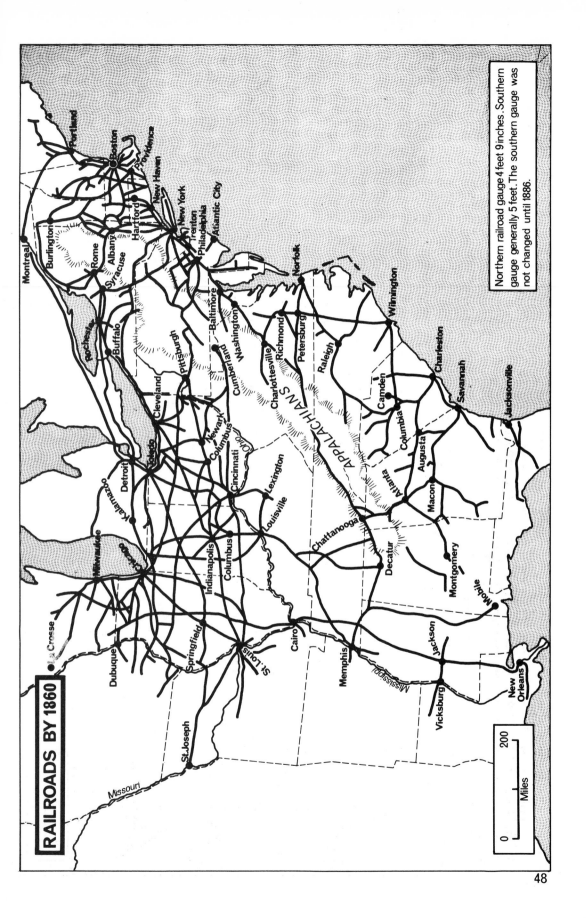

RAILROADS BY 1860

Northern railroad gauge 4 feet 9 inches. Southern gauge generally 5 feet. The southern gauge was not changed until 1886.

Montreal

Portland

Burlington

Boston

Providence

New Haven

Rome

Albany

Syracuse

Hartford

New York

Trenton

Philadelphia

Atlantic City

Buffalo

Pittsburgh

Baltimore

Washington

Cumberland

Charlottesville

Richmond

Norfolk

Petersburg

Raleigh

Wilmington

Cleveland

Newark

Columbus

Ohio

Cincinnati

Lexington

Camden

Charleston

Columbia

Augusta

Savannah

Detroit

Kalamazoo

Louisville

Atlanta

Macon

Jacksonville

Milwaukee

Toledo

Indianapolis

Columbus

Chattanooga

Decatur

Montgomery

Mobile

La Crosse

Dubuque

Springfield

St. Louis

Cairo

Memphis

Jackson

Vicksburg

New Orleans

St. Joseph

Missouri

Mississippi

APPALACHIANS

200

0

Miles

48

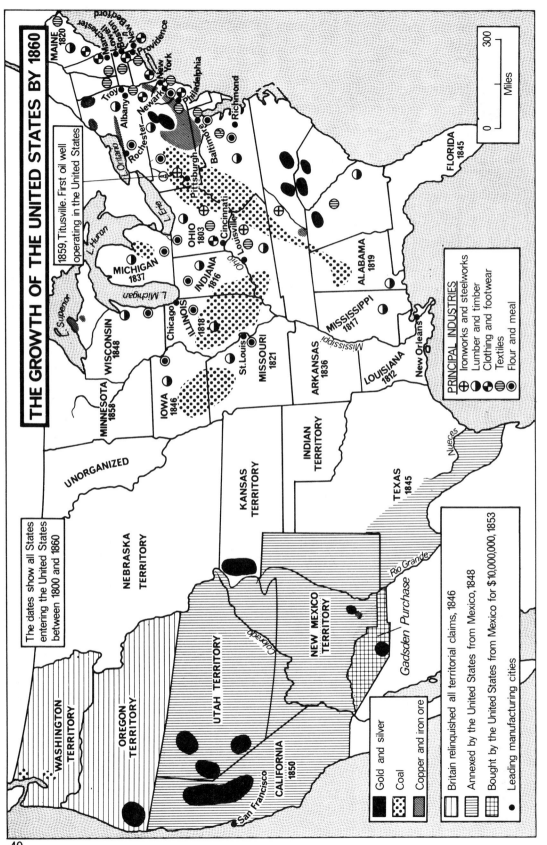

THE GROWTH OF THE UNITED STATES BY 1860

1859, Titusville. First oil well operating in the United States

The dates show all States entering the United States between 1800 and 1860

PRINCIPAL INDUSTRIES
Ironworks and steelworks
Lumber and timber
Clothing and footwear
Textiles
Flour and meal

Gold and silver
Coal
Copper and iron ore

Britain relinquished all territorial claims, 1846
Annexed by the United States from Mexico, 1848
Bought by the United States from Mexico for $10,000,000, 1853
Leading manufacturing cities

MAINE 1820
New Bedford
Troy
Albany
Newark
Philadelphia
Richmond
Baltimore
Rochester
Pittsburgh
OHIO 1803
Cincinnati
Louisville
MICHIGAN 1837
INDIANA 1816
ILLINOIS 1818
Chicago
ALABAMA 1819
MISSISSIPPI 1817
St.Louis
MISSOURI 1821
ARKANSAS 1836
LOUISIANA 1812
New Orleans
WISCONSIN 1848
MINNESOTA 1858
IOWA 1846

L. Ontario
L. Erie
L. Huron
L. Michigan
L. Superior
Ohio
Mississippi
Nueces
Rio Grande
Colorado

UNORGANIZED
NEBRASKA TERRITORY
KANSAS TERRITORY
INDIAN TERRITORY
TEXAS 1845
NEW MEXICO TERRITORY
UTAH TERRITORY
CALIFORNIA 1850
OREGON TERRITORY
WASHINGTON TERRITORY
San Francisco
Gadsden Purchase

FLORIDA 1845

300
0
Miles

49

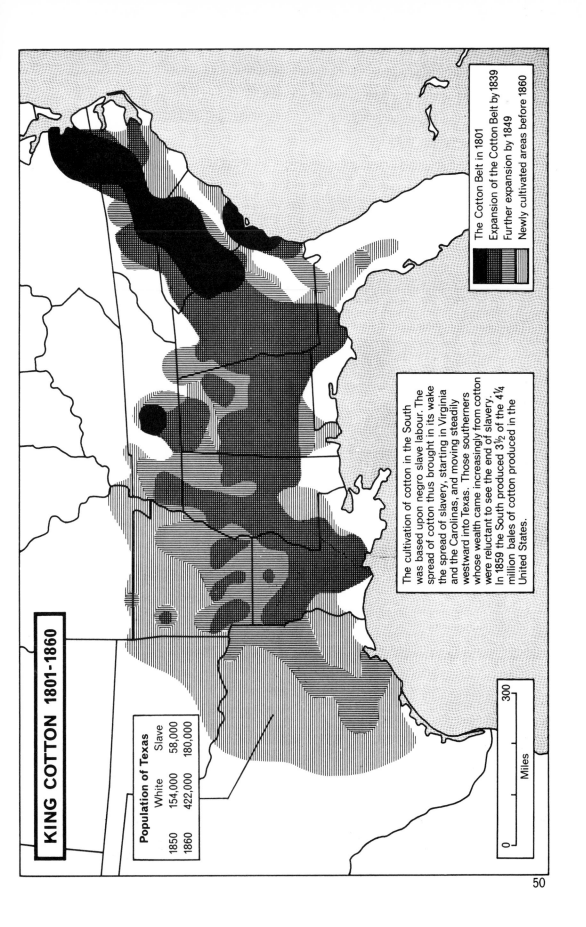

KING COTTON 1801-1860

Population of Texas

	White	Slave
1850	154,000	58,000
1860	422,000	180,000

The cultivation of cotton in the South was based upon negro slave labour. The spread of cotton thus brought in its wake the spread of slavery, starting in Virginia and the Carolinas, and moving steadily westward into Texas. Those southerners whose wealth came increasingly from cotton were reluctant to see the end of slavery. In 1859 the South produced 3½ of the 4¼ million bales of cotton produced in the United States.

The Cotton Belt in 1801
Expansion of the Cotton Belt by 1839
Further expansion by 1849
Newly cultivated areas before 1860

0   300
Miles

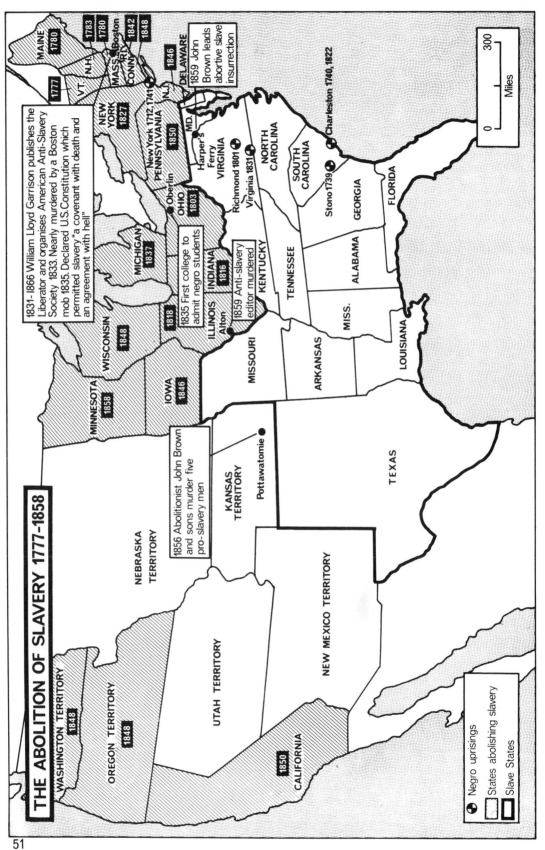

THE ABOLITION OF SLAVERY 1777-1858

1831- 1866 William Lloyd Garrison publishes the Liberator and organises American Anti-Slavery Society 1833. Nearly murdered by a Boston mob 1835. Declared U.S.Constitution which permitted slavery "a covenant with death and an agreement with hell"

1835 First college to admit negro students

1859 Anti-slavery editor murdered

1859 John Brown leads abortive slave insurrection

1856 Abolitionist John Brown and sons murder five pro-slavery men

MAINE 1780

N.H. 1783

VT. 1777

MASS. Boston 1780

R.I. 1842

CONN. 1848

DELAWARE 1846

NEW YORK 1827

New York 1712, 1741

N.J.

PENNSYLVANIA 1850

MD.

Harper's Ferry

VIRGINIA

Richmond 1801

Virginia 1831

NORTH CAROLINA

SOUTH CAROLINA

Stono 1739

Charleston 1740, 1822

GEORGIA

FLORIDA

ALABAMA

MISS.

LOUISIANA

ARKANSAS

TENNESSEE

KENTUCKY

Oberlin

OHIO 1803

INDIANA 1816

ILLINOIS 1818

Alton

MICHIGAN 1837

WISCONSIN 1848

IOWA 1846

MINNESOTA 1858

MISSOURI

Pottawatomie

KANSAS TERRITORY

TEXAS

NEBRASKA TERRITORY

NEW MEXICO TERRITORY

UTAH TERRITORY

OREGON TERRITORY 1848

WASHINGTON TERRITORY 1848

CALIFORNIA 1850

0 ___ 300

Miles

- Negro uprisings
- States abolishing slavery
- Slave States

51

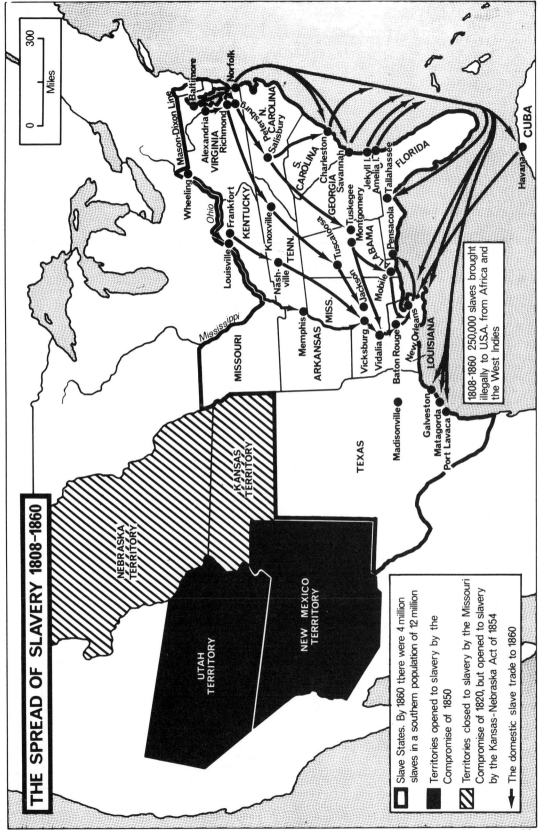

THE SPREAD OF SLAVERY 1808-1860

300 | Miles | 0

Mason-Dixon Line

Baltimore
Norfolk
Alexandria
VIRGINIA
Richmond
Petersburg
N. CAROLINA
Salisbury
S. CAROLINA
Charleston
Savannah
GEORGIA
Tuskegee
Jekyll I.
Amelia I.
FLORIDA
Pensacola
Tallahassee
Wheeling
Ohio
Frankfort
Louisville
KENTUCKY
Knoxville
Nash-ville
TENN.
Montgomery
ALABAMA
Mobile
Jackson
Memphis
MISS.
ARKANSAS
Vicksburg
Vidalia
Baton Rouge
New Orleans
LOUISIANA
Mississippi
MISSOURI
CUBA
Havana

1808-1860 250,000 slaves brought illegally to U.S.A. from Africa and the West Indies

Madisonville
Galveston
Matagorda
Port Lavaca
TEXAS

KANSAS TERRITORY

NEBRASKA TERRITORY

UTAH TERRITORY

NEW MEXICO TERRITORY

☐ Slave States. By 1860 there were 4 million slaves in a southern population of 12 million

■ Territories opened to slavery by the Compromise of 1850

▨ Territories closed to slavery by the Missouri Compromise of 1820, but opened to slavery by the Kansas-Nebraska Act of 1854

→ The domestic slave trade to 1860

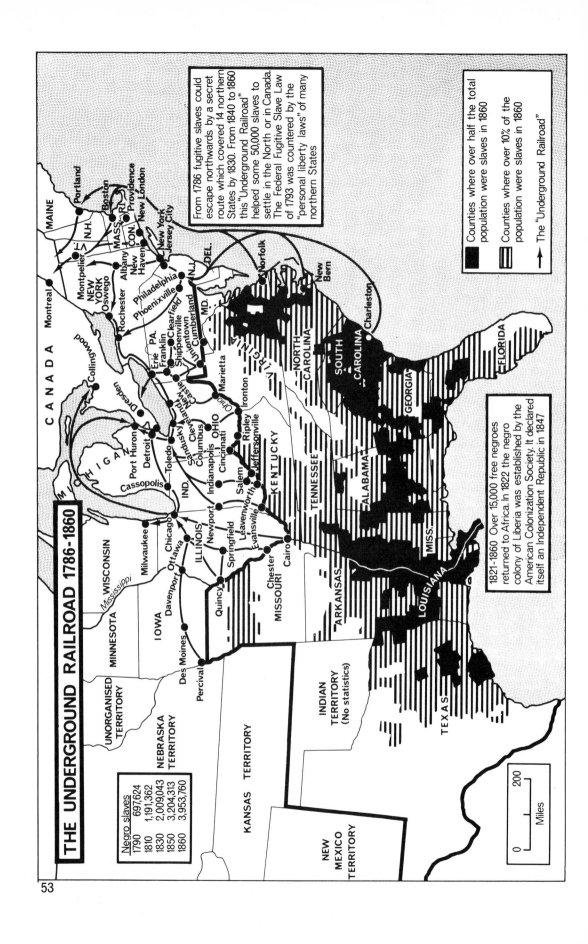

THE UNDERGROUND RAILROAD 1786-1860

Negro slaves
1790	697,624
1810	1,191,362
1830	2,009,043
1850	3,204,313
1860	3,953,760

From 1786 fugitive slaves could escape northwards by a secret route which covered 14 northern States by 1830. From 1840 to 1860 this "Underground Railroad" helped some 50,000 slaves to settle in the North or in Canada. The Federal Fugitive Slave Law of 1793 was countered by the "personal liberty laws" of many northern States

1821-1860 Over 15,000 free negroes returned to Africa. In 1822 the negro colony of Liberia was established by the American Colonization Society. It declared itself an Independent Republic in 1847

■ Counties where over half the total population were slaves in 1860

▥ Counties where over 10% of the population were slaves in 1860

→ The "Underground Railroad"

CANADA

Montreal

Collingwood

MICHIGAN
Port Huron
Detroit
Dresden
Toledo
Cassopolis

WISCONSIN
Milwaukee

MINNESOTA

UNORGANISED TERRITORY

NEBRASKA TERRITORY

IOWA
Davenport
Des Moines
Percival

ILLINOIS
Ottawa
Chicago
Quincy
Springfield

Mississippi

MAINE
Portland
N.H.
MASS.
Boston
Providence
New London
CON.
R.I.
New York
New Jersey City
N.J.
New Haven
Albany
Montpelier
NEW YORK
Rochester
Oswego
Philadelphia
Phoenixville
DEL.
MD.
Clearfield
Shippenville
Uniontown
Cumberland
Erie
PA.
Franklin

Norfolk
New Bern

VIRGINIA
NORTH CAROLINA
SOUTH CAROLINA
Charleston
GEORGIA
FLORIDA

Marietta
Ironton
OHIO
Cleveland
Sandusky
Columbus
Cincinnati
Ripley
Jeffersonville
Salem
Newport
IND.
Indianapolis
Leavenworth
Evansville

KENTUCKY
TENNESSEE
ALABAMA
MISS.

Chester
Cairo
MISSOURI
ARKANSAS
LOUISIANA

KANSAS TERRITORY

INDIAN TERRITORY
(No statistics)

TEXAS

NEW MEXICO TERRITORY

0   200
Miles

53

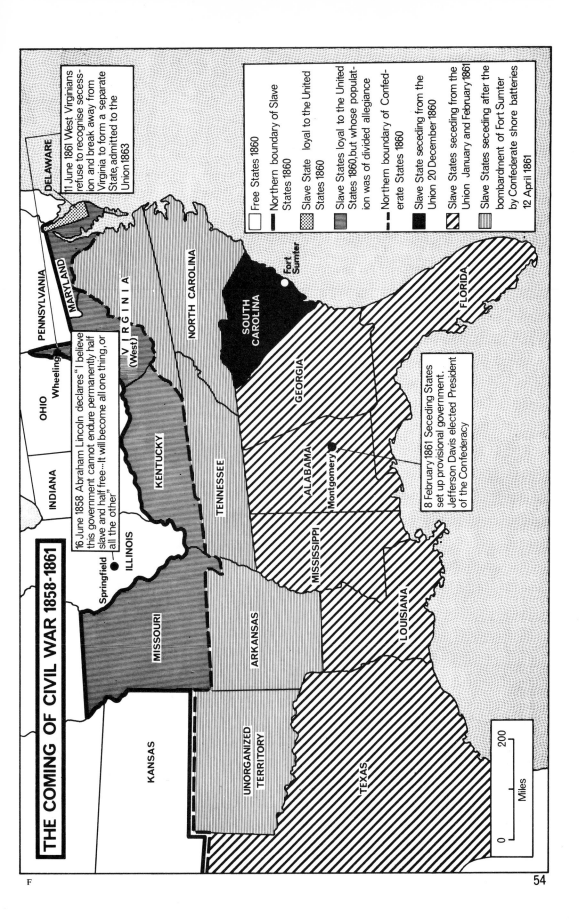

THE COMING OF CIVIL WAR 1858-1861

11 June 1861 West Virginians refuse to recognise secession and break away from Virginia to form a separate State, admitted to the Union 1863

Key:

	Free States 1860
	Northern boundary of Slave States 1860
	Slave State loyal to the United States 1860
	Slave States loyal to the United States 1860, but whose population was of divided allegiance
	Northern boundary of Confederate States 1860
	Slave State seceding from the Union 20 December 1860
	Slave States seceding from the Union January and February 1861
	Slave States seceding after the bombardment of Fort Sumter by Confederate shore batteries 12 April 1861

16 June 1858 Abraham Lincoln declares "I believe this government cannot endure permanently half slave and half free...It will become all one thing, or all the other"

8 February 1861 Seceding States set up provisional government. Jefferson Davis elected President of the Confederacy

DELAWARE

PENNSYLVANIA

MARYLAND

OHIO
Wheeling

INDIANA

ILLINOIS
Springfield

VIRGINIA

VIRGINIA (West)

NORTH CAROLINA

SOUTH CAROLINA

Fort Sumter

GEORGIA

FLORIDA

KENTUCKY

TENNESSEE

ALABAMA

Montgomery

MISSISSIPPI

MISSOURI

ARKANSAS

LOUISIANA

KANSAS

UNORGANIZED TERRITORY

TEXAS

Miles
0   200

F

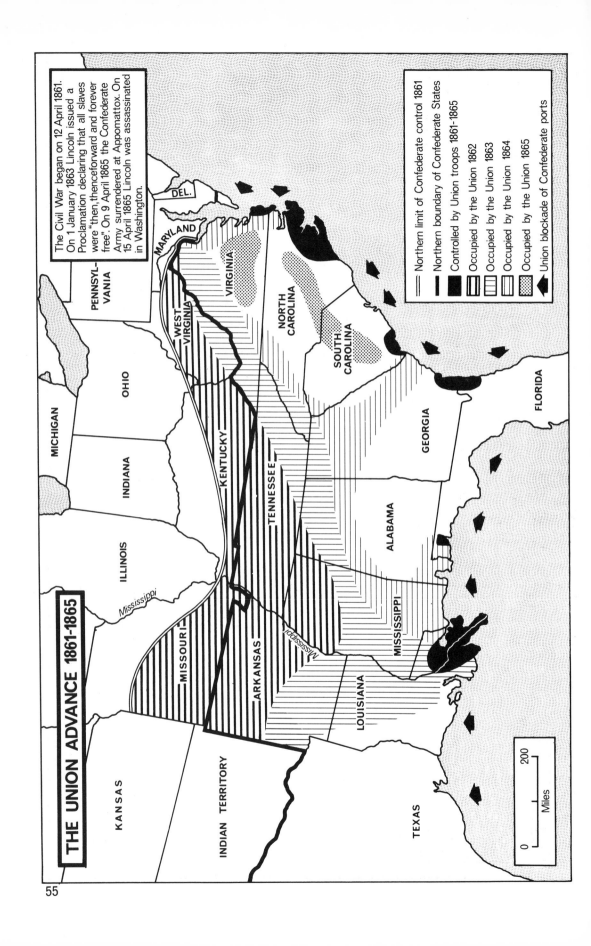

THE UNION ADVANCE 1861-1865

The Civil War began on 12 April 1861. On 1 January 1863 Lincoln issued a Proclamation declaring that all slaves were "then, thenceforward and forever free". On 9 April 1865 the Confederate Army surrendered at Appomattox. On 15 April 1865 Lincoln was assassinated in Washington.

Northern limit of Confederate control 1861

Northern boundary of Confederate States

Controlled by Union troops 1861-1865

Occupied by the Union 1862

Occupied by the Union 1863

Occupied by the Union 1864

Occupied by the Union 1865

Union blockade of Confederate ports

MICHIGAN

PENNSYL-VANIA

DEL.

MARYLAND

WEST VIRGINIA

VIRGINIA

NORTH CAROLINA

SOUTH CAROLINA

OHIO

INDIANA

ILLINOIS

KENTUCKY

TENNESSEE

GEORGIA

ALABAMA

MISSISSIPPI

LOUISIANA

ARKANSAS

MISSOURI

KANSAS

INDIAN TERRITORY

TEXAS

FLORIDA

Mississippi

Mississippi

0   200

Miles

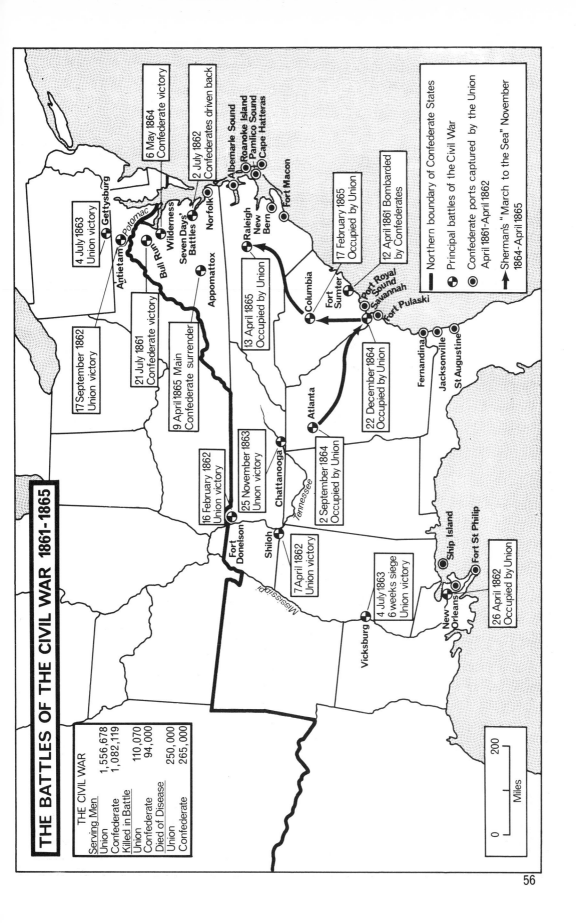

THE BATTLES OF THE CIVIL WAR 1861-1865

THE CIVIL WAR	
Serving Men	
Union	1,556,678
Confederate	1,082,119
Killed in Battle	
Union	110,070
Confederate	94,000
Died of Disease	
Union	250,000
Confederate	265,000

4 July 1863
Union victory
Gettysburg

17 September 1862
Union victory
Antietam

21 July 1861
Confederate victory
Bull Run

6 May 1864
Confederate victory
Wilderness

2 July 1862
Confederates driven back
**Seven Days'
Battles**

9 April 1865 Main
Confederate surrender
Appomattox

Norfolk

Albemarle Sound
Roanoke Island
Pamlico Sound
Cape Hatteras
Fort Macon

Raleigh
**New
Bern**

13 April 1865
Occupied by Union

17 February 1865
Occupied by Union
Columbia

**Fort
Sumter**

12 April 1861 Bombarded
by Confederates

**Fort Royal
Sound**
Savannah
Fort Pulaski

22 December 1864
Occupied by Union

Fernandina
Jacksonville
St Augustine

2 September 1864
Occupied by Union
Atlanta

16 February 1862
Union victory
**Fort
Donelson**

25 November 1863
Union victory
Chattanooga

7 April 1862
Union victory
Shiloh

Tennessee

Mississippi

4 July 1863
6 weeks siege
Union victory
Vicksburg

Ship Island
Fort St Philip

**New
Orleans**

26 April 1862
Occupied by Union

Potomac

— Northern boundary of Confederate States

⊕ Principal battles of the Civil War

◉ Confederate ports captured by the Union
April 1861–April 1862

↑ Sherman's "March to the Sea" November
1864–April 1865

0   200
Miles

56

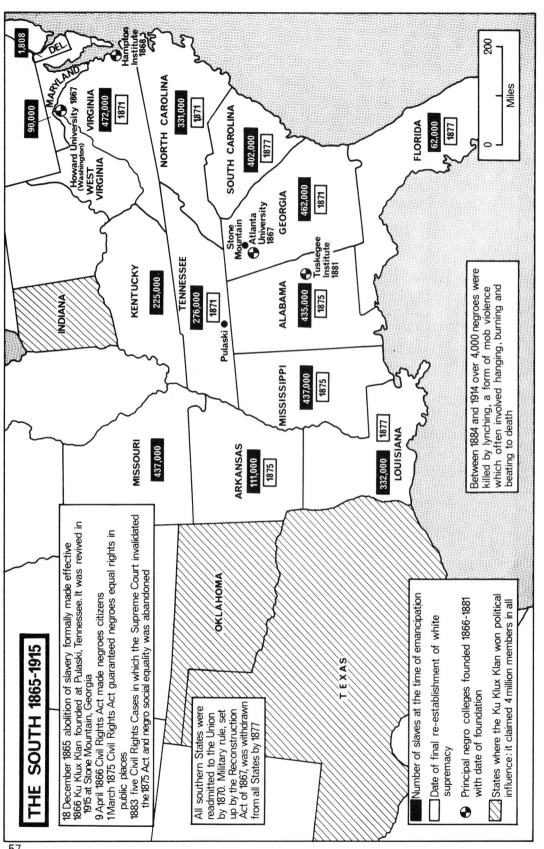

THE SOUTH 1865-1915

18 December 1865 abolition of slavery formally made effective
1866 Ku Klux Klan founded at Pulaski, Tennessee. It was revived in 1915 at Stone Mountain, Georgia
9 April 1866 Civil Rights Act made negroes citizens
1 March 1875 Civil Rights Act guaranteed negroes equal rights in public places
1883 five Civil Rights Cases in which the Supreme Court invalidated the 1875 Act and negro social equality was abandoned

All southern States were readmitted to the Union by 1870. Military rule, set up by the Reconstruction Act of 1867, was withdrawn from all States by 1877

Between 1884 and 1914 over 4,000 negroes were killed by lynching, a form of mob violence which often involved hanging, burning and beating to death

■ Number of slaves at the time of emancipation

□ Date of final re-establishment of white supremacy

◕ Principal negro colleges founded 1866-1881 with date of foundation

▨ States where the Ku Klux Klan won political influence: it claimed 4 million members in all

DEL. 1,808

MARYLAND 90,000

Howard University 1867 (Washington)

WEST VIRGINIA

VIRGINIA 472,000 1871

Hampton Institute 1868

NORTH CAROLINA 331,000 1871

SOUTH CAROLINA 402,000 1877

GEORGIA 462,000 1871

FLORIDA 62,000 1877

Stone Mountain

Atlanta University 1867

Tuskegee Institute 1881

KENTUCKY 225,000

TENNESSEE 276,000 1871

Pulaski

ALABAMA 435,000 1875

MISSISSIPPI 437,000 1875

INDIANA

MISSOURI 437,000

ARKANSAS 111,000 1875

LOUISIANA 332,000 1877

OKLAHOMA

TEXAS

0 200 Miles

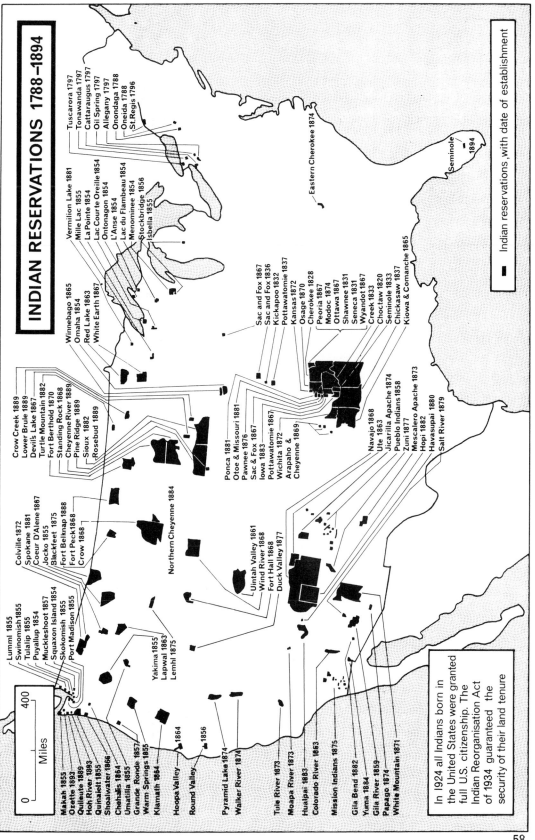

INDIAN RESERVATIONS 1788–1894

Miles
0   400

Tuscarora 1797
Tonawanda 1797
Cattaraugus 1797
Oil Spring 1797
Allegany 1797
Onondaga 1788
Oneida 1788
St Regis 1796

Eastern Cherokee 1874

Seminole 1894

■ Indian reservations, with date of establishment

Vermilion Lake 1881
Mille Lac 1855
La Pointe 1854
Lac Courte Oreille 1854
Ontonagon 1854
L'Anse 1854
Lac du Flambeau 1854
Menominee 1854
Stockbridge 1856
Isbella 1855

Winnebago 1865
Omaha 1854
Red Lake 1863
White Earth 1867

Sac and Fox 1867
Sac and Fox 1836
Kickapoo 1832
Pottawatomie 1837
Kansas 1872
Osage 1870
Cherokee 1828
Peoria 1867
Modoc 1874
Ottawa 1867
Shawnee 1831
Seneca 1831
Wyandot 1867
Creek 1833
Choctaw 1820
Seminole 1833
Chickasaw 1837
Kiowa & Comanche 1865

Crow Creek 1889
Lower Brule 1889
Devils Lake 1867
Turtle Mountain 1882
Fort Berthold 1870
Standing Rock 1868
Cheyenne River 1889
Pine Ridge 1889
Sioux 1882
Rosebud 1889

Ponca 1881
Otoe & Missouri 1881
Pawnee 1876
Sac & Fox 1867
Iowa 1883
Pottawatomie 1867
Wichita 1872
Arapaho &
Cheyenne 1869

Navajo 1868
Ute 1863
Jicarilla Apache 1874
Pueblo Indians 1858
Zuni 1877
Mescalero Apache 1873
Hopi 1882
Havasupai 1880
Salt River 1879

Colville 1872
SpoKane 1881
Coeur D'Alene 1867
Jocko 1855
Blackfeet 1855
Fort Belknap 1888
Fort Peck 1868
Crow 1868

Northern Cheyenne 1884

Uintah Valley 1861
Wind River 1868
Fort Hall 1868
Duck Valley 1877

Lumml 1855
Swinomish 1855
Tulalip 1855
Puyallup 1854
Muckleshoot 1857
Squaxon Island 1854
Skokomish 1855
Port Madison 1855

Makah 1855
Ozette 1893
Quileute 1889
Hoh River 1893
Quinalelt 1855
Shoalwater 1866
Chehalis 1864
Umatilla 1855
Grande Ronde 1857
Warm Springs 1855
Klamath 1864

Hoopa Valley
Round Valley

Yakima 1855
Lapwal 1863
Lemhi 1875

1864
1856

Pyramid Lake 1874
Walker River 1874

Tule River 1873
Moapa River 1873

Hualpai 1883
Colorado River 1863
Mission Indians 1875

Gila Bend 1882
Yuma 1884
Gila River 1859
Papago 1874
White Mountain 1871

In 1924 all Indians born in
the United States were granted
full U.S. citizenship. The
Indian Reorganisation Act
of 1934 guaranteed the
security of their land tenure

58

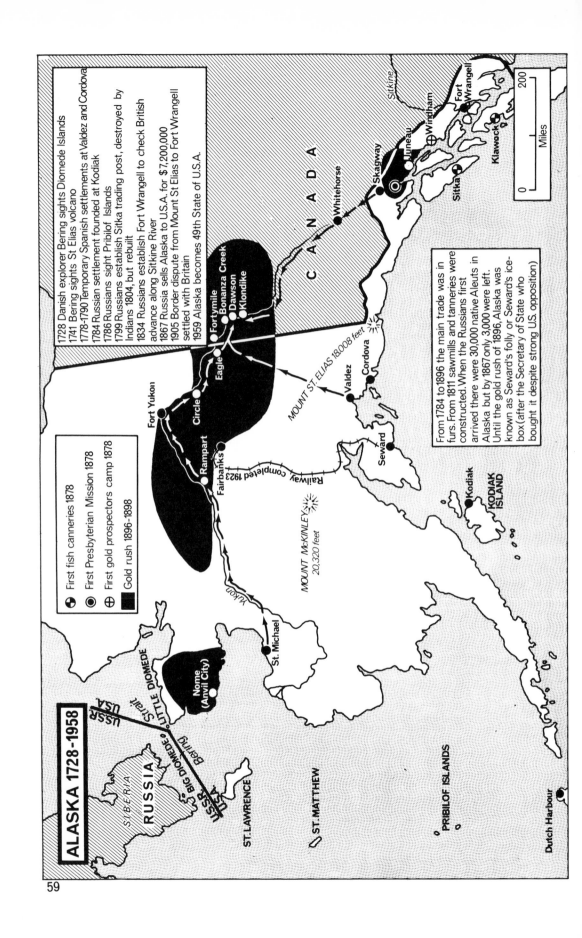

ALASKA 1728-1958

1728 Danish explorer Bering sights Diomede Islands
1741 Bering sights St Elias volcano
1778-1790 Temporary Spanish settlements at Valdez and Cordova
1784 Russian settlement founded at Kodiak
1786 Russians sight Pribilof Islands
1799 Russians establish Sitka trading post, destroyed by Indians 1804, but rebuilt
1834 Russians establish Fort Wrangell to check British advance along Sitkine River
1867 Russia sells Alaska to U.S.A. for $7,200,000
1905 Border dispute from Mount St Elias to Fort Wrangell settled with Britain
1959 Alaska becomes 49th State of U.S.A.

From 1784 to 1896 the main trade was in furs. From 1811 sawmills and tanneries were constructed. When the Russians first arrived there were 30,000 native Aleuts in Alaska but by 1867 only 3,000 were left. Until the gold rush of 1896, Alaska was known as Seward's folly or Seward's icebox (after the Secretary of State who bought it despite strong U.S. opposition)

○ First fish canneries 1878
◉ First Presbyterian Mission 1878
⊕ First gold prospectors camp 1878
■ Gold rush 1896-1898

0 _____ 200
Miles

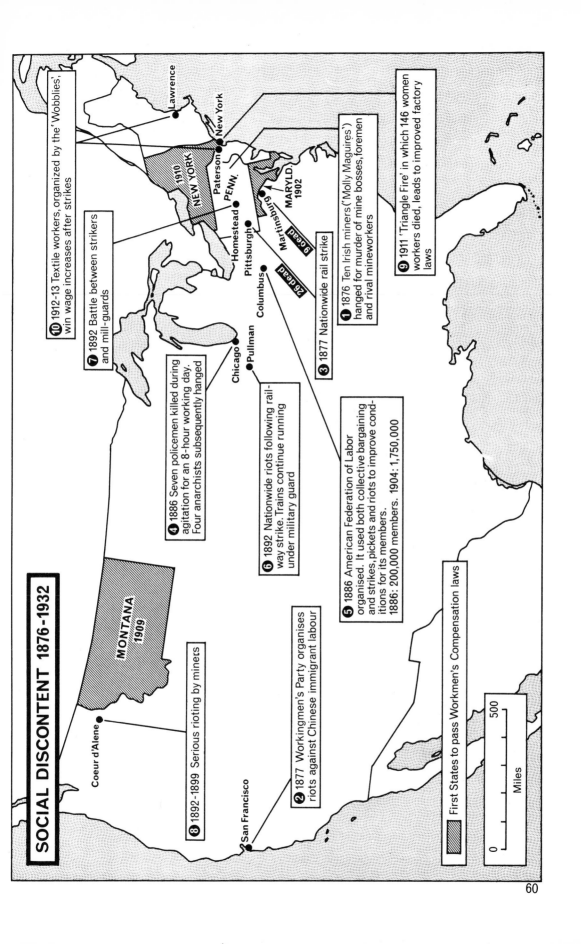

SOCIAL DISCONTENT 1876-1932

MONTANA 1909

NEW YORK 1910

⑩ 1912-13 Textile workers, organized by the 'Wobblies', win wage increases after strikes

⑦ 1892 Battle between strikers and mill-guards

① 1876 Ten Irish miners ('Molly Maguires') hanged for murder of mine bosses, foremen and rival mineworkers

⑨ 1911 'Triangle Fire' in which 146 women workers died, leads to improved factory laws

③ 1877 Nationwide rail strike

④ 1886 Seven policemen killed during agitation for an 8-hour working day. Four anarchists subsequently hanged

⑥ 1892 Nationwide riots following railway strike. Trains continue running under military guard

⑤ 1886 American Federation of Labor organised. It used both collective bargaining and strikes, pickets and riots to improve conditions for its members. 1886: 200,000 members. 1904: 1,750,000

② 1877 Workingmen's Party organises riots against Chinese immigrant labour

⑧ 1892-1899 Serious rioting by miners

Lawrence

New York

Paterson

Homestead

Pittsburgh

Columbus

Chicago

Pullman

Coeur d'Alene

San Francisco

PENN.

MARYLD. 1902

Martinsburg
9 dead

28 dead

First States to pass Workmen's Compensation laws

Miles
0   500

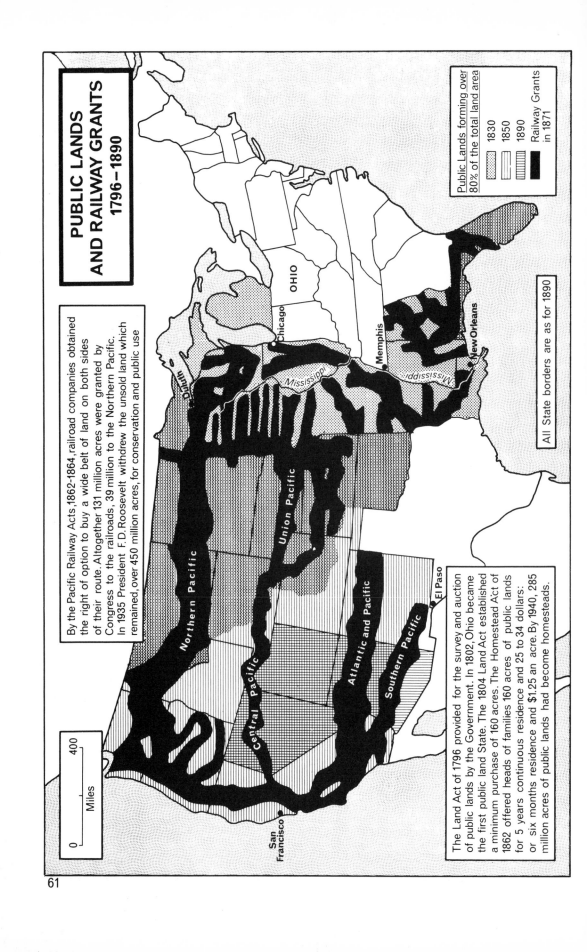

PUBLIC LANDS AND RAILWAY GRANTS 1796–1890

By the Pacific Railway Acts,1862-1864, railroad companies obtained the right of option to buy a wide belt of land on both sides of their route. Altogether 131 million acres were granted by Congress to the railroads, 39 million to the Northern Pacific. In 1935 President F.D.Roosevelt withdrew the unsold land which remained, over 450 million acres, for conservation and public use

The Land Act of 1796 provided for the survey and auction of public lands by the Government. In 1802, Ohio became the first public land State. The 1804 Land Act established a minimum purchase of 160 acres. The Homestead Act of 1862 offered heads of families 160 acres of public lands for 5 years continuous residence and 25 to 34 dollars; or six months residence and $1.25 an acre. By 1940, 285 million acres of public lands had become homesteads.

Public Lands forming over 80% of the total land area
- 1830
- 1850
- 1890
- Railway Grants in 1871

All State borders are as for 1890

Northern Pacific

Union Pacific

Central Pacific

Atlantic and Pacific

Southern Pacific

San Francisco

El Paso

Duluth

Chicago

OHIO

Memphis

New Orleans

Mississippi

Mississippi

0   400
Miles

61

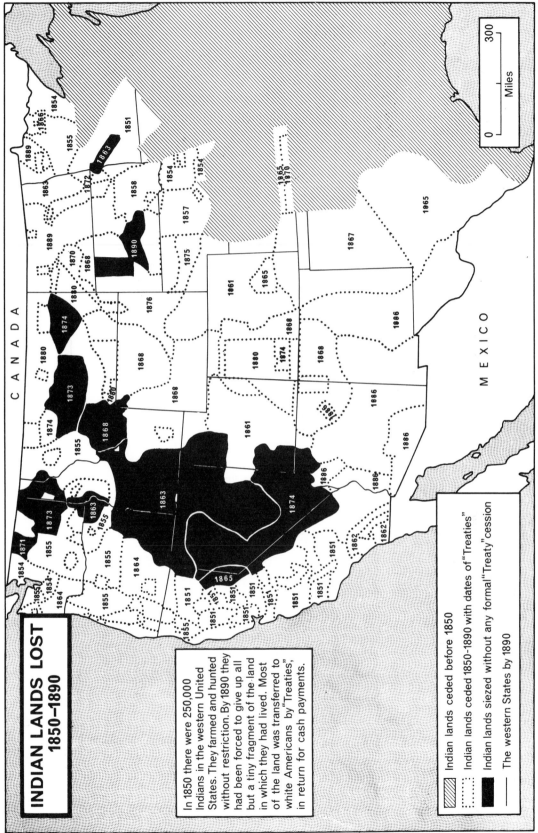

INDIAN LANDS LOST 1850–1890

In 1850 there were 250,000 Indians in the western United States. They farmed and hunted without restriction. By 1890 they had been forced to give up all but a tiny fragment of the land in which they had lived. Most of the land was transferred to white Americans by "Treaties", in return for cash payments.

C A N A D A

M E X I C O

300

0

Miles

Indian lands ceded before 1850

Indian lands ceded 1850–1890 with dates of "Treaties"

Indian lands siezed without any formal "Treaty" cession

The western States by 1890

62

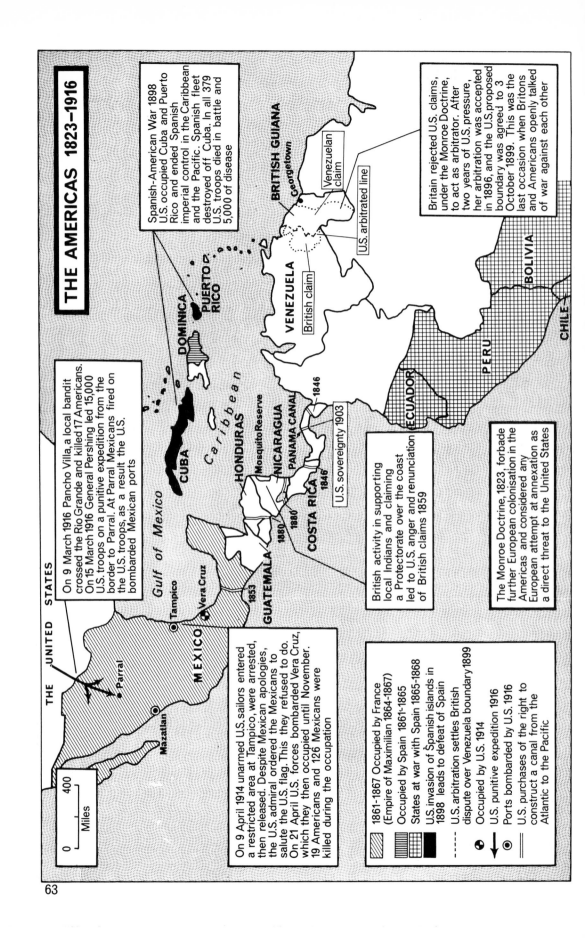

THE AMERICAS 1823–1916

THE UNITED STATES

MEXICO

Mazatlan

Parral

Tampico

Vera Cruz

Gulf of Mexico

GUATEMALA 1853

HONDURAS

MosquitoReserve

1860

NICARAGUA

COSTA RICA 1846

PANAMA CANAL

U.S. sovereignty 1903

1846

Caribbean

CUBA

DOMINICA

PUERTO RICO

ECUADOR

PERU

BOLIVIA

CHILE

VENEZUELA

British claim

Venezuelan claim

U.S. arbitrated line

BRITISH GUIANA

Georgetown

On 9 March 1916 Pancho Villa, a local bandit crossed the Rio Grande and killed 17 Americans. On 15 March 1916 General Pershing led 15,000 U.S. troops on a punitive expedition from the border to Parral. At Parral Mexicans fired on the U.S. troops, as a result the U.S. bombarded Mexican ports

On 9 April 1914 unarmed U.S. sailors entered a restricted area at Tampico, were arrested, then released. Despite Mexican apologies, the U.S. admiral ordered the Mexicans to salute the U.S. flag. This they refused to do. On 21 April U.S. forces bombarded Vera Cruz, which they then occupied until November. 19 Americans and 126 Mexicans were killed during the occupation

Spanish-American War 1898 U.S. occupied Cuba and Puerto Rico and ended Spanish imperial control in the Caribbean and the Pacific. Spanish fleet destroyed off Cuba. In all 379 U.S. troops died in battle and 5,000 of disease

Britain rejected U.S. claims, under the Monroe Doctrine, to act as arbitrator. After two years of U.S. pressure, her arbitration was accepted in 1896, and the U.S.proposed boundary was agreed to 3 October 1899. This was the last occasion when Britons and Americans openly talked of war against each other

British activity in supporting local Indians and claiming a Protectorate over the coast led to U.S. anger and renunciation of British claims 1859

The Monroe Doctrine, 1823, forbade further European colonisation in the Americas and considered any European attempt at annexation as a direct threat to the United States

1861-1867 Occupied by France (Empire of Maximilian 1864-1867)

Occupied by Spain 1861-1865

States at war with Spain 1865-1868

U.S. invasion of Spanish islands in 1898 leads to defeat of Spain

U.S. arbitration settles British dispute over Venezuela boundary1899

Occupied by U.S. 1914

U.S. punitive expedition 1916

Ports bombarded by U.S. 1916

U.S. purchases of the right to construct a canal from the Atlantic to the Pacific

0   400
Miles

63

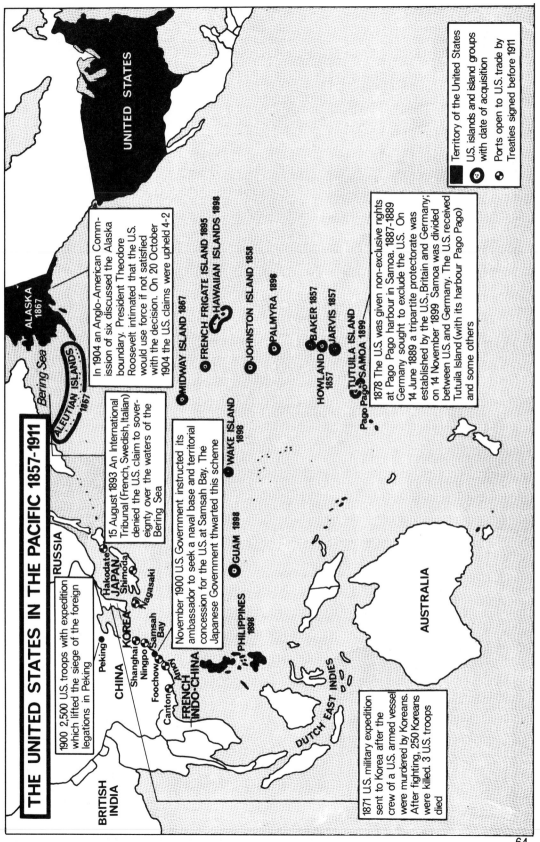

THE UNITED STATES IN THE PACIFIC 1857-1911

BRITISH INDIA

RUSSIA

Bering Sea

ALASKA
1867

ALEUTIAN ISLANDS
1867

UNITED STATES

CHINA

Peking ●

Hakodate
Shimoda
JAPAN
KOREA
Shanghai ●
Ningpo ●
Nagasaki
Foochow ●
Samsah Bay
Canton ● Amoy
**FRENCH
INDO-CHINA**

PHILIPPINES
1898

○ GUAM 1898

○ WAKE ISLAND
1898

○ MIDWAY ISLAND 1867

○ FRENCH FRIGATE ISLAND 1895
⊙ HAWAIIAN ISLANDS 1898

○ JOHNSTON ISLAND 1858

○ PALMYRA 1898

● HOWLAND
1857
● BAKER 1857
● JARVIS 1857

TUTUILA ISLAND
Pago Pago ● SAMOA 1899

DUTCH EAST INDIES

AUSTRALIA

1900 2,500 U.S. troops with expedition which lifted the siege of the foreign legations in Peking

15 August 1893 An International Tribunal (French, Swedish, Italian) denied the U.S. claim to sovereignty over the waters of the Bering Sea

November 1900 U.S. Government instructed its ambassador to seek a naval base and territorial concession for the U.S. at Samsah Bay. The Japanese Government thwarted this scheme

1871 U.S. military expedition sent to Korea after the crew of a U.S. armed vessel were murdered by Koreans. After fighting, 250 Koreans were killed. 3 U.S. troops died

In 1904 an Anglo-American Commission of six discussed the Alaska boundary. President Theodore Roosevelt intimated that the U.S. would use force if not satisfied with the decision. On 20 October 1904 the U.S. claims were upheld 4-2

1878 The U.S. was given non-exclusive rights at Pago Pago harbour in Samoa. 1887-1889 Germany sought to exclude the U.S. On 14 June 1889 a tripartite protectorate was established by the U.S., Britain and Germany; on 14 November 1899 Samoa was divided between U.S. and Germany. The U.S. received Tutuila Island (with its harbour Pago Pago) and some others

■ Territory of the United States
◉ U.S. islands and island groups with date of acquisition
● Ports open to U.S. trade by Treaties signed before 1911

64

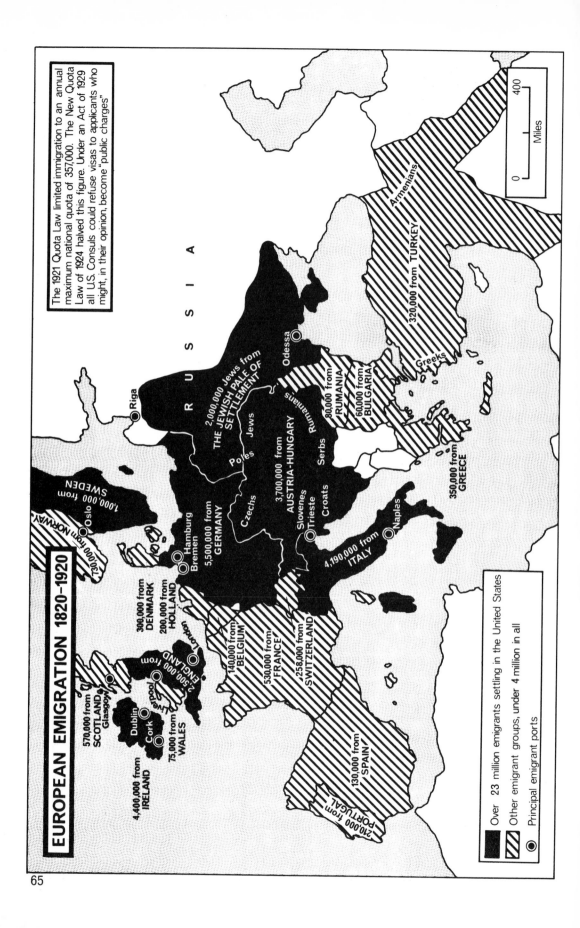

EUROPEAN EMIGRATION 1820–1920

The 1921 Quota Law limited immigration to an annual maximum national quota of 357,000. The New Quota Law of 1924 halved this figure. Under an Act of 1929 all U.S. Consuls could refuse visas to applicants who might, in their opinion, become "public charges"

R U S S I A

2,000,000 Jews from THE JEWISH PALE OF SETTLEMENT

Riga

Odessa

Jews

Poles

Czechs

3,700,000 from AUSTRIA-HUNGARY

Serbs

Slovenes

Croats

Rumanians

Trieste

80,000 from RUMANIA

60,000 from BULGARIA

320,000 from TURKEY

Armenians

Greeks

350,000 from GREECE

SWEDEN
1,000,000 from

NORWAY
730,000 from

Oslo

Hamburg

Bremen

5,500,000 from GERMANY

300,000 from DENMARK

200,000 from HOLLAND

140,000 from BELGIUM

530,000 from FRANCE

258,000 from SWITZERLAND

4,190,000 from ITALY

Naples

130,000 from SPAIN

210,000 from PORTUGAL

SCOTLAND
570,000 from

Glasgow

ENGLAND
2,500,000 from

London

Liverpool

Dublin

Cork

IRELAND
4,400,000 from

75,000 from WALES

0   400
Miles

- Over 23 million emigrants settling in the United States
- Other emigrant groups, under 4 million in all
- Principal emigrant ports

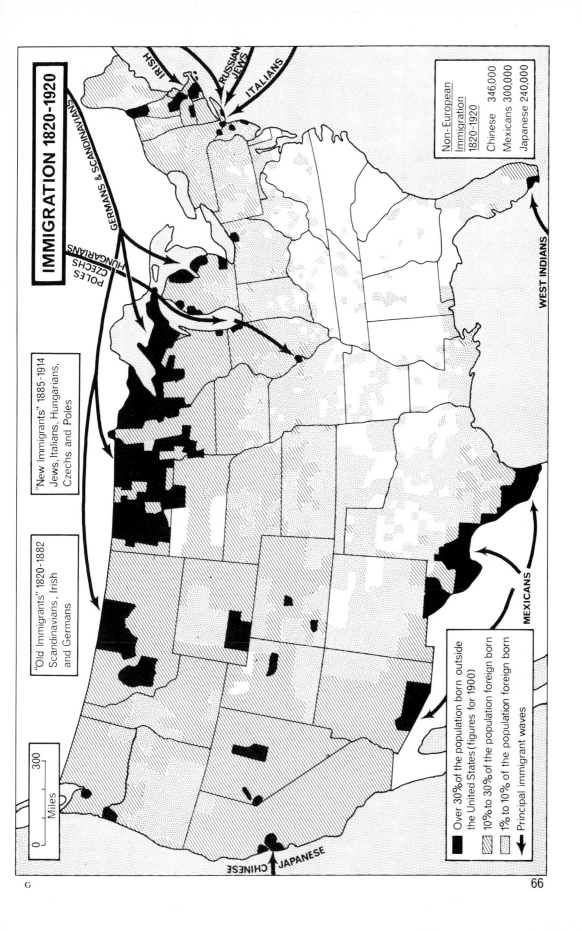

IMMIGRATION 1820-1920

Non-European
Immigration
1820-1920

Chinese   346,000
Mexicans 300,000
Japanese 240,000

IRISH

RUSSIAN JEWS

ITALIANS

GERMANS & SCANDINAVIANS

POLES CZECHS HUNGARIANS

WEST INDIANS

"New Immigrants" 1885-1914
Jews, Italians, Hungarians,
Czechs and Poles

"Old Immigrants" 1820-1882
Scandinavians, Irish
and Germans

MEXICANS

JAPANESE   CHINESE

Over 30% of the population born outside
the United States (figures for 1900)

10% to 30% of the population foreign born

1% to 10% of the population foreign born

Principal immigrant waves

300
Miles
0

G

66

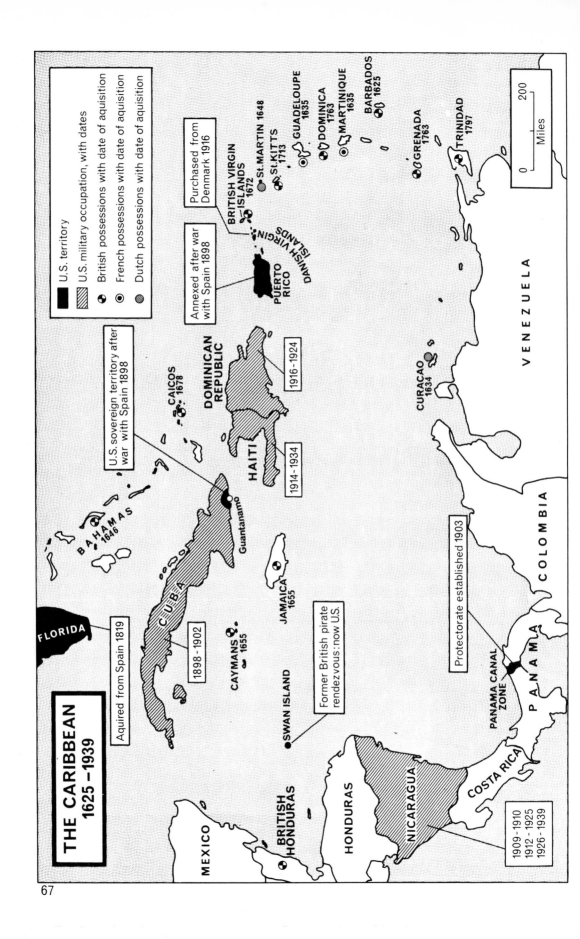

THE CARIBBEAN 1625–1939

U.S. territory
U.S. military occupation, with dates
British possessions with date of aquisition
French possessions with date of aquisition
Dutch possessions with date of aquisition

Aquired from Spain 1819

FLORIDA

MEXICO

BRITISH HONDURAS

HONDURAS

NICARAGUA

COSTA RICA

PANAMA

COLOMBIA

VENEZUELA

1909-1910
1912-1925
1926-1939

Protectorate established 1903

PANAMA CANAL ZONE

SWAN ISLAND

Former British pirate rendez vous: now U.S.

CAYMANS 1655

JAMAICA 1655

CUBA

1898-1902

BAHAMAS 1646

Guantanamo

CAICOS 1678

U.S. sovereign territory after war with Spain 1898

HAITI

DOMINICAN REPUBLIC

1914-1934

1916-1924

CURACAO 1634

PUERTO RICO

DANISH VIRGIN ISLANDS

BRITISH VIRGIN ISLANDS 1672

Annexed after war with Spain 1898

Purchased from Denmark 1916

St.MARTIN 1648

St.KITTS 1713

GUADELOUPE 1635

DOMINICA 1763

MARTINIQUE 1635

GRENADA 1763

BARBADOS 1625

TRINIDAD 1797

0   200
Miles

67

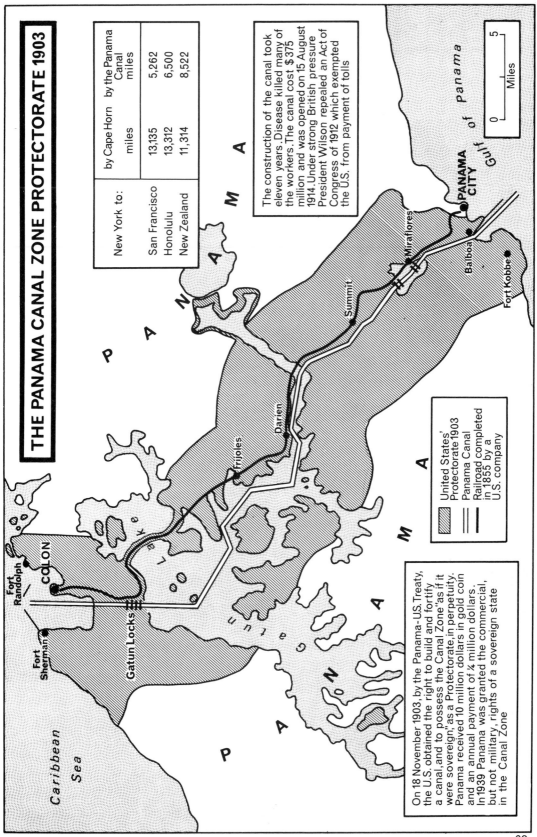

THE PANAMA CANAL ZONE PROTECTORATE 1903

New York to:	by Cape Horn miles	by the Panama Canal miles
San Francisco	13,135	5,262
Honolulu	13,312	6,500
New Zealand	11,314	8,522

The construction of the canal took eleven years. Disease killed many of the workers. The canal cost $375 million and was opened on 15 August 1914. Under strong British pressure President Wilson repealed an Act of Congress of 1912 which exempted the U.S. from payment of tolls

PANAMA

Gulf of Panama

PANAMA CITY

Miraflores

Balboa

Fort Kobbe

Summit

Darien

Frijoles

P A N A M A

P A N A M A

Caribbean Sea

Fort Randolph

COLON

Fort Sherman

Gatun Locks

United States' Protectorate 1903

Panama Canal

Railroad completed in 1855 by a U.S. company

0   5
Miles

On 18 November 1903, by the Panama-U.S.Treaty, the U.S. obtained the right to build and fortify a canal, and to possess the Canal Zone "as if it were sovereign," as a Protectorate, in perpetuity. Panama received 10 million dollars in gold coin and an annual payment of ¼ million dollars. In 1939 Panama was granted the commercial, but not military, rights of a sovereign state in the Canal Zone

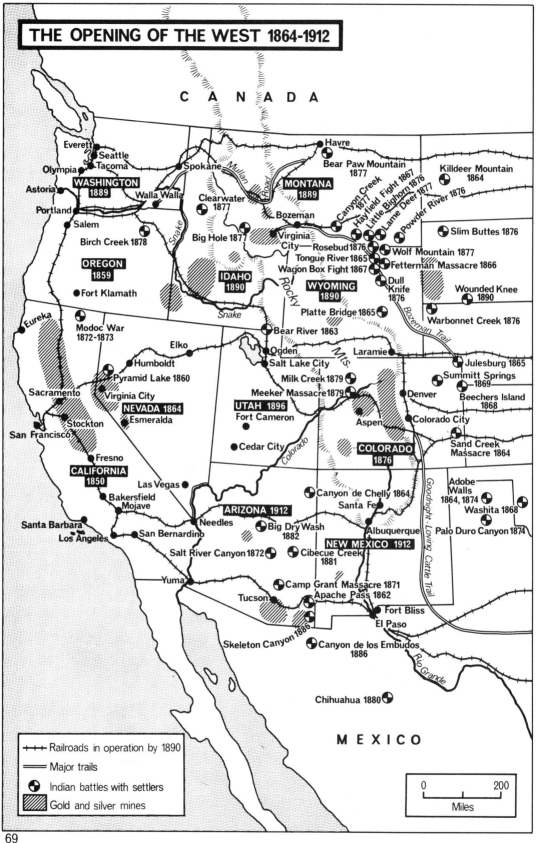

THE OPENING OF THE WEST 1864-1912

CANADA

Everett
Seattle
Olympia
Tacoma
WASHINGTON 1889
Astoria
Walla Walla
Portland
Salem
Birch Creek 1878
OREGON 1859
Fort Klamath

Spokane
Mullan Road
Clearwater 1877
Bozeman
Big Hole 1877
Virginia City
IDAHO 1890
Snake
Snake

Havre
Bear Paw Mountain 1877
MONTANA 1889
Canyon Creek 1877
Hayfield Fight 1867
Little Bighorn 1876
Lame Deer 1877
Powder River 1876
Rosebud 1876
Tongue River 1865
Wagon Box Fight 1867
WYOMING 1890
Platte Bridge 1865
Wolf Mountain 1877
Fetterman Massacre 1866
Dull Knife 1876

Killdeer Mountain 1864
Slim Buttes 1876
Wounded Knee 1890
Warbonnet Creek 1876

Eureka
Modoc War 1872-1873
Humboldt
Pyramid Lake 1860
Virginia City
Sacramento
NEVADA 1864
Esmeralda
Stockton
San Francisco
Fresno
CALIFORNIA 1850
Bakersfield
Mojave
Santa Barbara
Los Angeles
San Bernardino
Needles
Yuma

Elko
Bear River 1863
Ogden
Salt Lake City
Milk Creek 1879
Meeker Massacre 1879
UTAH 1896
Fort Cameron
Cedar City
Colorado
Las Vegas
Salt River Canyon 1872
ARIZONA 1912
Big Dry Wash 1882
Cibecue Creek 1881
Camp Grant Massacre 1871
Apache Pass 1862
Tucson
Skeleton Canyon 1886

Laramie
Julesburg 1865
Summitt Springs 1869
Beechers Island 1868
Denver
Aspen
Colorado City
COLORADO 1876
Sand Creek Massacre 1864
Rocky Mts.
Bozeman Trail

Adobe Walls 1864, 1874
Washita 1868
Santa Fe
Canyon de Chelly 1864
Albuquerque
NEW MEXICO 1912
Palo Duro Canyon 1874
Goodnight-Loving Cattle Trail
Fort Bliss
El Paso
Canyon de los Embudos 1886
Rio Grande
Chihuahua 1880

MEXICO

Railroads in operation by 1890
Major trails
Indian battles with settlers
Gold and silver mines

0   200
Miles

69

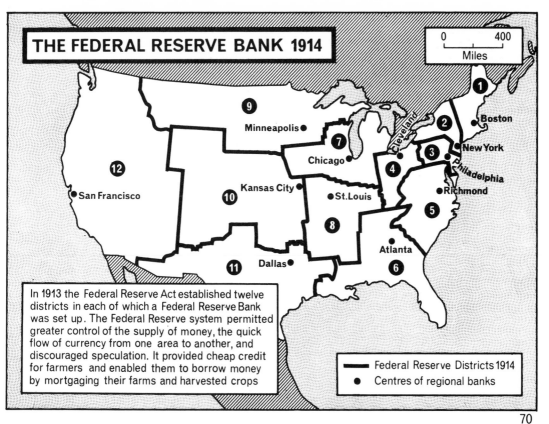

THE FEDERAL RESERVE BANK 1914

0 — 400
Miles

In 1913 the Federal Reserve Act established twelve districts in each of which a Federal Reserve Bank was set up. The Federal Reserve system permitted greater control of the supply of money, the quick flow of currency from one area to another, and discouraged speculation. It provided cheap credit for farmers and enabled them to borrow money by mortgaging their farms and harvested crops

— Federal Reserve Districts 1914
● Centres of regional banks

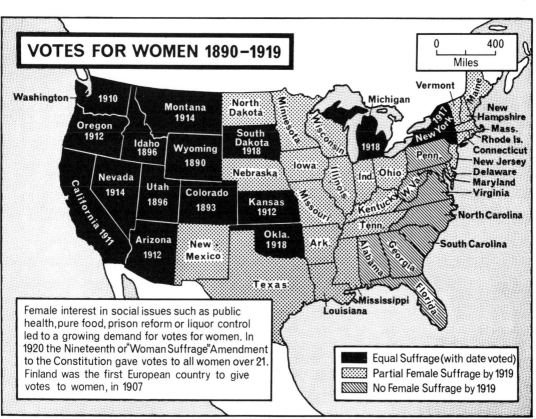

VOTES FOR WOMEN 1890–1919

0 — 400
Miles

Female interest in social issues such as public health, pure food, prison reform or liquor control led to a growing demand for votes for women. In 1920 the Nineteenth or "Woman Suffrage" Amendment to the Constitution gave votes to all women over 21. Finland was the first European country to give votes to women, in 1907

Equal Suffrage (with date voted)
Partial Female Suffrage by 1919
No Female Suffrage by 1919

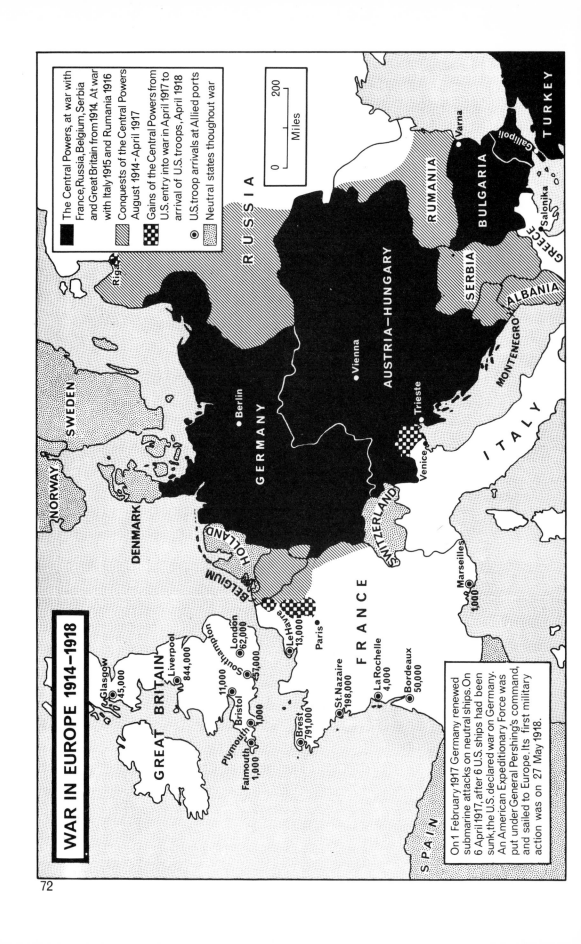

WAR IN EUROPE 1914-1918

The Central Powers, at war with France, Russia, Belgium, Serbia and Great Britain from 1914. At war with Italy 1915 and Rumania 1916

Conquests of the Central Powers August 1914 - April 1917

Gains of the Central Powers from U.S. entry into war in April 1917 to arrival of U.S. troops, April 1918

⊚ U.S. troop arrivals at Allied ports

Neutral states throughout war

0   200
Miles

On 1 February 1917 Germany renewed submarine attacks on neutral ships. On 6 April 1917, after 6 U.S. ships had been sunk, the U.S. declared war on Germany. An American Expeditionary Force was put under General Pershing's command, and sailed to Europe. Its first military action was on 27 May 1918.

NORWAY

SWEDEN

DENMARK

RUSSIA

Riga

Berlin

GERMANY

HOLLAND

BELGIUM

SWITZERLAND

AUSTRIA-HUNGARY

Vienna

Trieste

Venice

ITALY

MONTENEGRO

ALBANIA

SERBIA

RUMANIA

Varna

BULGARIA

Gallipoli

GREECE

Salonika

TURKEY

GREAT BRITAIN

Glasgow
45,000

Liverpool
844,000

Southampton
57,000

London
62,000

Bristol
11,000

Plymouth
1,000

Falmouth
1,000

LeHavre
13,000

Paris

FRANCE

Brest
791,000

St.Nazaire
198,000

La Rochelle
4,000

Bordeaux
50,000

Marseilles
1,000

SPAIN

72

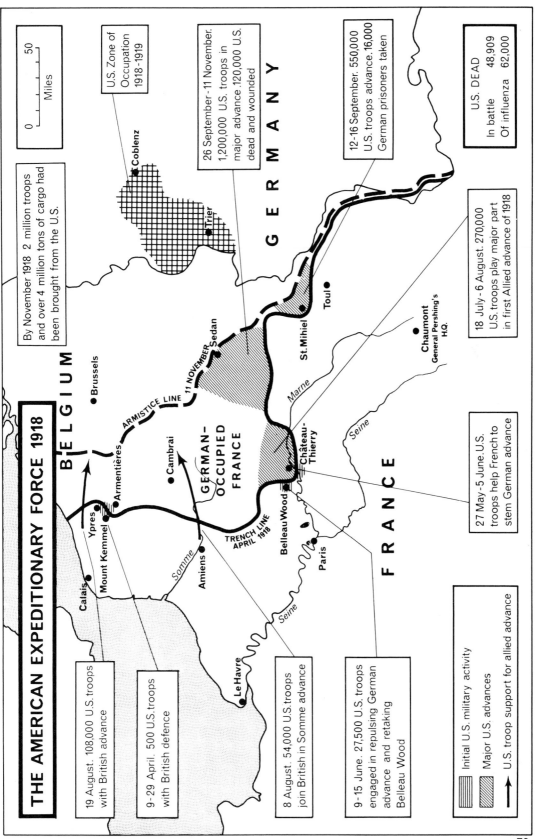

THE AMERICAN EXPEDITIONARY FORCE 1918

0 50
Miles

U.S. Zone of Occupation 1918-1919

26 September - 11 November. 1,200,000 U.S. troops in major advance. 120,000 U.S. dead and wounded

12-16 September. 550,000 U.S. troops advance. 16,000 German prisoners taken

U.S. DEAD
In battle   48,909
Of influenza 62,000

By November 1918 2 million troops and over 4 million tons of cargo had been brought from the U.S.

18 July - 6 August. 270,000 U.S. troops play major part in first Allied advance of 1918

27 May-5 June. U.S. troops help French to stem German advance

19 August. 108,000 U.S. troops with British advance

9-29 April. 500 U.S. troops with British defence

8 August. 54,000 U.S. troops join British in Somme advance

9-15 June. 27,500 U.S. troops engaged in repulsing German advance and retaking Belleau Wood

GERMANY

BELGIUM

FRANCE

GERMAN-OCCUPIED FRANCE

ARMISTICE LINE

11 NOVEMBER

TRENCH LINE APRIL 1918

Coblenz
Trier
Sedan
St. Mihiel
Toul
Chaumont
General Pershing's H.Q.
Brussels
Armentières
Cambrai
Ypres
Mount Kemmel
Calais
Amiens
Le Havre
Belleau Wood
Château-Thierry
Paris
Marne
Seine
Seine
Somme

Initial U.S. military activity

Major U.S. advances

U.S. troop support for allied advance

73

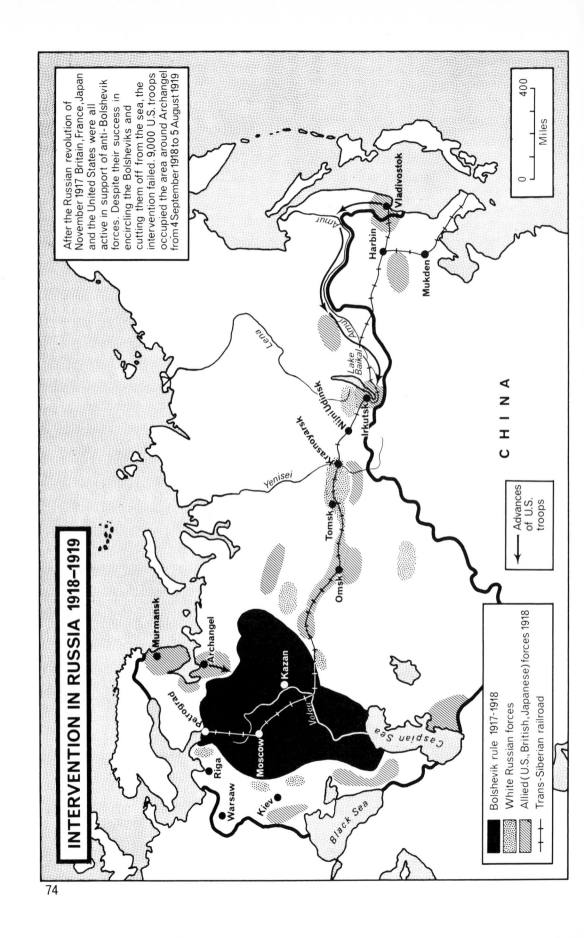

INTERVENTION IN RUSSIA 1918–1919

After the Russian revolution of November 1917 Britain, France, Japan and the United States were all active in support of anti-Bolshevik forces. Despite their success in encircling the Bolsheviks and cutting them off from the sea, the intervention failed. 9,000 U.S. troops occupied the area around Archangel from 4 September 1918 to 5 August 1919

0   400
Miles

Vladivostok
Harbin
Mukden

CHINA

Amur

Lena

Lake Baikal

Nijni Udinsk
Irkutsk

Krasnoyarsk

Yenisei

Tomsk

Omsk

Murmansk
Archangel

Petrograd

Kazan

Volga

Moscow

Riga

Warsaw
Kiev

Black Sea

Caspian Sea

Advances of U.S. troops

Bolshevik rule 1917-1918
White Russian forces
Allied (U.S., British, Japanese) forces 1918
Trans-Siberian railroad

74

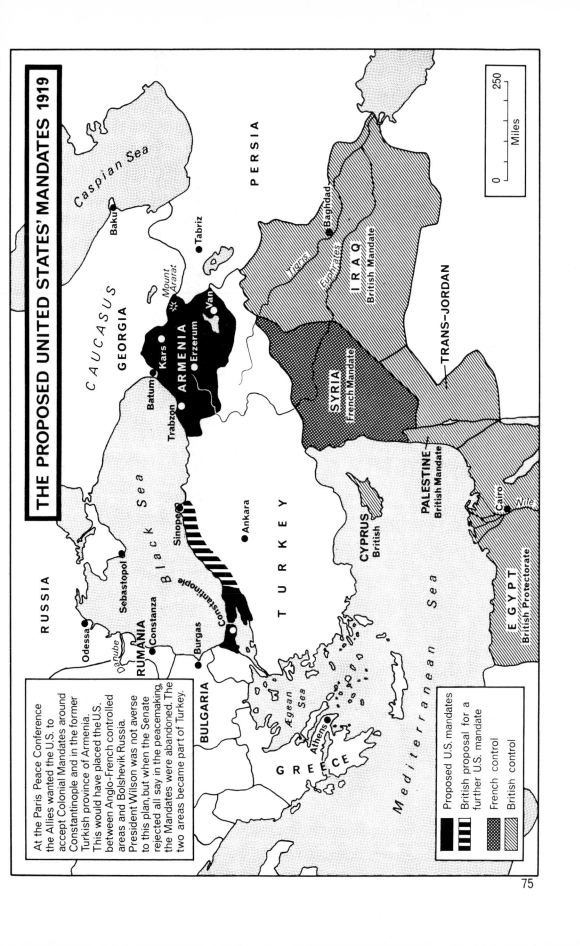

THE PROPOSED UNITED STATES' MANDATES 1919

At the Paris Peace Conference the Allies wanted the U.S. to accept Colonial Mandates around Constantinople and in the former Turkish province of Armenia. This would have placed the U.S. between Anglo-French controlled areas and Bolshevik Russia. President Wilson was not averse to this plan, but when the Senate rejected all say in the peacemaking, the Mandates were abandoned. The two areas became part of Turkey.

RUSSIA

Odessa

Sebastopol

Constanza

RUMANIA

Danube

Burgas

BULGARIA

Constantinople

Black Sea

Sinope

Trabzon

Batum

Ankara

TURKEY

Caspian Sea

Baku

Tabriz

Mount *Ararat*

Van

ARMENIA

Kars

Erzerum

CAUCASUS

GEORGIA

PERSIA

Baghdad

Tigris

Euphrates

IRAQ
British Mandate

SYRIA
French Mandate

TRANS-JORDAN

PALESTINE
British Mandate

CYPRUS
British

Cairo

Nile

EGYPT
British Protectorate

Mediterranean Sea

Aegean Sea

Athens

GREECE

Proposed U.S. mandates

British proposal for a further U.S. mandate

French control

British control

0   250
Miles

75

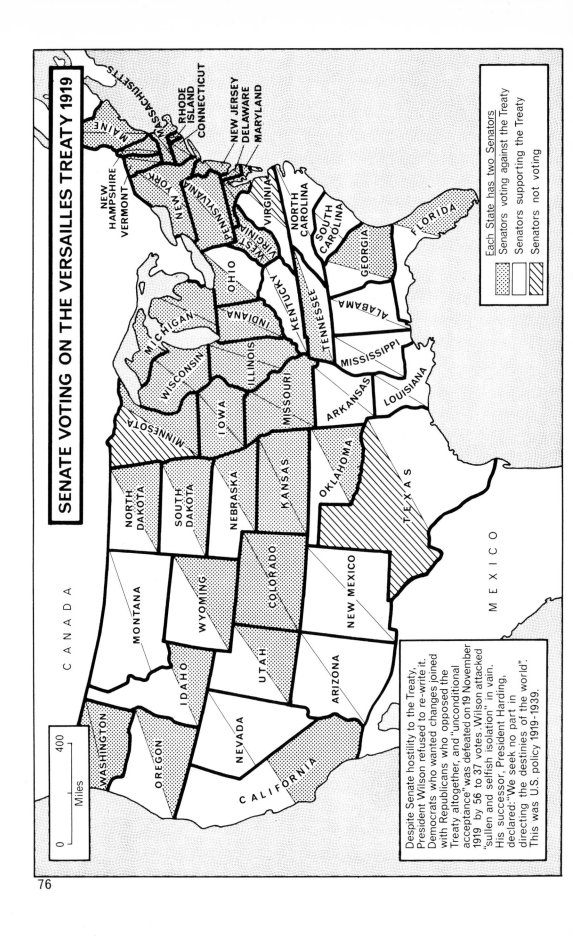

SENATE VOTING ON THE VERSAILLES TREATY 1919

CANADA

M E X I C O

Each State has two Senators

Senators voting against the Treaty

Senators supporting the Treaty

Senators not voting

WASHINGTON

OREGON

CALIFORNIA

NEVADA

IDAHO

MONTANA

WYOMING

UTAH

ARIZONA

NEW MEXICO

COLORADO

NORTH DAKOTA

SOUTH DAKOTA

NEBRASKA

KANSAS

OKLAHOMA

TEXAS

MINNESOTA

IOWA

MISSOURI

ARKANSAS

LOUISIANA

WISCONSIN

ILLINOIS

MICHIGAN

INDIANA

OHIO

KENTUCKY

TENNESSEE

MISSISSIPPI

ALABAMA

GEORGIA

FLORIDA

SOUTH CAROLINA

NORTH CAROLINA

VIRGINIA

WEST VIRGINIA

PENNSYLVANIA

NEW YORK

MAINE

NEW HAMPSHIRE

VERMONT

MASSACHUSETTS

RHODE ISLAND

CONNECTICUT

NEW JERSEY

DELAWARE

MARYLAND

0   400

Miles

Despite Senate hostility to the Treaty,
President Wilson refused to re-write it.
Democrats who wanted changes joined
with Republicans who opposed the
Treaty altogether, and "unconditional
acceptance" was defeated on 19 November
1919 by 56 to 37 votes. Wilson attacked
"sullen and selfish isolation" in vain.
His successor, President Harding,
declared: "We seek no part in
directing the destinies of the world".
This was U.S. policy 1919-1939.

76

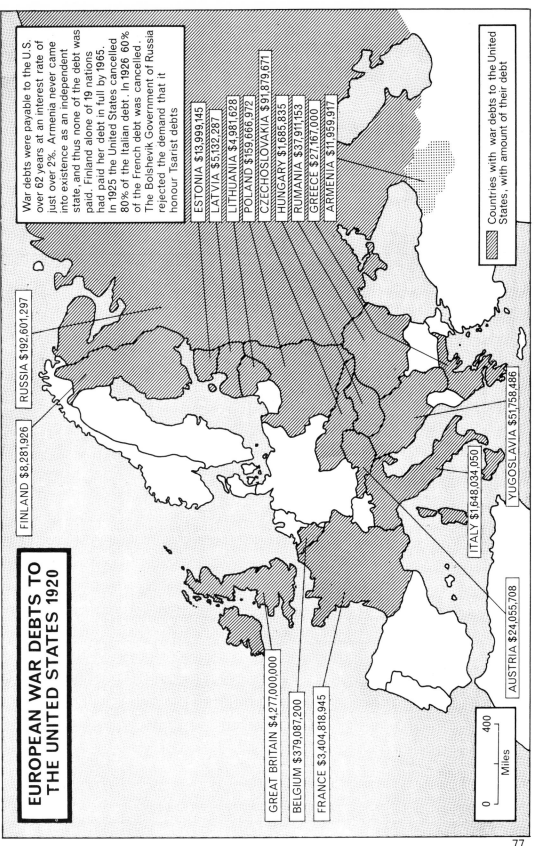

EUROPEAN WAR DEBTS TO THE UNITED STATES 1920

War debts were payable to the U.S. over 62 years at an interest rate of just over 2%. Armenia never came into existence as an independent state, and thus none of the debt was paid. Finland alone of 19 nations had paid her debt in full by 1965. In 1925 the United States cancelled 80% of the Italian debt. In 1926 60% of the French debt was cancelled. The Bolshevik Government of Russia rejected the demand that it honour Tsarist debts

ESTONIA $13,999,145
LATVIA $5,132,287
LITHUANIA $4,981,628
POLAND $159,666,972
CZECHOSLOVAKIA $91,879,671
HUNGARY $1,685,835
RUMANIA $37,911,153
GREECE $27,167,000
ARMENIA $11,959,917

Countries with war debts to the United States, with amount of their debt

RUSSIA $192,601,297

FINLAND $8,281,926

ITALY $1,648,034,050

YUGOSLAVIA $51,758,486

AUSTRIA $24,055,708

GREAT BRITAIN $4,277,000,000

BELGIUM $379,087,200

FRANCE $3,404,818,945

0   400
Miles

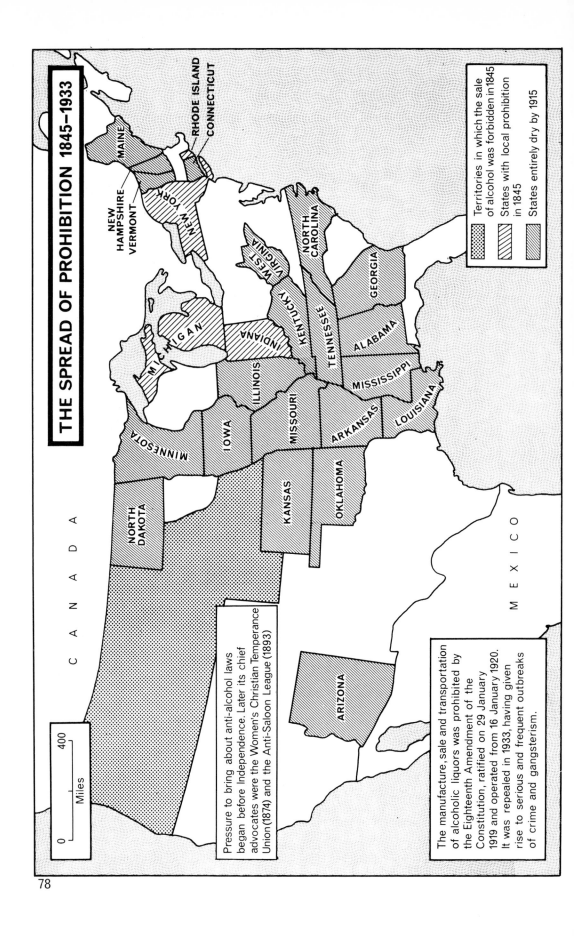

THE SPREAD OF PROHIBITION 1845–1933

CANADA

MEXICO

NORTH DAKOTA

MINNESOTA

MICHIGAN

IOWA

KANSAS

OKLAHOMA

MISSOURI

ARKANSAS

LOUISIANA

ILLINOIS

INDIANA

KENTUCKY

TENNESSEE

MISSISSIPPI

ALABAMA

GEORGIA

NORTH CAROLINA

WEST VIRGINIA

NEW YORK

VERMONT

NEW HAMPSHIRE

MAINE

RHODE ISLAND

CONNECTICUT

ARIZONA

Territories in which the sale
of alcohol was forbidden in1845

States with local prohibition
in 1845

States entirely dry by 1915

Pressure to bring about anti-alcohol laws
began before Independence. Later its chief
advocates were the Women's Christian Temperance
Union(1874) and the Anti-Saloon League (1893)

The manufacture, sale and transportation
of alcoholic liquors was prohibited by
the Eighteenth Amendment of the
Constitution, ratified on 29 January
1919 and operated from 16 January 1920.
It was repealed in 1933, having given
rise to serious and frequent outbreaks
of crime and gangsterism.

0   400
Miles

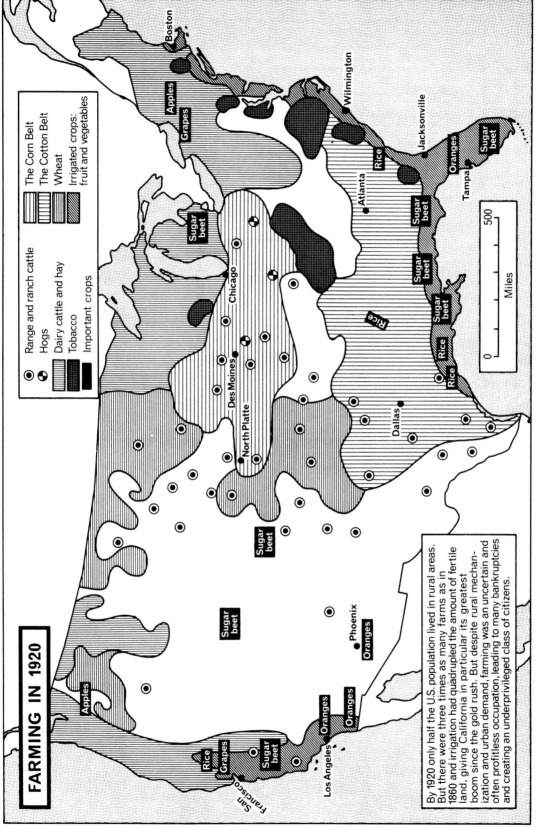

FARMING IN 1920

Legend:
- ◉ Range and ranch cattle
- ◐ Hogs
- Dairy cattle and hay
- Tobacco
- Important crops

- The Corn Belt
- The Cotton Belt
- Wheat
- Irrigated crops: fruit and vegetables

Boston
Apples
Grapes
Wilmington
Jacksonville
Rice
Oranges
Sugar beet
Atlanta
Sugar beet
Sugar beet
Tampa
Sugar beet
Chicago
Des Moines
North Platte
Rice
Sugar beet
Rice
Rice
Rice
Dallas
Sugar beet
Phoenix
Oranges
Sugar beet
Los Angeles
Oranges
Oranges
San Francisco
Rice
Grapes
Sugar beet
Apples

Miles
0   500

By 1920 only half the U.S. population lived in rural areas. But there were three times as many farms as in 1860 and irrigation had quadrupled the amount of fertile land, giving California in particular its greatest boom since the gold rush. But despite rural mechanization and urban demand, farming was an uncertain and often profitless occupation, leading to many bankruptcies and creating an underprivileged class of citizens.

H

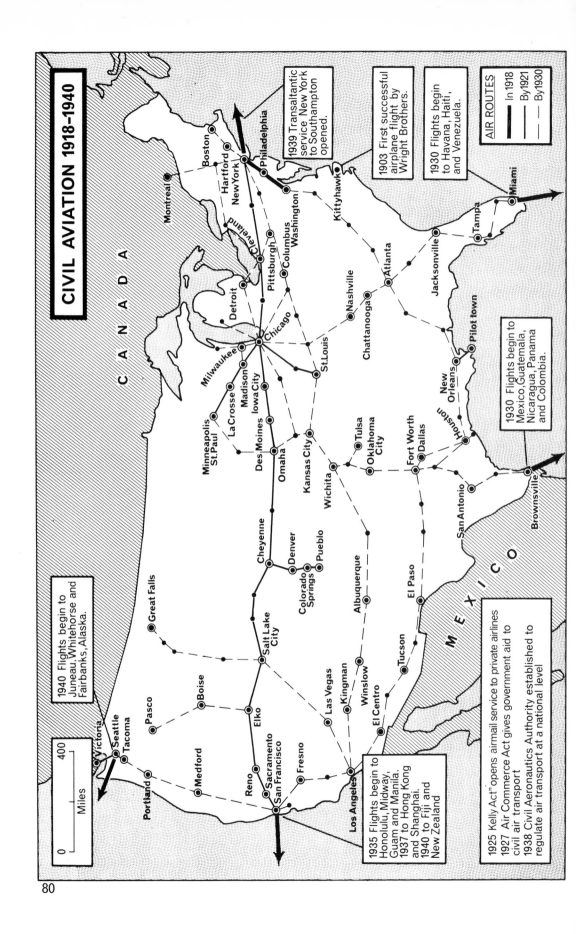

CIVIL AVIATION 1918–1940

AIR ROUTES
— In 1918
— By1921
--- By1930

1939 Transatlantic service New York to Southampton opened.

1903 First successful airplane flight by Wright Brothers.

1930 Flights begin to Havana, Haiti, and Venezuela.

1930 Flights begin to Mexico, Guatemala, Nicaragua, Panama and Colombia.

1940 Flights begin to Juneau, Whitehorse and Fairbanks, Alaska.

1935 Flights begin to Honolulu, Midway, Guam and Manila. 1937 to Hong Kong and Shanghai. 1940 to Fiji and New Zealand

1925 Kelly Act opens airmail service to private airlines
1927 Air Commerce Act gives government aid to civil air transport
1938 Civil Aeronautics Authority established to regulate air transport at a national level

CANADA

MEXICO

Miles
0   400

Boston
Hartford
New York
Philadelphia
Washington
Columbus
Kittyhawk
Montreal
Cleveland
Pittsburgh
Detroit
Nashville
Atlanta
Chattanooga
Jacksonville
Tampa
Miami
Pilot town
New Orleans
Houston
Chicago
Milwaukee
Madison
Iowa City
La Crosse
Des Moines
Minneapolis St.Paul
St.Louis
Kansas City
Omaha
Wichita
Tulsa
Oklahoma City
Fort Worth
Dallas
San Antonio
Brownsville
Cheyenne
Denver
Pueblo
Colorado Springs
Albuquerque
El Paso
Tucson
Winslow
Kingman
El Centro
Las Vegas
Salt Lake City
Great Falls
Boise
Pasco
Elko
Reno
Sacramento
San Francisco
Fresno
Los Angeles
Medford
Portland
Seattle
Tacoma
Victoria

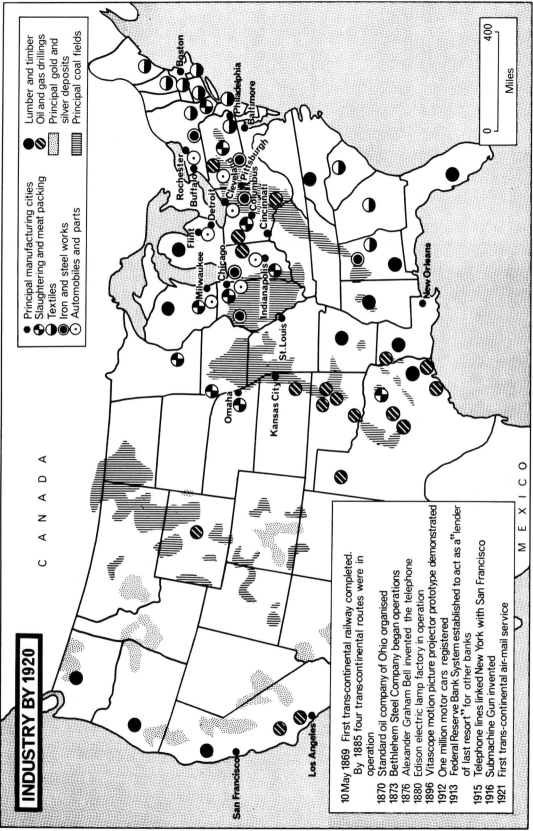

INDUSTRY BY 1920

Legend:
- Principal manufacturing cities
- Slaughtering and meat packing
- Textiles
- Iron and steel works
- Automobiles and parts
- Lumber and timber
- Oil and gas drillings
- Principal gold and silver deposits
- Principal coal fields

CANADA

MEXICO

San Francisco

Los Angeles

Omaha

Kansas City

St. Louis

Milwaukee

Chicago

Indianapolis

Flint

Detroit

Rochester

Buffalo

Cleveland

Pittsburgh

Columbus

Cincinnati

Boston

Philadelphia

Baltimore

New Orleans

Miles
0   400

10 May 1869 First trans-continental railway completed.
By 1885 four trans-continental routes were in operation

1870 Standard oil company of Ohio organised
1873 Bethlehem Steel Company began operations
1876 Alexander Graham Bell invented the telephone
1880 Edison electric lamp factory in operation
1896 Vitascope motion picture projector prototype demonstrated
1912 One million motor cars registered
1913 Federal Reserve Bank System established to act as a "lender of last resort" for other banks
1915 Telephone lines linked New York with San Francisco
1916 Submachine Gun invented
1921 First trans-continental air-mail service

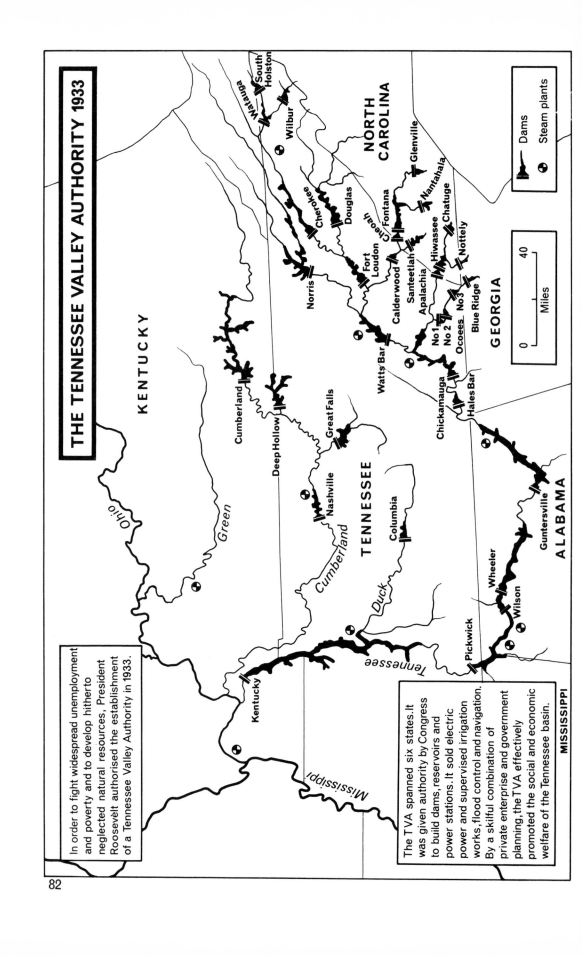

THE TENNESSEE VALLEY AUTHORITY 1933

In order to fight widespread unemployment and poverty and to develop hitherto neglected natural resources, President Roosevelt authorised the establishment of a Tennessee Valley Authority in 1933.

The TVA spanned six states. It was given authority by Congress to build dams, reservoirs and power stations. It sold electric power and supervised irrigation works, flood control and navigation. By a skilful combination of private enterprise and government planning, the TVA effectively promoted the social and economic welfare of the Tennessee basin.

Dams

Steam plants

40

Miles

0

KENTUCKY

NORTH CAROLINA

TENNESSEE

GEORGIA

ALABAMA

MISSISSIPPI

Ohio

Green

Cumberland

Mississippi

Duck

Tennessee

Kentucky

Pickwick

Wilson

Wheeler

Guntersville

Columbia

Nashville

Great Falls

Deep Hollow

Chickamauga

Hales Bar

Watts Bar

Norris

Fort Loudon

Cherokee

Douglas

Cheoah

Fontana

Calderwood

Santeetlah

Apalachia

Hiwassee

Nantahala

Chatuge

Nottely

Glenville

No 1

No 2

Ocoees No 3

Blue Ridge

Watauga

South Holston

Wilbur

THE UNITED STATES 1914–1945

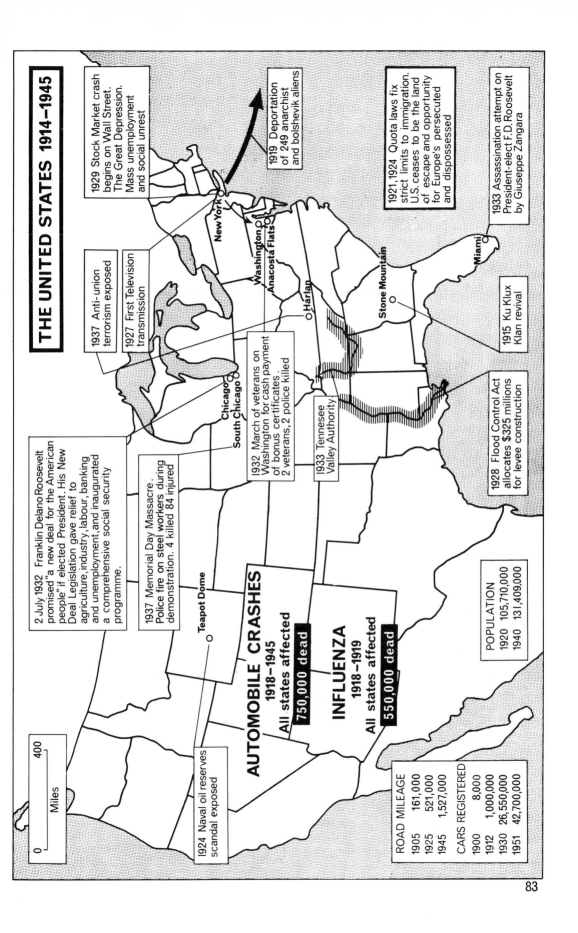

1929 Stock Market crash begins on Wall Street. The Great Depression. Mass unemployment and social unrest

1919 Deportation of 249 anarchist and bolshevik aliens

1921, 1924 Quota laws fix strict limits to immigration. U.S. ceases to be the land of escape and opportunity for Europe's persecuted and dispossessed

1933 Assassination attempt on President-elect F.D. Roosevelt by Giuseppe Zangara

1937 Anti-union terrorism exposed

1927 First Television transmission

1915 Ku Klux Klan revival

2 July 1932 Franklin Delano Roosevelt promised "a new deal for the American people" if elected President. His New Deal Legislation gave relief to agriculture, industry, labour, banking and unemployment, and inaugurated a comprehensive social security programme.

1932 March of veterans on Washington for cash payment of bonus certificates. 2 veterans, 2 police killed

1933 Tennessee Valley Authority

1928 Flood Control Act allocates $325 millions for levee construction

1937 Memorial Day Massacre. Police fire on steel workers during demonstration. 4 killed 84 injured

1924 Naval oil reserves scandal exposed

New York
Washington
Anacosta Flats
Harlan
Stone Mountain
Miami
Chicago
South Chicago
Teapot Dome

AUTOMOBILE CRASHES
1918–1945
All states affected
750,000 dead

INFLUENZA
1918–1919
All states affected
550,000 dead

POPULATION
1920 105,710,000
1940 131,409,000

ROAD MILEAGE	
1905	161,000
1925	521,000
1945	1,527,000

CARS REGISTERED	
1900	8,000
1912	1,000,000
1930	26,550,000
1951	42,700,000

0 ___ 400
Miles

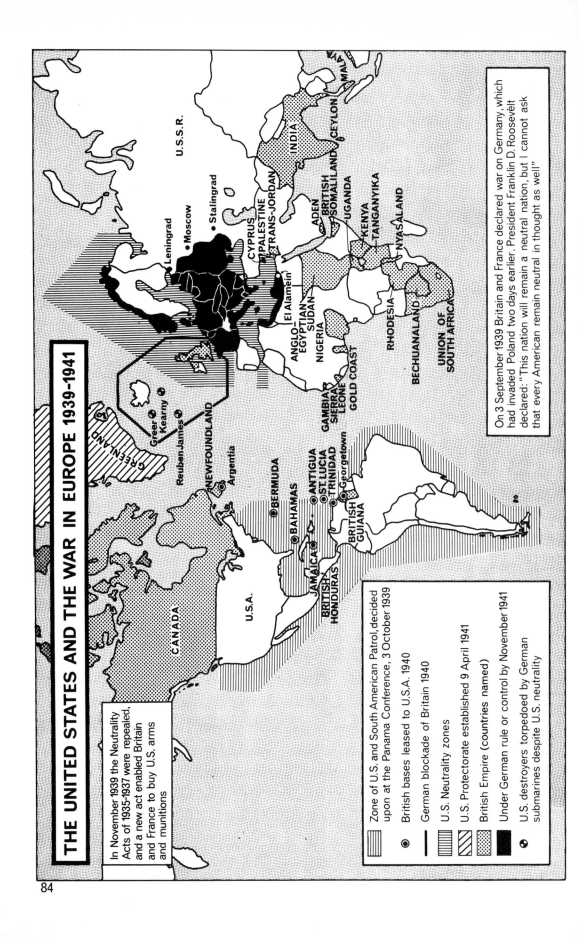

THE UNITED STATES AND THE WAR IN EUROPE 1939-1941

In November 1939 the Neutrality Acts of 1935-1937 were repealed, and a new act enabled Britain and France to buy U.S. arms and munitions

On 3 September 1939 Britain and France declared war on Germany, which had invaded Poland two days earlier. President Franklin D. Roosevelt declared: "This nation will remain a neutral nation, but I cannot ask that every American remain neutral in thought as well"

Zone of U.S. and South American Patrol, decided upon at the Panama Conference, 3 October 1939

British bases leased to U.S.A. 1940

German blockade of Britain 1940

U.S. Neutrality zones

U.S. Protectorate established 9 April 1941

British Empire (countries named)

Under German rule or control by November 1941

U.S. destroyers torpedoed by German submarines despite U.S. neutrality

GREENLAND

Greer
Kearny
Reuben James
NEWFOUNDLAND
Argentia

CANADA

U.S.A.

BERMUDA
BAHAMAS
JAMAICA
BRITISH HONDURAS
ANTIGUA
ST LUCIA
TRINIDAD
Georgetown
BRITISH GUIANA

U.S.S.R.

Leningrad
Moscow
Stalingrad

CYPRUS
PALESTINE
TRANS-JORDAN
ANGLO-EGYPTIAN SUDAN
El Alamein
NIGERIA
GAMBIA
SIERRA LEONE
GOLD COAST
ADEN
BRITISH SOMALILAND
UGANDA
KENYA
TANGANYIKA
NYASALAND
RHODESIA
BECHUANALAND
UNION OF SOUTH AFRICA

INDIA
CEYLON

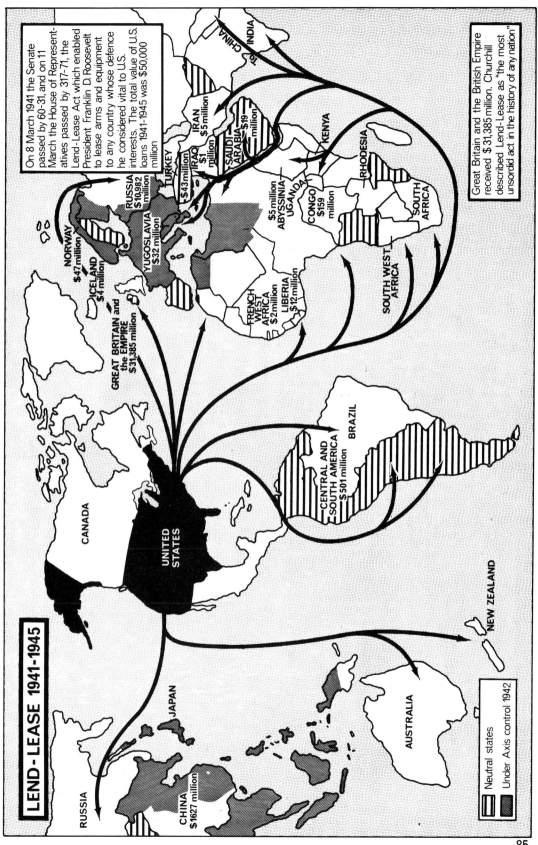

LEND-LEASE 1941-1945

On 8 March 1941 the Senate passed by 60-31, and on 11 March the House of Representatives passed by 317-71, the Lend-Lease Act which enabled President Franklin D Roosevelt to lease arms and equipment to any country whose defence he considered vital to U.S. interests. The total value of U.S. loans 1941-1945 was $50,000 million

Great Britain and the British Empire received $ 31,385 million. Churchill described Lend-Lease as "the most unsordid act in the history of any nation"

CHINA
INDIA
TURKEY
IRAN $5million
IRAQ $1 million
SAUDI ARABIA $19 million
KENYA
RHODESIA
SOUTH AFRICA
UGANDA $5million
CONGO $159 million
ABYSSINIA
RUSSIA $10,982 million
$43million
YUGOSLAVIA $32 million
NORWAY $47million
ICELAND $4 million
SOUTH WEST AFRICA
GREAT BRITAIN and the EMPIRE $31,385 million
FRENCH WEST AFRICA $2million
LIBERIA $12million
CANADA
UNITED STATES
BRAZIL
CENTRAL AND SOUTH AMERICA $501 million
NEW ZEALAND
AUSTRALIA
JAPAN
CHINA $1627 million
RUSSIA

Neutral states
Under Axis control 1942

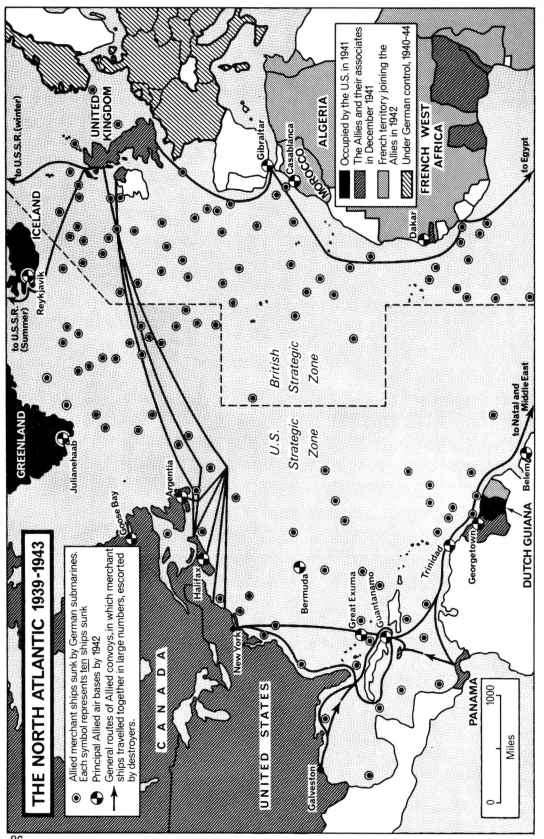

THE NORTH ATLANTIC 1939-1943

◉ Allied merchant ships sunk by German submarines. Each symbol represents *ten* ships sunk

◕ Principal Allied air bases by 1942

↑ General routes of Allied convoys, in which merchant ships travelled together in large numbers, escorted by destroyers.

Occupied by the U.S. in 1941

The Allies and their associates in December 1941

French territory joining the Allies in 1942

Under German control, 1940-44

GREENLAND

ICELAND

to U.S.S.R. (Summer)

to U.S.S.R. (winter)

Reykjavik

UNITED KINGDOM

Julianehaab

Goose Bay

Argentia

Gibraltar

Casablanca

MOROCCO

ALGERIA

FRENCH WEST AFRICA

Dakar

to Egypt

C A N A D A

Halifax

New York

U.S. Strategic Zone

British Strategic Zone

UNITED STATES

Galveston

Bermuda

Great Exuma

Guantanamo

Trinidad

Georgetown

DUTCH GUIANA

Belem

to Natal and Middle East

PANAMA

0   1000

Miles

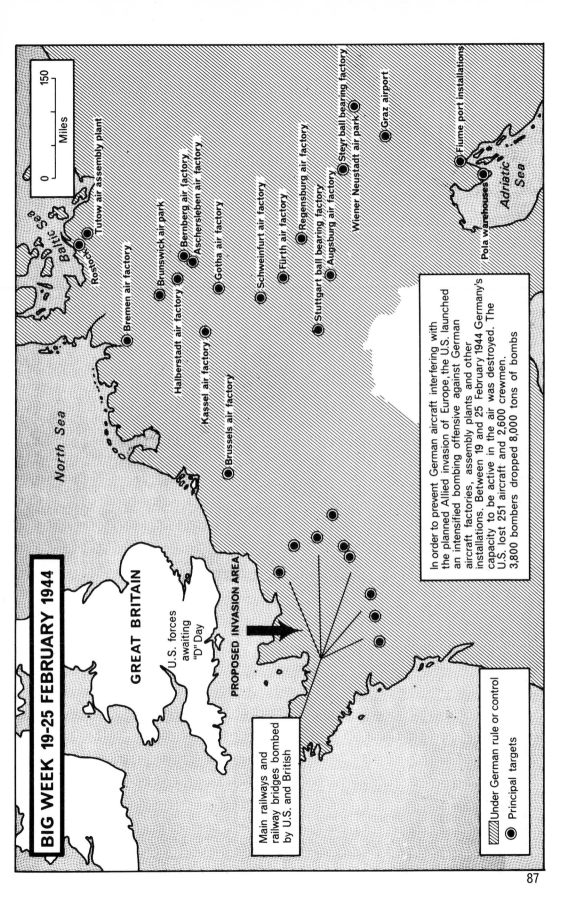

BIG WEEK 19-25 FEBRUARY 1944

GREAT BRITAIN

U.S. forces
awaiting
"D" Day

PROPOSED INVASION AREA

North Sea

Main railways and
railway bridges bombed
by U.S. and British

Baltic Sea

Rostock

Tutow air assembly plant

Bremen air factory

Brunswick air park

Bernberg air factory

Aschersleben air factory

Halberstadt air factory

Gotha air factory

Kassel air factory

Schweinfurt air factory

Fürth air factory

Regensburg air factory

Stuttgart ball bearing factory

Augsburg air factory

Steyr ball bearing factory

Wiener Neustadt air park

Graz airport

Brussels air factory

Pola warehouses

Fiume port installations

Adriatic Sea

0   150
Miles

In order to prevent German aircraft interfering with
the planned Allied invasion of Europe, the U.S. launched
an intensified bombing offensive against German
aircraft factories, assembly plants and other
installations. Between 19 and 25 February 1944 Germany's
capacity to be active in the air was destroyed. The
U.S. lost 251 aircraft and 2,600 crewmen.
3,800 bombers dropped 8,000 tons of bombs.

▨ Under German rule or control
◉ Principal targets

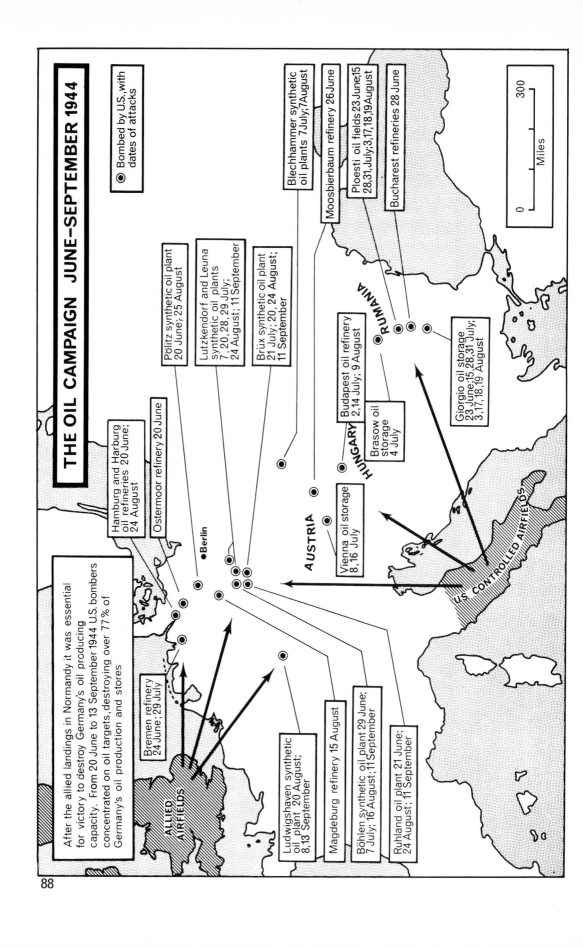

THE OIL CAMPAIGN JUNE–SEPTEMBER 1944

◉ Bombed by U.S.,with dates of attacks

After the allied landings in Normandy it was essential for victory to destroy Germany's oil producing capacity. From 20 June to 13 September 1944 U.S. bombers concentrated on oil targets, destroying over 77% of Germany's oil production and stores

0 ⊢———⊣ 300

Miles

Pölitz synthetic oil plant 20 June; 25 August

Lutzkendorf and Leuna synthetic oil plants 7, 20, 28, 29 July; 24 August; 11 September

Brüx synthetic oil plant 21 July; 20, 24 August; 11 September

Blechhammer synthetic oil plants 7 July; 7 August

Moosbierbaum refinery 26 June

Ploesti oil fields 23 June; 15 28, 31, July; 3, 17, 18, 19 August

Bucharest refineries 28 June

Hamburg and Harburg oil refineries 20 June; 24 August

Ostermoor refinery 20 June

•Berlin

RUMANIA

Budapest oil refinery 2, 14 July; 9 August

Brasov oil storage 4 July

Giorgio oil storage 23 June; 15, 28, 31 July; 3, 17, 18, 19 August

HUNGARY

AUSTRIA

Vienna oil storage 8, 16 July

U.S. CONTROLLED AIRFIELDS

Bremen refinery 24 June; 29 July

ALLIED AIRFIELDS

Ludwigshaven synthetic oil plant 20 August; 8, 13 September

Magdeburg refinery 15 August

Böhlen synthetic oil plant 29 June; 7 July; 16 August; 11 September

Ruhland oil plant 21 June; 24 August; 11 September

88

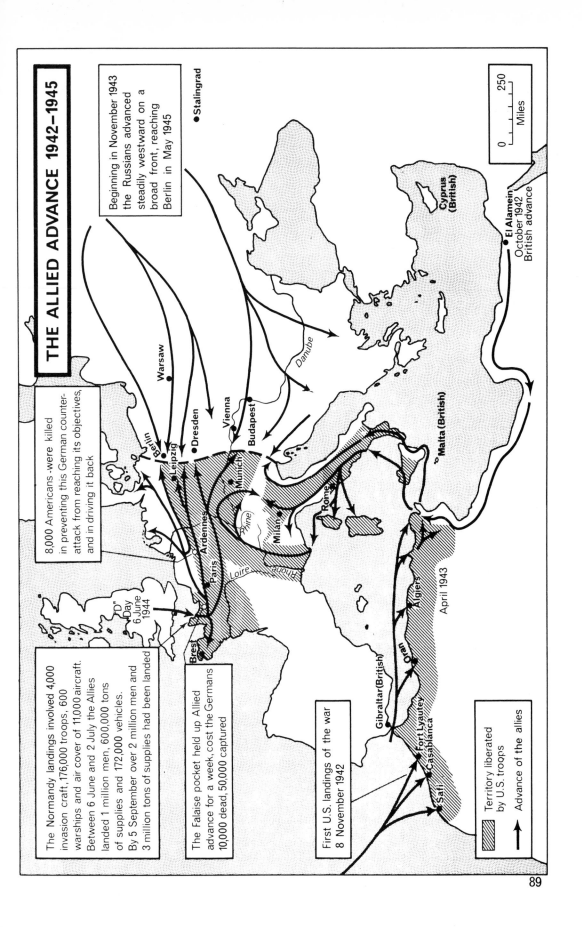

THE ALLIED ADVANCE 1942–1945

Beginning in November 1943 the Russians advanced steadily westward on a broad front, reaching Berlin in May 1945

•Stalingrad

0   250
Miles

Cyprus
(British)

El Alamein
October 1942
British advance

Danube

Warsaw

Vienna

Dresden

•Leipzig

Budapest

Berlin

Munich

Malta (British)

8,000 Americans -were killed in preventing this German counter-attack from reaching its objectives, and in driving it back

Ardennes

Rhine

Milan

Rome

April 1943

Paris

Loire

Rhône

The Normandy landings involved 4,000 invasion craft, 176,000 troops, 600 warships and air cover of 11,000 aircraft. Between 6 June and 2 July the Allies landed 1 million men, 600,000 tons of supplies and 172,000 vehicles. By 5 September over 2 million men and 3 million tons of supplies had been landed

"D" Day 6 June 1944

Brest

The Falaise pocket held up Allied advance for a week, cost the Germans 10,000 dead, 50,000 captured

Algiers

Oran

Gibraltar(British)

First U.S. landings of the war 8 November 1942

Fort Lyautey
Casablanca

Safi

Territory liberated by U.S. troops

Advance of the allies

89

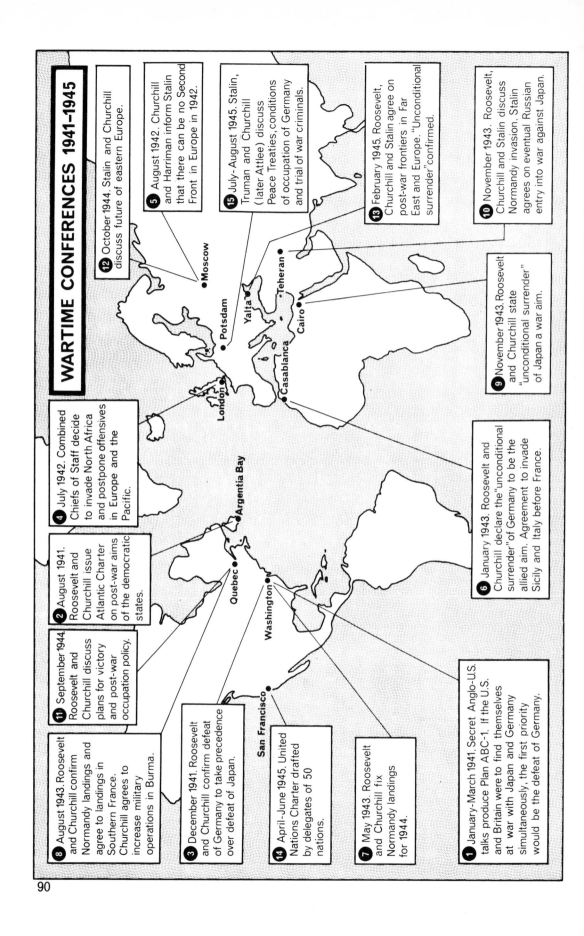

WARTIME CONFERENCES 1941–1945

12 October 1944. Stalin and Churchill discuss future of eastern Europe.

5 August 1942. Churchill and Harriman inform Stalin that there can be no Second Front in Europe in 1942.

15 July–August 1945. Stalin, Truman and Churchill (later Attlee) discuss Peace Treaties, conditions of occupation of Germany and trial of war criminals.

13 February 1945. Roosevelt, Churchill and Stalin agree on post-war frontiers in Far East and Europe. "Unconditional surrender" confirmed.

10 November 1943. Roosevelt, Churchill and Stalin discuss Normandy invasion. Stalin agrees on eventual Russian entry into war against Japan.

9 November 1943. Roosevelt and Churchill state "unconditional surrender" of Japan a war aim.

4 July 1942. Combined Chiefs of Staff decide to invade North Africa and postpone offensives in Europe and the Pacific.

2 August 1941. Roosevelt and Churchill issue Atlantic Charter on post-war aims of the democratic states.

11 September 1944. Roosevelt and Churchill discuss plans for victory and post-war occupation policy.

6 January 1943. Roosevelt and Churchill declare the "unconditional surrender" of Germany to be the allied aim. Agreement to invade Sicily and Italy before France.

8 August 1943. Roosevelt and Churchill confirm Normandy landings and agree to landings in Southern France. Churchill agrees to increase military operations in Burma.

3 December 1941. Roosevelt and Churchill confirm defeat of Germany to take precedence over defeat of Japan.

14 April–June 1945. United Nations Charter drafted by delegates of 50 nations.

7 May 1943. Roosevelt and Churchill fix Normandy landings for 1944.

1 January–March 1941. Secret Anglo-U.S. talks produce Plan ABC-1. If the U.S. and Britain were to find themselves at war with Japan and Germany simultaneously, the first priority would be the defeat of Germany.

Moscow

Potsdam

Yalta

Teheran

Casablanca

Cairo

London

Argentia Bay

Quebec

Washington

San Francisco

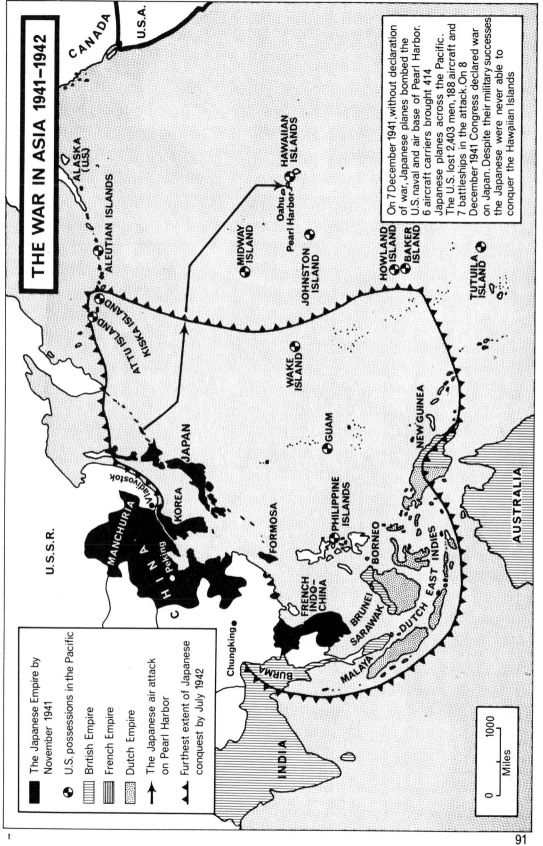

THE WAR IN ASIA 1941–1942

On 7 December 1941, without declaration of war, Japanese planes bombed the U.S. naval and air base of Pearl Harbor. 6 aircraft carriers brought 414 Japanese planes across the Pacific. The U.S. lost 2,403 men, 188 aircraft and 7 battleships in the attack. On 8 December 1941 Congress declared war on Japan. Despite their military successes the Japanese were never able to conquer the Hawaiian Islands

CANADA

U.S.A.

ALASKA (U.S.)

ALEUTIAN ISLANDS

KISKA ISLAND

ATTU ISLAND

U.S.S.R.

MANCHURIA

Vladivostok

KOREA

JAPAN

C H I N A

Peking

Chungking

FORMOSA

FRENCH INDO-CHINA

BURMA

INDIA

MALAYA

SARAWAK

BRUNEI

BORNEO

DUTCH EAST INDIES

PHILIPPINE ISLANDS

GUAM

WAKE ISLAND

NEW GUINEA

AUSTRALIA

MIDWAY ISLAND

Oahu
Pearl Harbor

HAWAIIAN ISLANDS

JOHNSTON ISLAND

HOWLAND ISLAND

BAKER ISLAND

TUTUILA ISLAND

Legend

- The Japanese Empire by November 1941
- U.S. possessions in the Pacific
- British Empire
- French Empire
- Dutch Empire
- The Japanese air attack on Pearl Harbor
- Furthest extent of Japanese conquest by July 1942

0   1000
Miles

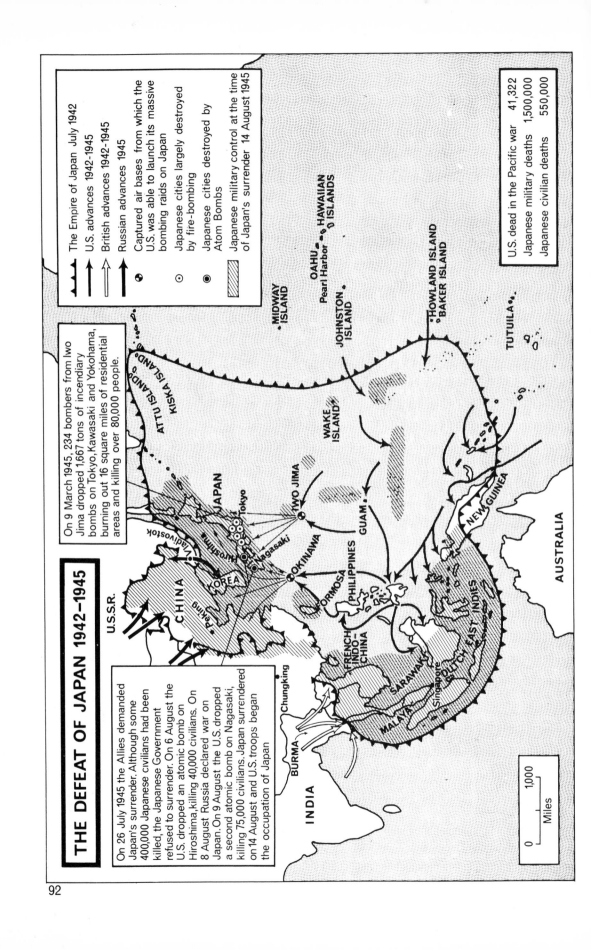

THE DEFEAT OF JAPAN 1942-1945

On 26 July 1945 the Allies demanded Japan's surrender. Although some 400,000 Japanese civilians had been killed, the Japanese Government refused to surrender. On 6 August the U.S. dropped an atomic bomb on Hiroshima, killing 40,000 civilians. On 8 August Russia declared war on Japan. On 9 August the U.S. dropped a second atomic bomb on Nagasaki, killing 75,000 civilians. Japan surrendered on 14 August and U.S. troops began the occupation of Japan

On 9 March 1945, 234 bombers from Iwo Jima dropped 1,667 tons of incendiary bombs on Tokyo, Kawasaki and Yokohama, burning out 16 square miles of residential areas and killing over 80,000 people.

The Empire of Japan July 1942

U.S. advances 1942-1945

British advances 1942-1945

Russian advances 1945

Captured air bases from which the U.S. was able to launch its massive bombing raids on Japan

Japanese cities largely destroyed by fire-bombing

Japanese cities destroyed by Atom Bombs

Japanese military control at the time of Japan's surrender 14 August 1945

U.S. dead in the Pacific war 41,322

Japanese military deaths 1,500,000

Japanese civilian deaths 550,000

INDIA
BURMA
Chungking
CHINA
U.S.S.R.
Vladivostok
Peking
KOREA
JAPAN
Tokyo
Hiroshima
Nagasaki
OKINAWA
FORMOSA
PHILIPPINES
FRENCH INDO-CHINA
MALAYA
Singapore
SARAWAK
DUTCH EAST INDIES
NEW GUINEA
AUSTRALIA
IWO JIMA
GUAM
WAKE ISLAND
MIDWAY ISLAND
OAHU HAWAIIAN ISLANDS
Pearl Harbor
JOHNSTON ISLAND
HOWLAND ISLAND
BAKER ISLAND
TUTUILA
OGASAWARA ISLANDS
ATTU ISLAND
KISKA ISLAND

0   1,000
Miles

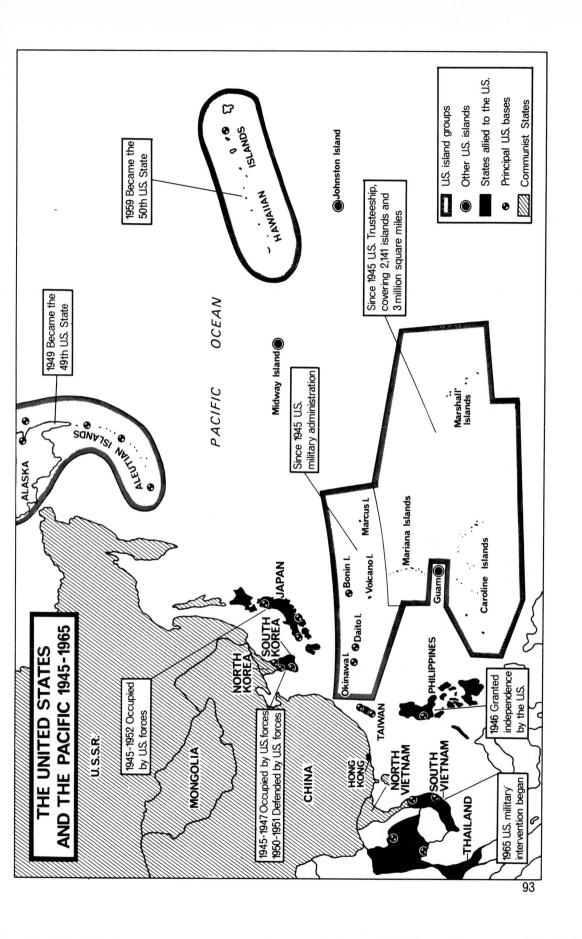

THE UNITED STATES
AND THE PACIFIC 1945-1965

1949 Became the 49th U.S. State

1959 Became the 50th U.S. State

Since 1945 U.S. Trusteeship, covering 2,141 islands and 3 million square miles

Since 1945 U.S. military administration

1945-1952 Occupied by U.S. forces

1945-1947 Occupied by U.S. forces
1950-1951 Defended by U.S. forces

1946 Granted independence by the U.S.

1965 U.S. military intervention began

U.S.S.R.

MONGOLIA

CHINA

ALASKA

ALEUTIAN ISLANDS

PACIFIC OCEAN

HAWAIIAN ISLANDS

Johnston Island

Midway Island

Marcus I.

Bonin I.

Volcano I.

Mariana Islands

Marshall Islands

Caroline Islands

Guam

Okinawa I.

Daito I.

JAPAN

NORTH KOREA

SOUTH KOREA

TAIWAN

HONG KONG

NORTH VIETNAM

SOUTH VIETNAM

THAILAND

PHILIPPINES

U.S. island groups

Other U.S. islands

States allied to the U.S.

Principal U.S. bases

Communist States

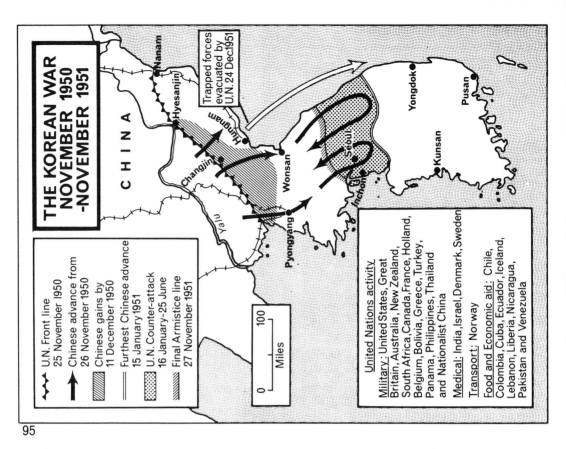

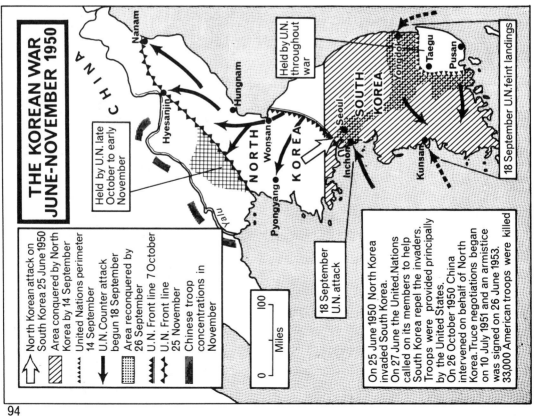

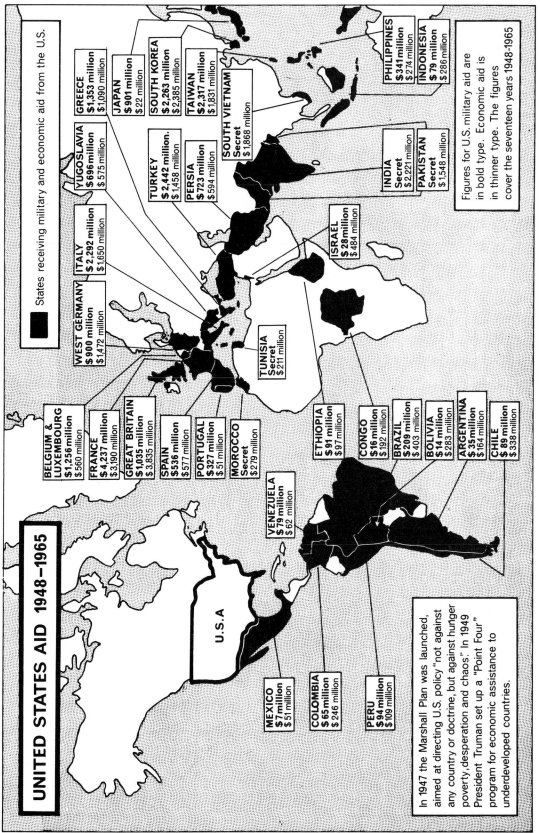

UNITED STATES AID 1948–1965

States receiving military and economic aid from the U.S.

In 1947 the Marshall Plan was launched, aimed at directing U.S. policy "not against any country or doctrine, but against hunger poverty, desperation and chaos." In 1949 President Truman set up a "Point Four" program for economic assistance to underdeveloped countries.

Figures for U.S. military aid are in bold type. Economic aid is in thinner type. The figures cover the seventeen years 1948-1965

U.S.A

MEXICO
$7million
$51 million

COLOMBIA
$65 million
$ 246 million

PERU
$94 million
$109 million

VENEZUELA
$79 million
$62 million

ETHIOPIA
$91 million
$97million

CONGO
$16 million
$ 192 million

BRAZIL
$209 million
$ 403 million

BOLIVIA
$14 million
$283 million

ARGENTINA
$35 million
$164 million

CHILE
$89 million
$ 338 million

BELGIUM &
LUXEMBOURG
$1,256million
$ 560 million

FRANCE
$4,237 million
$3,190 million

GREAT BRITAIN
$1,035 million
$3,835 million

SPAIN
$536 million
$577 million

PORTUGAL
$327 million
$ 51 million

MOROCCO
Secret
$279 million

WEST GERMANY
$900 million
$1,472 million

ITALY
$2,292 million
$1,650 million

TUNISIA
Secret
$211 million

GREECE
$1,353 million
$1,090 million

YUGOSLAVIA
$696million
$575 million

JAPAN
$901 million
$22 million

SOUTH KOREA
$2,263 million
$2,385 million

TURKEY
$2,442 million.
$1,458 million

PERSIA
$723 million
$594 million

TAIWAN
$2,317 million
$1,831 million

SOUTH VIETNAM
Secret
$1,868 million

ISRAEL
$28million
$484 million

INDIA
Secret
$2,221 million

PAKISTAN
Secret
$1,548 million

PHILIPPINES
$341million
$274 million

INDONESIA
$79 million
$286million

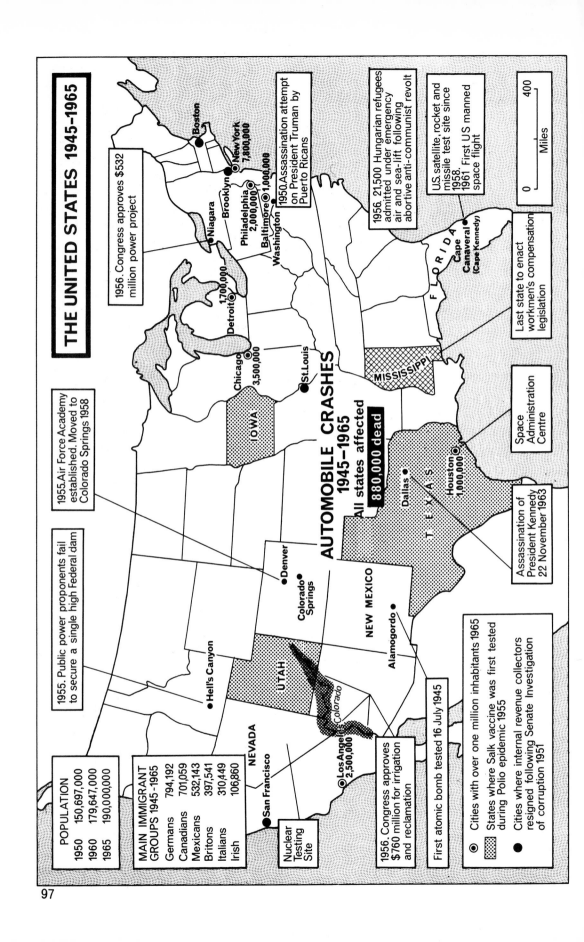

THE UNITED STATES 1945–1965

1956. Congress approves $532 million power project

1956. 21,500 Hungarian refugees admitted under emergency air and sea-lift following abortive anti-communist revolt

U.S. satellite, rocket and missile test site since 1958.
1961 First US manned space flight

1950.Assassination attempt on President Truman by Puerto Ricans

Last state to enact workmen's compensation legislation

Space Administration Centre

Assassination of President Kennedy 22 November 1963

1955.Air Force Academy established. Moved to Colorado Springs 1958

1955. Public power proponents fail to secure a single high Federal dam

1956. Congress approves $760 million for irrigation and reclamation

First atomic bomb tested 16 July 1945

AUTOMOBILE CRASHES
1945–1965
All states affected
880,000 dead

POPULATION
1950	150,697,000
1960	179,647,000
1965	190,000,000

MAIN IMMIGRANT GROUPS 1945–1965
Germans	794,192
Canadians	701,059
Mexicans	532,143
Britons	397,541
Italians	310,449
Irish	106,860

Nuclear Testing Site

Boston

New York 7,800,000

Brooklyn 2,000,000 ● Philadelphia 1,000,000

Niagara

Philadelphia 2,000,000

Baltimore 1,000,000

Washington

Detroit 1,700,000

Chicago 3,500,000

St.Louis

IOWA

MISSISSIPPI

FLORIDA

Cape Canaveral (Cape Kennedy)

TEXAS

Dallas ●

Houston 1,000,000 ●

Denver ●

Colorado Springs ●

NEW MEXICO

Alamogordo ●

Hell's Canyon ●

UTAH

Colorado

NEVADA

Los Angeles 2,500,000

San Francisco ●

◉ Cities with over one million inhabitants 1965

▒ States where Salk vaccine was first tested during Polio epidemic 1955

● Cities where internal revenue collectors resigned following Senate Investigation of corruption 1951

0   400
Miles

97

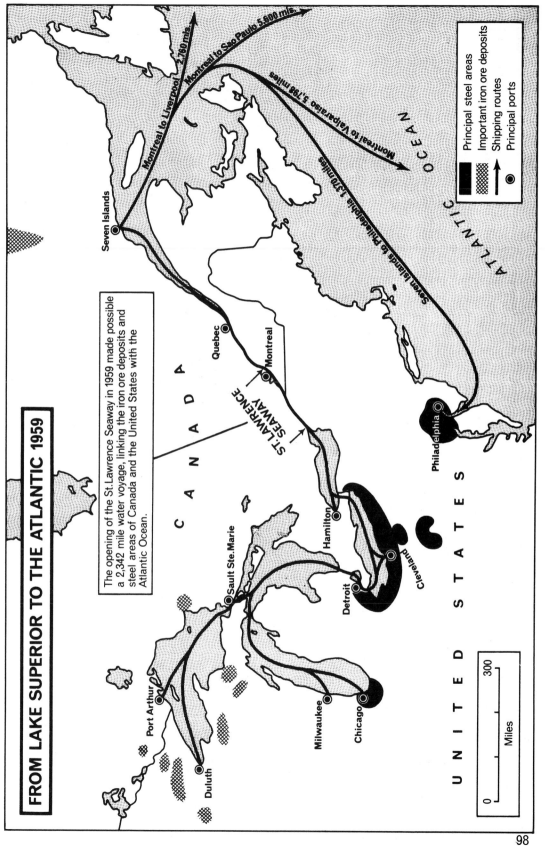

FROM LAKE SUPERIOR TO THE ATLANTIC 1959

The opening of the St.Lawrence Seaway in 1959 made possible a 2,342 mile water voyage, linking the iron ore deposits and steel areas of Canada and the United States with the Atlantic Ocean.

Montreal to Liverpool 2,760 miles

Montreal to Sao Paulo 5,800 miles

Montreal to Valparaiso 5,798 miles

Seven Islands to Philadelphia 1,370 miles

ATLANTIC OCEAN

ST. LAWRENCE SEAWAY

Seven Islands

Quebec

Montreal

Philadelphia

C A N A D A

Port Arthur

Duluth

Sault Ste.Marie

Milwaukee

Chicago

Detroit

Hamilton

Cleveland

U N I T E D   S T A T E S

Miles

0   300

Legend
- Principal steel areas
- Important iron ore deposits
- Shipping routes
- Principal ports

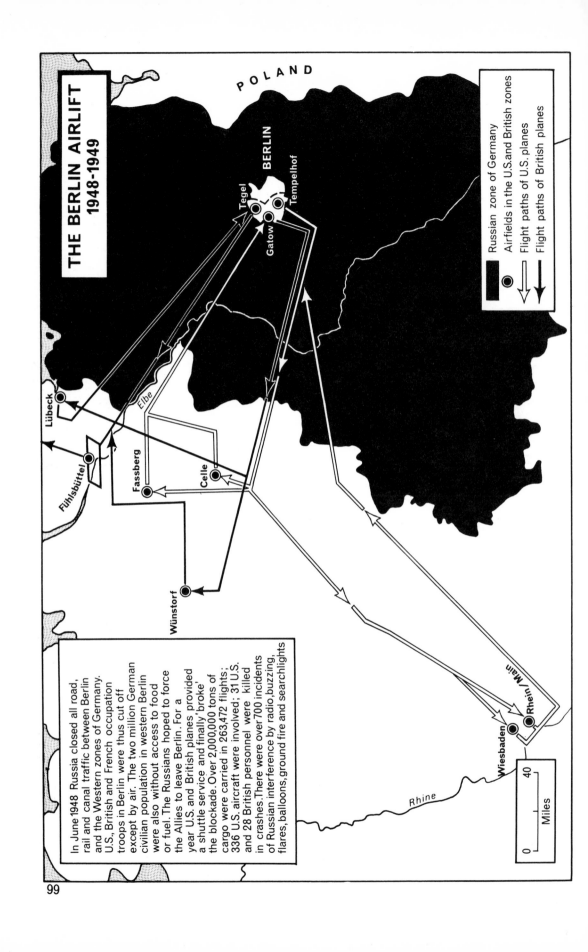

POLAND

THE BERLIN AIRLIFT
1948-1949

BERLIN

Tegel

Gatow

Tempelhof

Lübeck

Fühlsbüttel

Fassberg

Celle

Elbe

Wünstorf

Main

Rhein

Wiesbaden

Rhine

Russian zone of Germany

Airfields in the U.S.and British zones

Flight paths of U.S. planes

Flight paths of British planes

In June 1948 Russia closed all road, rail and canal traffic between Berlin and the Western zones of Germany. U.S., British and French occupation troops in Berlin were thus cut off except by air. The two million German civilian population in western Berlin were also without access to food or fuel. The Russians hoped to force the Allies to leave Berlin. For a year U.S. and British planes provided a shuttle service and finally 'broke' the blockade. Over 2,000,000 tons of cargo were carried in 263,472 flights; 336 U.S. aircraft were involved; 31 U.S. and 28 British personnel were killed in crashes.There were over700 incidents of Russian interference by radio,buzzing, flares, balloons,ground fire and searchlights

0   40
Miles

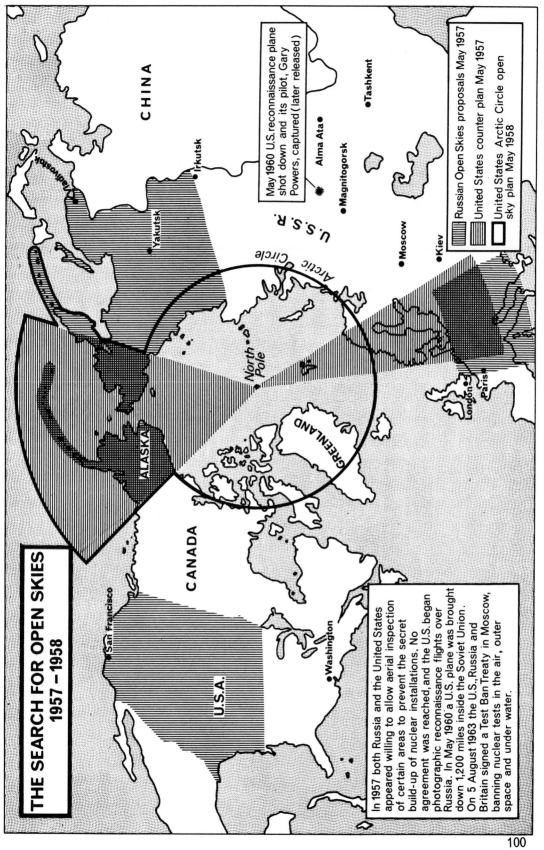

THE SEARCH FOR OPEN SKIES
1957 – 1958

CHINA

U.S.S.R.

●Tashkent

Alma Ata●

●Magnitogorsk

●Irkutsk

●Yakutsk

●Moscow

●Kiev

Vladivostok

Arctic Circle

North Pole

GREENLAND

ALASKA

CANADA

London● ●Paris

U.S.A.

●San Francisco

●Washington

May 1960 U.S. reconnaissance plane shot down and its pilot, Gary Powers, captured (later released)

Russian Open Skies proposals May 1957

United States counter plan May 1957

United States Arctic Circle open sky plan May 1958

In 1957 both Russia and the United States appeared willing to allow aerial inspection of certain areas to prevent the secret build-up of nuclear installations. No agreement was reached, and the U.S. began photographic reconnaissance flights over Russia. In May 1960 a U.S. plane was brought down 1,200 miles inside the Soviet Union. On 5 August 1963 the U.S., Russia and Britain signed a Test Ban Treaty in Moscow, banning nuclear tests in the air, outer space and under water.

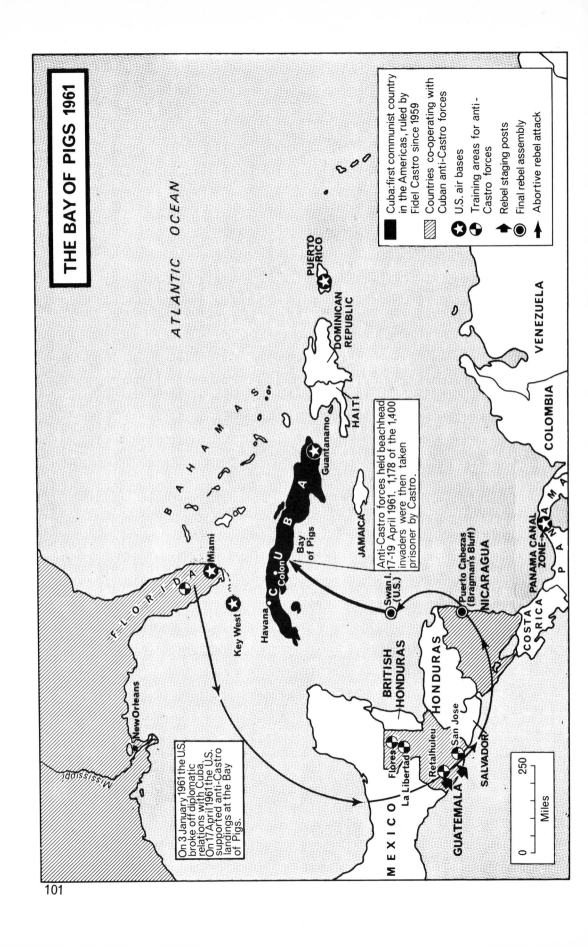

THE BAY OF PIGS 1961

ATLANTIC OCEAN

Legend:
- Cuba: first communist country in the Americas, ruled by Fidel Castro since 1959
- Countries co-operating with Cuban anti-Castro forces
- U.S. air bases
- Training areas for anti-Castro forces
- Rebel staging posts
- Final rebel assembly
- Abortive rebel attack

PUERTO RICO

DOMINICAN REPUBLIC

HAITI

JAMAICA

Swan I. (U.S.)

Anti-Castro forces held beachhead 17-19 April 1961. 1,178 of the 1,400 invaders were then taken prisoner by Castro.

Guantanamo

C U B A

Colon
Bay of Pigs
Havana

Miami

Key West

FLORIDA

New Orleans

Mississippi

BAHAMAS

On 3 January 1961 the U.S. broke off diplomatic relations with Cuba. On 17 April 1961 the U.S. supported anti-Castro landings at the Bay of Pigs.

MEXICO

BRITISH HONDURAS

Flores
La Libertad

HONDURAS

Retalhuleu
San Jose

GUATEMALA

SALVADOR

Puerto Cabezas (Bragman's Bluff)

NICARAGUA

COSTA RICA

PANAMA CANAL ZONE

PANAMA

COLOMBIA

VENEZUELA

0   250
Miles

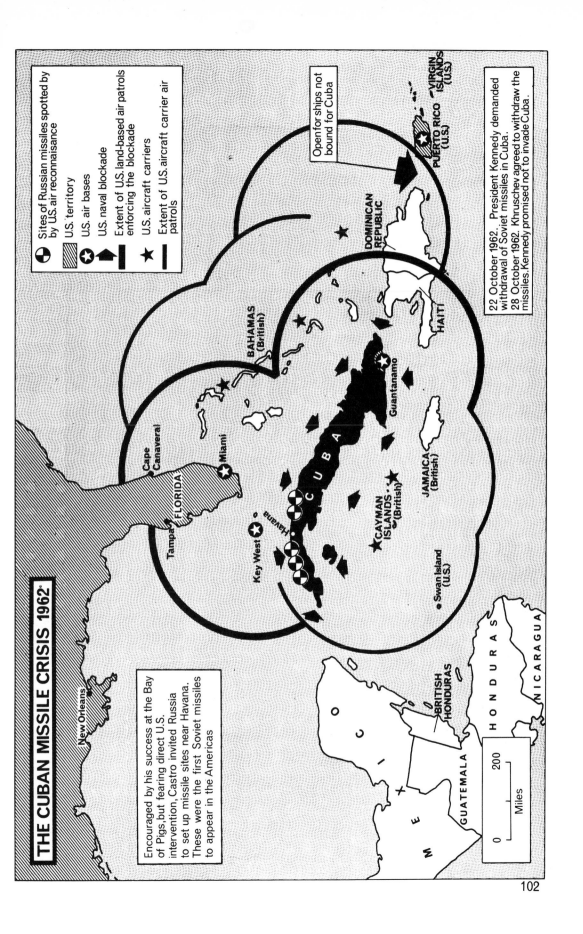

THE CUBAN MISSILE CRISIS 1962

Encouraged by his success at the Bay of Pigs, but fearing direct U.S. intervention, Castro invited Russia to set up missile sites near Havana. These were the first Soviet missiles to appear in the Americas

Open for ships not bound for Cuba

22 October 1962. President Kennedy demanded withdrawal of Soviet missiles in Cuba.
28 October 1962. Khruschev agreed to withdraw the missiles. Kennedy promised not to invade Cuba.

Legend:
- Sites of Russian missiles spotted by U.S. air reconnaissance
- U.S. territory
- U.S. air bases
- U.S. naval blockade
- Extent of U.S. land-based air patrols enforcing the blockade
- U.S. aircraft carriers
- Extent of U.S. aircraft carrier air patrols

New Orleans

FLORIDA
Tampa
Cape Canaveral
Miami
Key West

C U B A
Havana
Guantanamo

BAHAMAS (British)

DOMINICAN REPUBLIC
HAITI
PUERTO RICO (U.S.)
VIRGIN ISLANDS (U.S.)

CAYMAN ISLANDS (British)
JAMAICA (British)
Swan Island (U.S.)

M E X I C O
GUATEMALA
BRITISH HONDURAS
H O N D U R A S
N I C A R A G U A

0   200
Miles

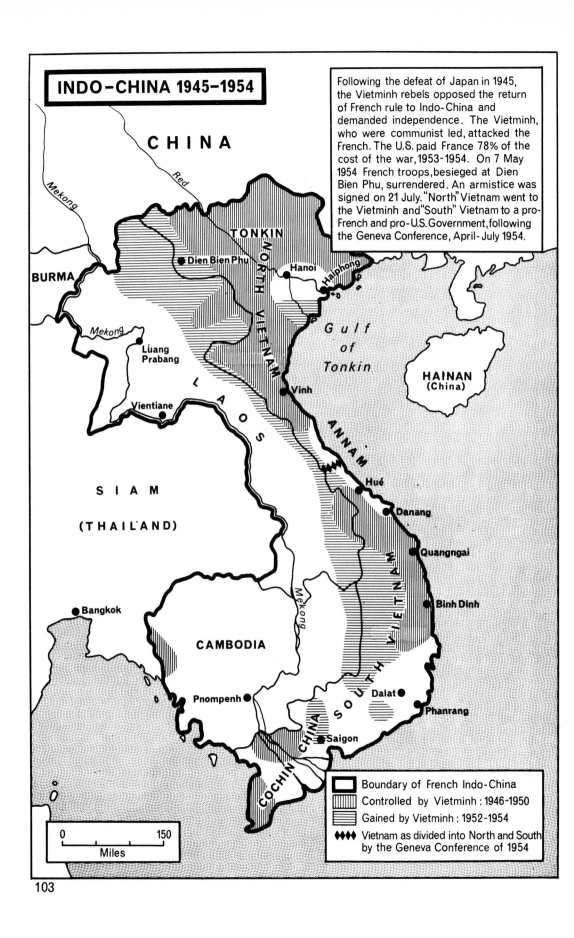

INDO-CHINA 1945-1954

Following the defeat of Japan in 1945, the Vietminh rebels opposed the return of French rule to Indo-China and demanded independence. The Vietminh, who were communist led, attacked the French. The U.S. paid France 78% of the cost of the war, 1953-1954. On 7 May 1954 French troops, besieged at Dien Bien Phu, surrendered. An armistice was signed on 21 July. "North" Vietnam went to the Vietminh and "South" Vietnam to a pro-French and pro-U.S. Government, following the Geneva Conference, April-July 1954.

CHINA

BURMA

TONKIN

● Dien Bien Phu

● Hanoi

Haiphong

NORTH VIETNAM

Red

Mekong

Mekong

● Luang Prabang

● Vientiane

L A O S

Gulf of Tonkin

HAINAN (China)

● Vinh

ANNAM

S I A M

(T H A I L A N D)

Hué

● Danang

● Quangngai

● Bangkok

CAMBODIA

Mekong

SOUTH VIETNAM

● Binh Dinh

● Dalat

● Phanrang

● Pnompenh

COCHIN CHINA

● Saigon

0   150

Miles

Boundary of French Indo-China

Controlled by Vietminh : 1946-1950

Gained by Vietminh : 1952-1954

◆◆◆◆ Vietnam as divided into North and South by the Geneva Conference of 1954

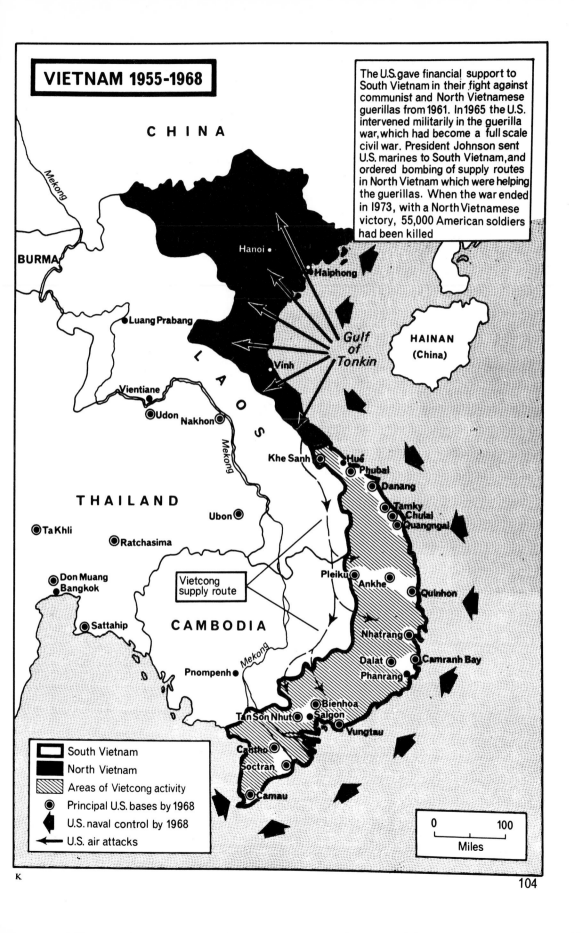

VIETNAM 1955-1968

CHINA

The U.S. gave financial support to South Vietnam in their fight against communist and North Vietnamese guerillas from 1961. In 1965 the U.S. intervened militarily in the guerilla war, which had become a full scale civil war. President Johnson sent U.S. marines to South Vietnam, and ordered bombing of supply routes in North Vietnam which were helping the guerillas. When the war ended in 1973, with a North Vietnamese victory, 55,000 American soldiers had been killed

BURMA

Hanoi

Haiphong

Luang Prabang

HAINAN
(China)

Gulf
of
Tonkin

Vinh

Vientiane

Udon
Nakhon

L A O S

Khe Sanh
Hué
Phubal
Danang
Tamky
Chulai
Quangngai

THAILAND

Ubon

Ta Khli

Ratchasima

Pleiku
Ankhe
Quinhon

Don Muang
Bangkok

Vietcong
supply route

CAMBODIA

Sattahip

Nhatrang

Dalat
Camranh Bay
Phanrang

Pnompenh

Mekong

Bienhoa
Tan Son Nhut
Saigon
Vungtau

Cantho
Soctran

Camau

	South Vietnam
	North Vietnam
	Areas of Vietcong activity
◉	Principal U.S. bases by 1968
◄	U.S. naval control by 1968
←	U.S. air attacks

0   100
Miles

K

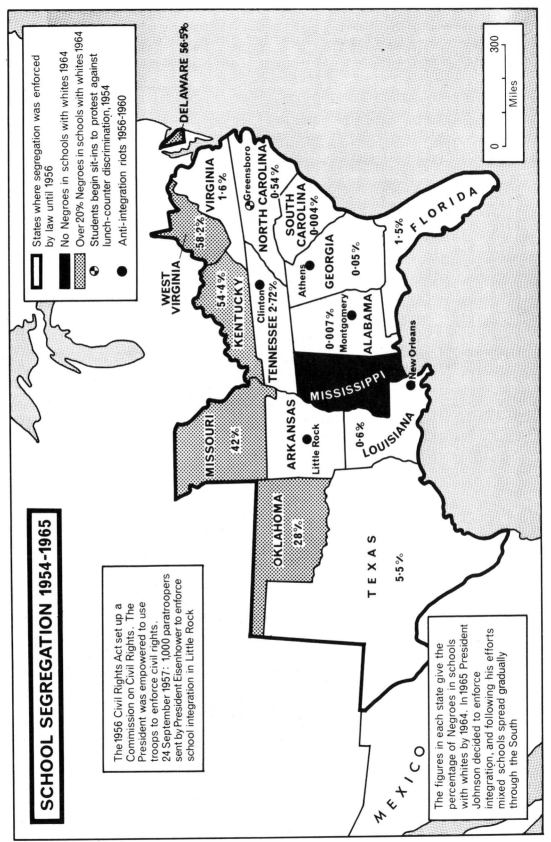

SCHOOL SEGREGATION 1954–1965

The 1956 Civil Rights Act set up a Commission on Civil Rights. The President was empowered to use troops to enforce civil rights.
24 September 1957: 1,000 paratroopers sent by President Eisenhower to enforce school integration in Little Rock

The figures in each state give the percentage of Negroes in schools with whites by 1964. In 1965 President Johnson decided to enforce integration, and following his efforts mixed schools spread gradually through the South

Legend:
- States where segregation was enforced by law until 1956
- No Negroes in schools with whites 1964
- Over 20% Negroes in schools with whites 1964
- ◑ Students begin sit-ins to protest against lunch-counter discrimination, 1954
- ● Anti-integration riots 1956–1960

DELAWARE 56·5%

VIRGINIA 1·6%

●Greensboro

NORTH CAROLINA 0·54%

SOUTH CAROLINA 0·004%

WEST VIRGINIA 58·2%

KENTUCKY 54·4%

●Clinton

TENNESSEE 2·72%

Athens

GEORGIA 0·05%

1·5%

FLORIDA

0·007%

Montgomery

ALABAMA

●New Orleans

MISSOURI 42%

ARKANSAS

●Little Rock

0·6%

LOUISIANA

MISSISSIPPI

OKLAHOMA 28%

TEXAS 5·5%

MEXICO

0   300
Miles

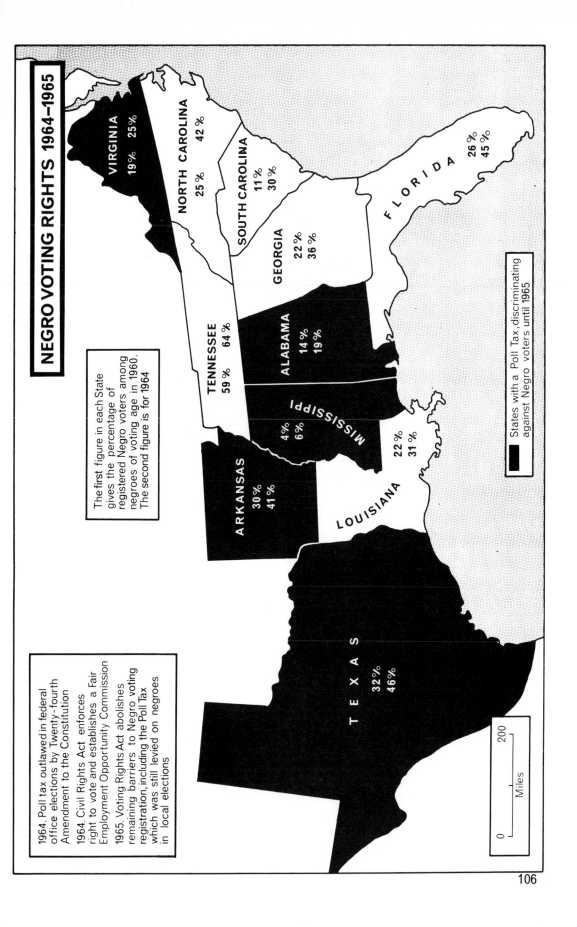

NEGRO VOTING RIGHTS 1964–1965

The first figure in each State gives the percentage of registered Negro voters among negroes of voting age in 1960. The second figure is for 1964

1964. Poll tax outlawed in federal office elections by Twenty-fourth Amendment to the Constitution

1964. Civil Rights Act enforces right to vote and establishes a Fair Employment Opportunity Commission

1965. Voting Rights Act abolishes remaining barriers to Negro voting registration, including the Poll Tax which was still levied on negroes in local elections

VIRGINIA
19% 25%

NORTH CAROLINA
25% 42%

SOUTH CAROLINA
11% 30%

GEORGIA
22% 36%

FLORIDA
26% 45%

TENNESSEE
59% 64%

ALABAMA
14% 19%

MISSISSIPPI
4% 6%

ARKANSAS
30% 41%

LOUISIANA
22% 31%

TEXAS
32% 46%

States with a Poll Tax, discriminating against Negro voters until 1965

0   200
Miles

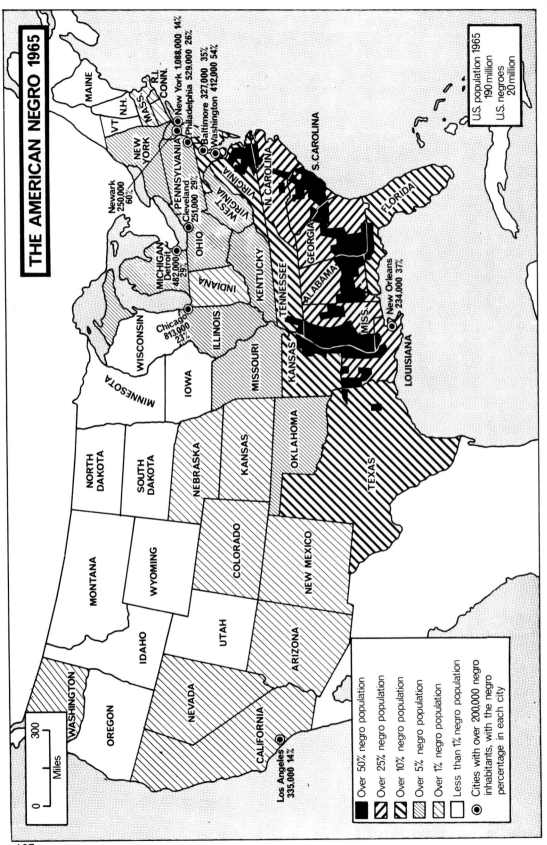

THE AMERICAN NEGRO 1965

U.S. population 1965 190 million
U.S. negroes 20 million

New York 1,088,000 14%
Philadelphia 529,000 26%
Baltimore 327,000 35%
Washington 412,000 54%

Newark 250,000 60%
Cleveland 251,000 29%
Detroit 482,000 29%
Chicago 813,000 23%
New Orleans 234,000 37%

Los Angeles 335,000 14%

Miles 0 300

- Over 50% negro population
- Over 25% negro population
- Over 10% negro population
- Over 5% negro population
- Over 1% negro population
- Less than 1% negro population
- Cities with over 200,000 negro inhabitants, with the negro percentage in each city

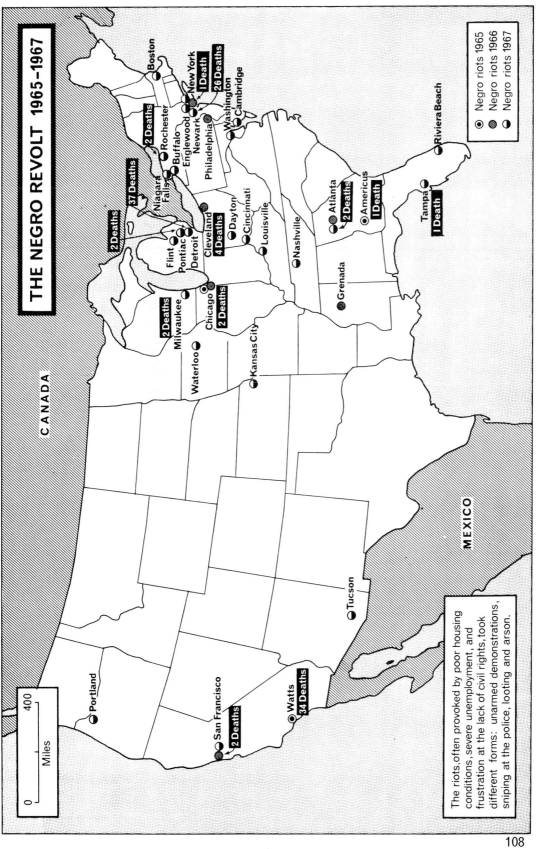

THE NEGRO REVOLT 1965-1967

CANADA

MEXICO

Portland

San Francisco **2 Deaths**

Watts **34 Deaths**

Tucson

Waterloo

Milwaukee **2 Deaths**

Chicago **2 Deaths**

Kansas City

Flint
Pontiac
Detroit **2 Deaths**

Cleveland **4 Deaths**

Dayton

Cincinnati

Louisville

Nashville

Grenada

Atlanta **2 Deaths**

Americus **I Death**

Niagara
Falls **37 Deaths**

Buffalo

Rochester **2 Deaths**

Englewood

Newark **26 Deaths**

Philadelphia

Washington

Cambridge

New York **I Death**

Boston

Tampa **I Death**

Riviera Beach

0   400
Miles

- ◉ Negro riots 1965
- ◍ Negro riots 1966
- ◐ Negro riots 1967

The riots, often provoked by poor housing
conditions, severe unemployment, and
frustration at the lack of civil rights, took
different forms: unarmed demonstrations,
sniping at the police, looting and arson.

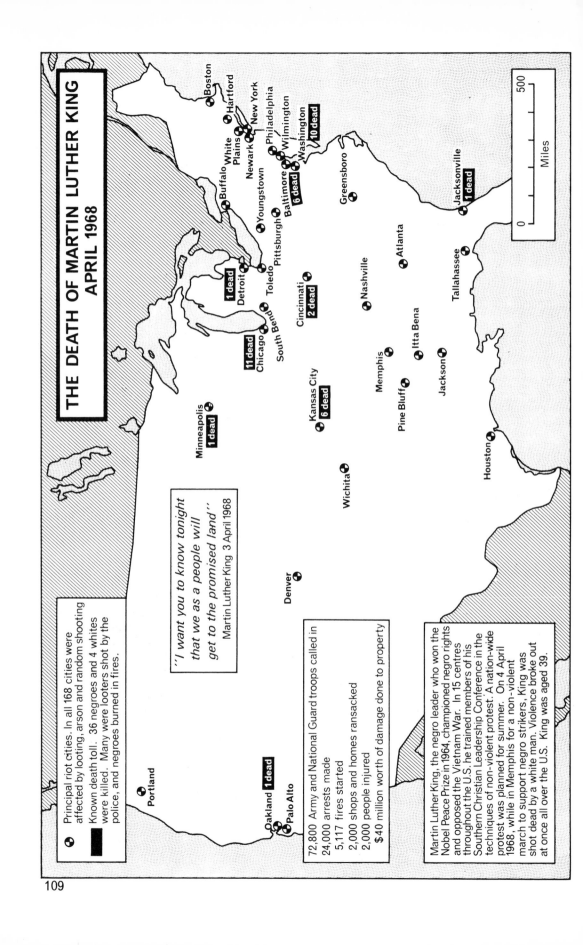

THE DEATH OF MARTIN LUTHER KING
APRIL 1968

Boston

Hartford
Buffalo   White   New York
          Plains
Newark   Philadelphia
Youngstown   Wilmington
Pittsburgh   Baltimore   Washington **10 dead**
                         6 dead
                                    Greensboro

Detroit **1 dead**
Toledo
Cincinnati **2 dead**   Nashville
Chicago **11 dead**
South Bend   Atlanta

Kansas City **6 dead**   Tallahassee
                                    Jacksonville **1 dead**
Minneapolis **1 dead**
                        Memphis
                        Pine Bluff   Itta Bena
Wichita   Jackson

                        Houston

Denver

Portland

Oakland **1 dead**
Palo Alto

0   500
        Miles

*"I want you to know tonight
that we as a people will
get to the promised land"*
Martin Luther King 3 April 1968

Principal riot cities. In all 168 cities were
affected by looting, arson and random shooting

Known death toll. 36 negroes and 4 whites
were killed. Many were looters shot by the
police, and negroes burned in fires.

72,800 Army and National Guard troops called in
24,000 arrests made
5,117 fires started
2,000 shops and homes ransacked
2,000 people injured
$40 million worth of damage done to property

Martin Luther King, the negro leader who won the
Nobel Peace Prize in 1964, championed negro rights
and opposed the Vietnam War. In 15 centres
throughout the U.S. he trained members of his
Southern Christian Leadership Conference in the
techniques of non-violent protest. A nation-wide
protest was planned for summer. On 4 April
1968, while in Memphis for a non-violent
march to support negro strikers, King was
shot dead by a white man. Violence broke out
at once all over the U.S. King was aged 39.

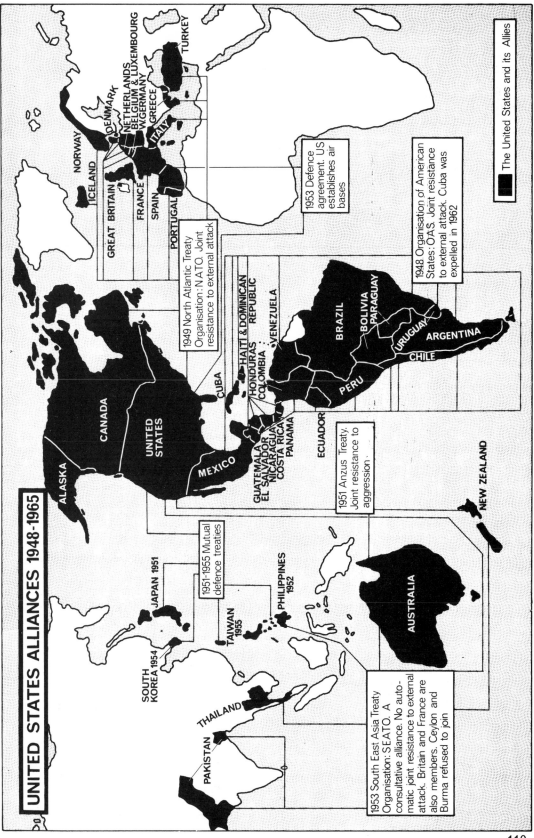

UNITED STATES ALLIANCES 1948-1965

NORWAY
ICELAND
GREAT BRITAIN
FRANCE
SPAIN
PORTUGAL
DENMARK
NETHERLANDS, BELGIUM & LUXEMBOURG
W.GERMANY
ITALY
GREECE
TURKEY

1949 North Atlantic Treaty Organisation: N.A.T.O. Joint resistance to external attack

1953 Defence agreement. US establishes air bases

1948 Organisation of American States: O.A.S. Joint resistance to external attack. Cuba was expelled in 1962

ALASKA
CANADA
UNITED STATES
MEXICO
GUATEMALA
EL SALVADOR
NICARAGUA
COSTA RICA
PANAMA
CUBA
HAITI & DOMINICAN REPUBLIC
HONDURAS
COLOMBIA
VENEZUELA
ECUADOR
PERU
BRAZIL
BOLIVIA
PARAGUAY
CHILE
URUGUAY
ARGENTINA

1951 Anzus Treaty. Joint resistance to aggression.

1951-1955 Mutual defence treaties

JAPAN 1951
SOUTH KOREA 1954
TAIWAN 1955
PHILIPPINES 1952

PAKISTAN
THAILAND

NEW ZEALAND
AUSTRALIA

1953 South East Asia Treaty Organisation: SEATO. A consultative alliance. No automatic joint resistance to external attack. Britain and France are also members. Ceylon and Burma refused to join

■ The United States and its Allies

110

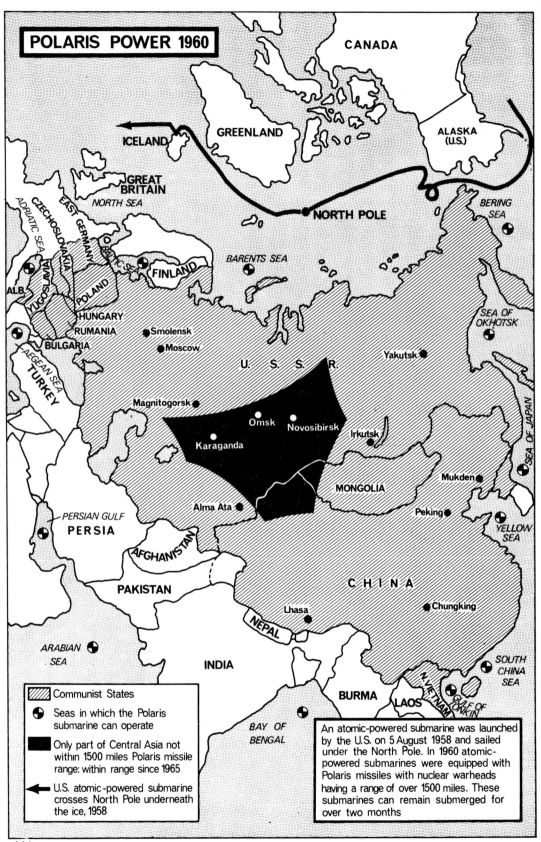

POLARIS POWER 1960

CANADA

ICELAND
GREENLAND
ALASKA (U.S.)

NORTH SEA
GREAT BRITAIN

EAST GERMANY
CZECHOSLOVAKIA
ADRIATIC SEA
ALB.
YUGOSLAVIA
POLAND
FINLAND
HUNGARY
RUMANIA
BULGARIA
AEGEAN SEA
TURKEY

BARENTS SEA

NORTH POLE

BERING SEA

SEA OF OKHOTSK

Smolensk
Moscow

U. S. S. R.

Yakutsk

Magnitogorsk

Omsk
Novosibirsk
Irkutsk

Karaganda

Alma Ata

MONGOLIA

Mukden

Peking

SEA OF JAPAN

YELLOW SEA

PERSIAN GULF
PERSIA

AFGHANISTAN

PAKISTAN

NEPAL
Lhasa

C H I N A

Chungking

SOUTH CHINA SEA

ARABIAN SEA

INDIA

BURMA

LAOS
N. VIETNAM
GULF OF TONKIN

BAY OF BENGAL

/// Communist States

✪ Seas in which the Polaris submarine can operate

■ Only part of Central Asia not within 1500 miles Polaris missile range: within range since 1965

← U.S. atomic-powered submarine crosses North Pole underneath the ice, 1958

An atomic-powered submarine was launched by the U.S. on 5 August 1958 and sailed under the North Pole. In 1960 atomic-powered submarines were equipped with Polaris missiles with nuclear warheads having a range of over 1500 miles. These submarines can remain submerged for over two months

AMERICAN PREPAREDNESS 1960

S.VIETNAM
Tan Son Nhut
Bienhoa
Chulai
Camranh Bay
Nhatrang
Danang
Ankhe
Ubon
Udon THAILAND
Nakhon
Ratchasima
Sattahip
Bangkok
Ta Khli

❼

PHILIPPINES
Sangley Point
Subic Bay
Clark

Tainan
Taipei
TAIWAN
Kadena Naha
OKINAWA

Andersen
Agana
Apra
Harbour
Iwo Jima
JAPAN
Yokosuka
Misawa
Tachikawa
Atsugi
Yokota

❼

S.KOREA
Kunsan
Sasebo
Iwakuni
Osan
Kimpo

CHINA

MONGOLIA

U.S.S.R.

PAKISTAN
Peshawar

SAUDI
ARABIA
Dhahran

TURKEY
Incirlik
Ankara
Cigli
Iraklion
GREECE
❻
Wheelus
Naples
ITALY
Ramstein
Aviano
Villefranche
W.GERMANY
Wiesbaden
New Amsterdam
FRANCE
HOLLAND
Prestwick
London
High
Wycombe
UNITED
KINGDOM
SPAIN
Zaragoza
Torrejon
Moron
Rota
Kenitra
MOROCCO
LIBYA

❼

Shemya

Adak

Midway

NORTH
POLE

ICELAND
Keflavik Airport

Thule

GREENLAND
Sondrestrom

Lajes Field
AZORES

ALASKA
Eielson
Elmendorf
Kodiak

DISTANT EARLY WARNING LINE

❷
Goose
Argentia

Johnston

HAWAIIAN IS
Pearl Harbor
Hickam
Wheeler
Bellows

MID-CANADA LINE
CANADA
PINETREE LINE

❶

UNITED STATES

U.S. NAVAL SPACE
SURVEILLANCE SYSTEM

Kindley
Bermuda

Ramey
Roosevelt
Roads
PUERTO RICO

CUBA
Guantanamo Bay

PANAMA
Coco Solo

	Communist States
	Major U.S. bases
	Ballistic Missile Early Warning System
	Radar coverage
	Other warning lines
	U.S. Fleets with numbers

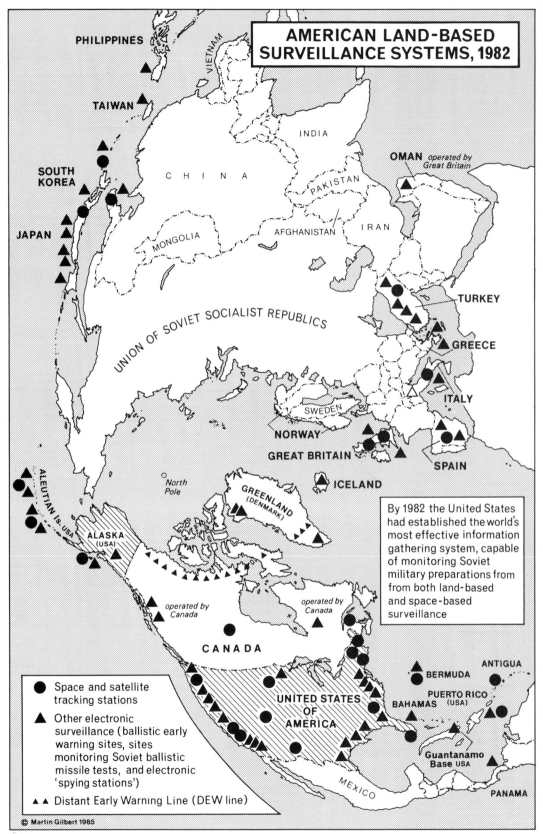

AMERICAN LAND-BASED SURVEILLANCE SYSTEMS, 1982

PHILIPPINES

TAIWAN

SOUTH KOREA

JAPAN

VIETNAM

INDIA

CHINA

PAKISTAN

MONGOLIA

AFGHANISTAN

IRAN

OMAN *operated by Great Britain*

TURKEY

GREECE

UNION OF SOVIET SOCIALIST REPUBLICS

ITALY

SWEDEN

NORWAY

GREAT BRITAIN

SPAIN

ALEUTIAN IS. USA

North Pole

ICELAND

ALASKA (USA)

GREENLAND (DENMARK)

By 1982 the United States had established the world's most effective information gathering system, capable of monitoring Soviet military preparations from from both land-based and space-based surveillance

operated by Canada

operated by Canada

CANADA

ANTIGUA

BERMUDA

PUERTO RICO (USA)

BAHAMAS

UNITED STATES OF AMERICA

● Space and satellite tracking stations

▲ Other electronic surveillance (ballistic early warning sites, sites monitoring Soviet ballistic missile tests, and electronic 'spying stations')

▲▲ Distant Early Warning Line (DEW line)

Guantanamo Base USA

MEXICO

PANAMA

© Martin Gilbert 1985

THE UNITED STATES AND THE SOVIET UNION IN OUTER SPACE

Between 1957 and 1981 a total of 2,725 satellites were launched, most of them by the United States and the Soviet Union. Some of the principal satellites in orbit in 1981 are shown here. In March 1981 the US National Aeronautics and Space Administration (NASA) launched its Columbia Orbiter, the first re-usable space vehicle (44 missions planned by the end of 1985, nine of them military)

SATELLITES

Early Warning
USA   22
USSR 25

Communications
USA   118
USSR 366
NATO   5
UK   4
France 2

Photographic reconnaisance
USA   235
USSR   538
China   3

Electronic reconnaisance
USA   790
USSR   125

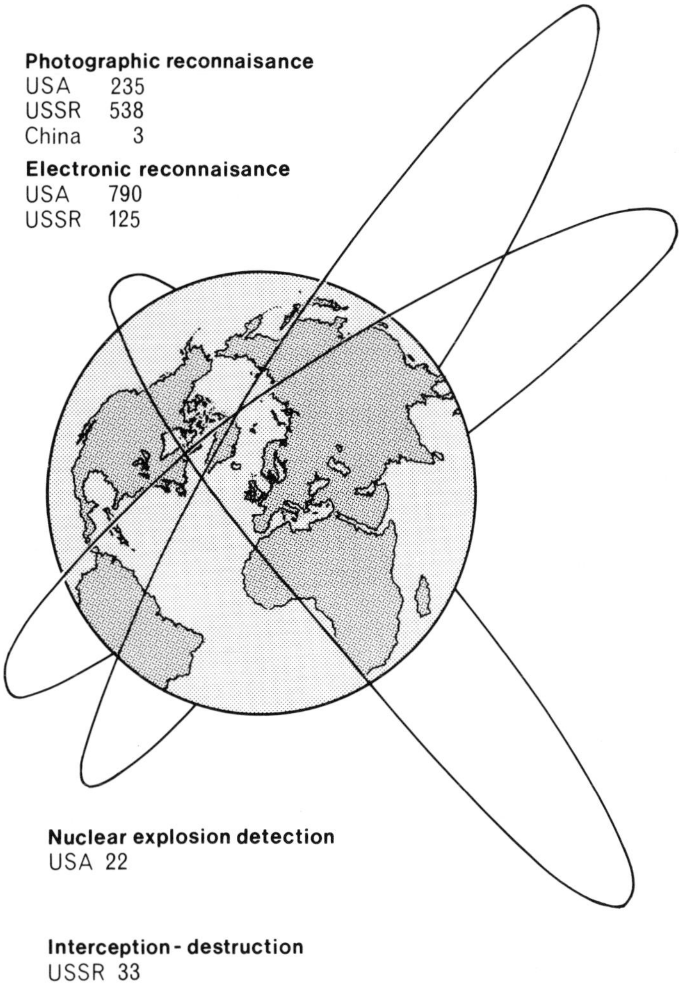

Navigation
USA   39
USSR 25

Nuclear explosion detection
USA 22

Ocean surveillance
USA   18
USSR   32

Interception - destruction
USSR 33

In January 1985, at Geneva, the United States and the Soviet Union agreed to begin talks aimed at an agreement over the restriction of warfare in outer space. The United States was involved in the development of anti-satellite missiles and anti-missile lasers, and the Soviet Union in anti-satellite satellites

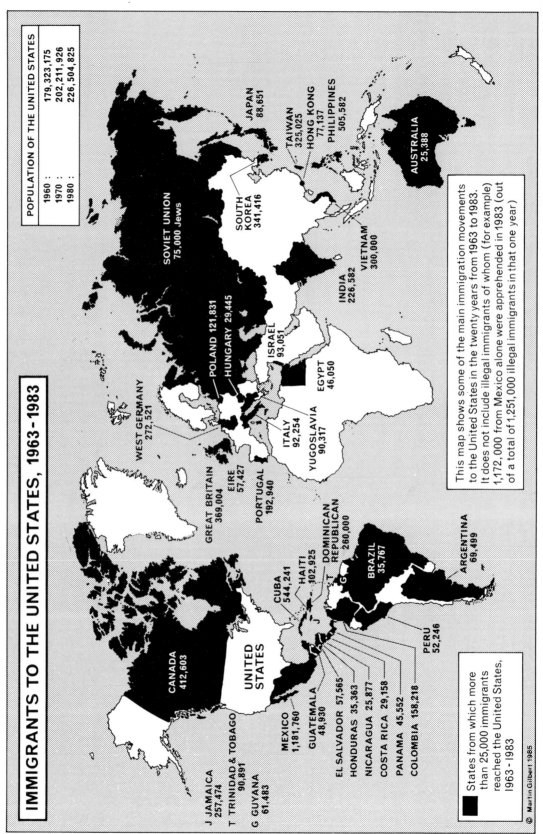

IMMIGRANTS TO THE UNITED STATES, 1963 - 1983

POPULATION OF THE UNITED STATES	
1960 :	179,323,175
1970 :	202,211,926
1980 :	226,504,825

SOVIET UNION
75,000 Jews

JAPAN
88,651

TAIWAN
325,025

HONG KONG
77,137

PHILIPPINES
505,582

SOUTH KOREA
341,416

AUSTRALIA
25,388

VIETNAM
300,000

INDIA
226,582

POLAND 121,831

HUNGARY 29,445

ISRAEL
93,051

EGYPT
46,050

WEST GERMANY
272,521

ITALY
92,254

YUGOSLAVIA
90,317

GREAT BRITAIN
369,004

EIRE
57,427

PORTUGAL
192,940

DOMINICAN
REPUBLIC
260,000

BRAZIL
35,767

ARGENTINA
69,499

CUBA
544,241

HAITI
102,925

PERU
52,246

CANADA
412,603

UNITED
STATES

MEXICO
1,181,760

GUATEMALA
48,930

EL SALVADOR 57,565

HONDURAS 35,363

NICARAGUA 25,877

COSTA RICA 29,158

PANAMA 45,552

COLOMBIA 158,218

J JAMAICA
257,474

T TRINIDAD & TOBAGO
90,891

G GUYANA
61,483

This map shows some of the main immigration movements
to the United States in the twenty years from 1963 to 1983.
It does not include illegal immigrants of whom (for example)
1,172,000 from Mexico alone were apprehended in 1983 (out
of a total of 1,251,000 illegal immigrants in that one year)

States from which more
than 25,000 immigrants
reached the United States,
1963 - 1983

© Martin Gilbert 1985

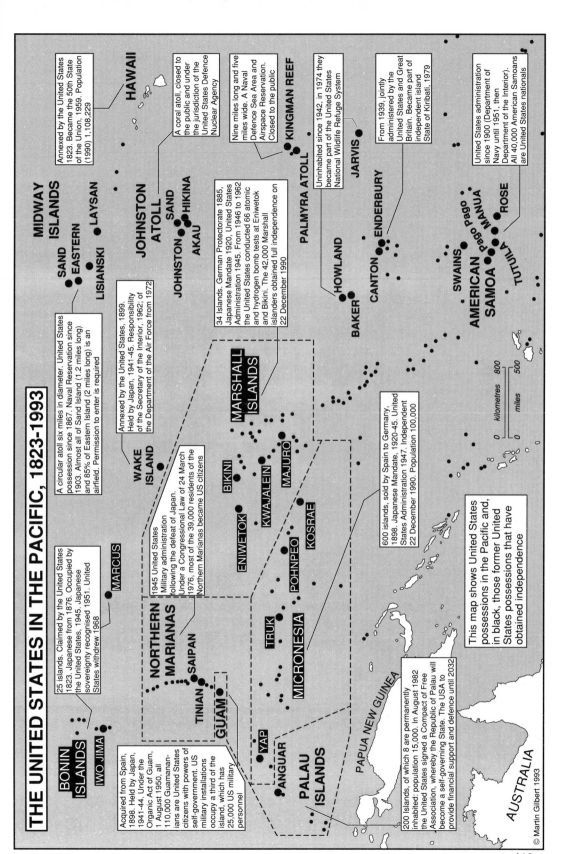

THE UNITED STATES IN THE PACIFIC, 1823-1993

BONIN ISLANDS

IWO JIMA

HAWAII

Annexed by the United States 1823. Became the 50th State of the Union, 1959. Population (1990) 1,108,229

25 islands. Claimed by the United States 1823. Japanese from 1876. Occupied by the United States, 1945. Japanese sovereignty recognised 1951. United States withdrew 1968

MARCUS

MIDWAY ISLANDS

SAND
EASTERN

A circular atoll six miles in diameter. United States possession since 1867. Naval Reservation since 1903. Almost all of Sand Island (1.2 miles long) and 85% of Eastern Island (2 miles long) is an airfield. Permission to enter is required

LAYSAN
LISIANSKI

JOHNSTON ATOLL

SAND
JOHNSTON   HIKINA
AKAU

A coral atoll, closed to the public and under the jurisdiction of the United States Defence Nuclear Agency

KINGMAN REEF

Nine miles long and five miles wide. A Naval Defence Sea Area and Airspace Reservation. Closed to the public

PALMYRA ATOLL

Uninhabited since 1942; in 1974 they became part of the United States National Wildlife Refuge System

JARVIS

From 1939, jointly administered by the United States and Great Britain. Became part of independent island State of Kiribati, 1979

ENDERBURY

CANTON

HOWLAND

BAKER

United States administration since 1900 (Department of Navy until 1951, then Department of the Interior). All 40,000 American Samoans are United States nationals

ROSE
MANUA
Pago Pago
AMERICAN SAMOA
TUTUILA
SWAINS

34 Islands. German Protectorate 1885, Japanese Mandate 1920, United States Administration 1945. From 1946 to 1962 the United States conducted 66 atomic and hydrogen bomb tests at Eniwetok and Bikini. The 42,000 Marshall islanders obtained full independence on 22 December 1990

MARSHALL ISLANDS

Annexed by the United States, 1899. Held by Japan, 1941-45. Responsibility of the Secretary of the Interior, 1962; of the Department of the Air Force from 1972

WAKE ISLAND

1945 United States Military administration following the defeat of Japan. Under a Congressional Law of 24 March 1976, most of the 39,000 residents of the Northern Marianas became US citizens

BIKINI

KWAJALEIN

MAJURO

ENIWETOK

POHNPEO

KOSRAE

MICRONESIA

TRUK

600 islands, sold by Spain to Germany, 1898. Japanese Mandate, 1920-45. United States Administration 1947. Independent 22 December 1990. Population 100,000

NORTHERN MARIANAS

SAIPAN
TINIAN
GUAM

Acquired from Spain, 1898. Held by Japan, 1941-44. Under the Organic Act of Guam, 1 August 1950, all 110,000 Guamananians are United States citizens with powers of self-government. US military installations occupy a third of the island, which has 25,000 US military personnel

YAP

ANGUAR

PALAU ISLANDS

200 islands, of which 8 are permanently inhabited: population 15,000. In August 1982 the United States signed a Compact of Free Association, whereby the Republic of Palau will become a self-governing State. The USA to provide financial support and defence until 2032

PAPUA NEW GUINEA

This map shows United States possessions in the Pacific and, in black, those former United States possessions that have obtained independence

0   500   miles
0   800   kilometres

AUSTRALIA

© Martin Gilbert 1993

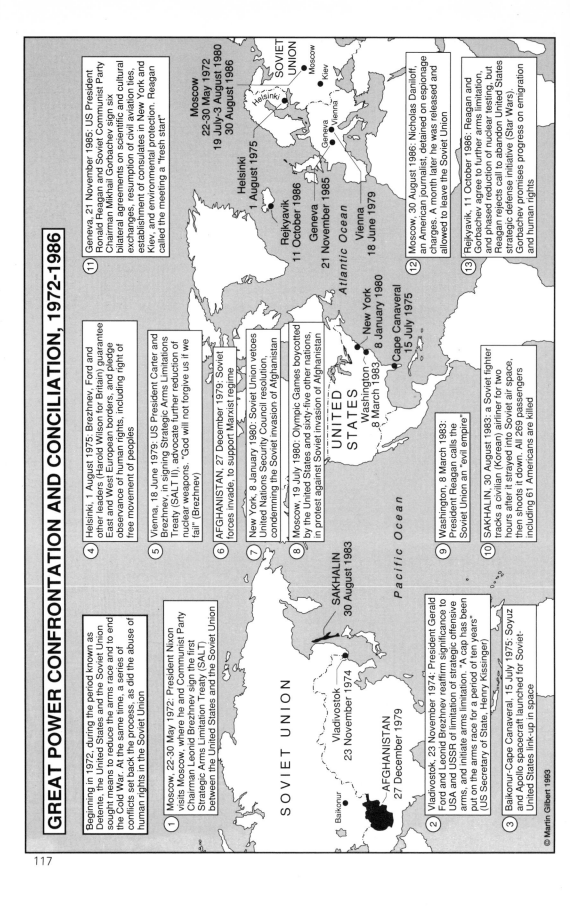

GREAT POWER CONFRONTATION AND CONCILIATION, 1972-1986

Beginning in 1972, during the period known as Detente, the United States and the Soviet Union sought means to reduce the arms race and to end the Cold War. At the same time, a series of conflicts set back the process, as did the abuse of human rights in the Soviet Union

(1) Moscow, 22-30 May 1972: President Nixon visits Moscow, where he and Communist Party Chairman Leonid Brezhnev sign the first Strategic Arms Limitation Treaty (SALT) between the United States and the Soviet Union

(2) Vladivostok, 23 November 1974: President Gerald Ford and Leonid Brezhnev reaffirm significance to USA and USSR of limitation of strategic offensive arms, and initiate arms limitation. "A cap has been put on the arms race for a period of ten years" (US Secretary of State, Henry Kissinger)

(3) Baikonur-Cape Canaveral, 15 July 1975: Soyuz and Apollo spacecraft launched for Soviet-United States link-up in space

(4) Helsinki, 1 August 1975: Brezhnev, Ford and other leaders (Harold Wilson for Britain) guarantee East and West European borders, and pledge observance of human rights, including right of free movement of peoples

(5) Vienna, 18 June 1979: US President Carter and Brezhnev, in signing Strategic Arms Limitations Treaty (SALT II), advocate further reduction of nuclear weapons. "God will not forgive us if we fail" (Brezhnev)

(6) AFGHANISTAN, 27 December 1979: Soviet forces invade, to support Marxist regime

(7) New York, 8 January 1980: Soviet Union vetoes United Nations Security Council resolution, condemning the Soviet invasion of Afghanistan

(8) Moscow, 19 July 1980: Olympic Games boycotted by the United States and sixty-five other nations, in protest against Soviet invasion of Afghanistan

(9) Washington, 8 March 1983: President Reagan calls the Soviet Union an "evil empire"

(10) SAKHALIN, 30 August 1983: a Soviet fighter tracks a civilian (Korean) airliner for two hours after it strayed into Soviet air space, then shoots it down. All 269 passengers including 61 Americans are killed

(11) Geneva, 21 November 1985: US President Ronald Reagan and Soviet Communist Party Chairman Mikhail Gorbachev sign six bilateral agreements on scientific and cultural exchanges, resumption of civil aviation ties, establishment of consulates in New York and Kiev, and environmental protection. Reagan called the meeting a "fresh start"

(12) Moscow, 30 August 1986: Nicholas Daniloff, an American journalist, detained on espionage charges. A month later he was released and allowed to leave the Soviet Union

(13) Rejkyavik, 11 October 1986: Reagan and Gorbachev agree to further arms limitation, and phased reduction of nuclear testing, but Reagan rejects call to abandon United States strategic defense initiative (Star Wars). Gorbachev promises progress on emigration and human rights

Moscow
22-30 May 1972
19 July-3 August 1980
30 August 1986

SOVIET UNION
● Moscow
● Kiev

Helsinki
● Helsinki
Vienna
● Vienna
● Geneva

Helsinki
1 August 1975

Rejkyavik
11 October 1986

Geneva
21 November 1985

Vienna
18 June 1979

Atlantic Ocean

New York
8 January 1980

Washington
8 March 1983

● Cape Canaveral
15 July 1975

UNITED STATES

SOVIET UNION

Baikonur ●

AFGHANISTAN
27 December 1979

Vladivostok ●
Vladivostok
23 November 1974

SAKHALIN
30 August 1983

Pacific Ocean

© Martin Gilbert 1993

117

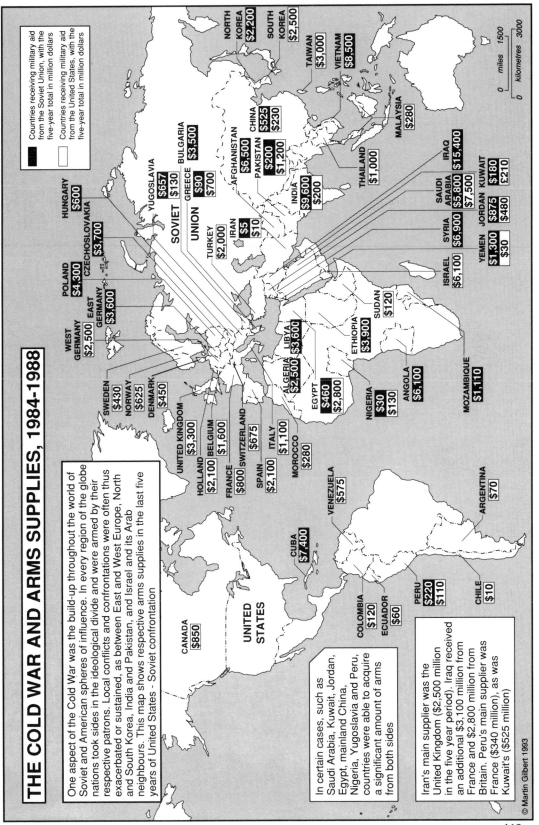

THE COLD WAR AND ARMS SUPPLIES, 1984-1988

One aspect of the Cold War was the build-up throughout the world of Soviet and American spheres of influence. In every region of the globe nations took sides in the ideological divide and were armed by their respective patrons. Local conflicts and confrontations were often thus exacerbated or sustained, as between East and West Europe, North and South Korea, India and Pakistan, and Israel and its Arab neighbours. This map shows respective arms supplies in the last five years of United States - Soviet confrontation

In certain cases, such as Saudi Arabia, Kuwait, Jordan, Egypt, mainland China, Nigeria, Yugoslavia and Peru, countries were able to acquire a significant amount of arms from both sides

Iran's main supplier was the United Kingdom ($2,500 million in the five year period). Iraq received an additional $3,100 million from France and $2,800 million from Britain. Peru's main supplier was France ($340 million), as was Kuwait's ($525 million)

Legend:
- ■ Countries receiving military aid from the Soviet Union, with the five-year total in million dollars
- □ Countries receiving military aid from the United States, with the five-year total in million dollars

Country figures:

- CANADA $850
- UNITED STATES
- CUBA $7,400
- VENEZUELA $575
- COLOMBIA $120
- ECUADOR $60
- PERU $220 / $110
- CHILE $10
- ARGENTINA $70
- UNITED KINGDOM $3,300
- HOLLAND $2,100
- BELGIUM $1,600
- FRANCE $800
- SWITZERLAND $675
- SPAIN $2,100
- ITALY $1,100
- MOROCCO $280
- SWEDEN $430
- NORWAY $625
- DENMARK $450
- WEST GERMANY $2,500
- EAST GERMANY $3,600
- POLAND $4,300
- CZECHOSLOVAKIA $3,700
- HUNGARY $600
- YUGOSLAVIA $657 / $130
- BULGARIA $3,500
- GREECE $90 / $700
- SOVIET UNION
- TURKEY $2,000
- IRAN $5 / $10
- AFGHANISTAN $6,500
- PAKISTAN $200 / $1,200
- CHINA $525 / $230
- INDIA $9,600 / $200
- THAILAND $1,000
- MALAYSIA $280
- NORTH KOREA $2,200
- SOUTH KOREA $2,500
- TAIWAN $3,000
- VIETNAM $8,500
- ALGERIA $2,500
- LIBYA $3,600
- EGYPT $460 / $2,800
- NIGERIA $30 / $130
- SUDAN $120
- ETHIOPIA $3,900
- ANGOLA $6,100
- MOZAMBIQUE $1,110
- ISRAEL $6,100
- SYRIA $6,900
- SAUDI ARABIA $5,800 / $7,500
- IRAQ $15,400
- JORDAN $875 / $480
- KUWAIT $180 / £210
- YEMEN $1,300 / $30

Scale: 0 miles 1500 / 0 kilometres 3000

© Martin Gilbert 1993

118

THE END OF THE COLD WAR, 1987-1993

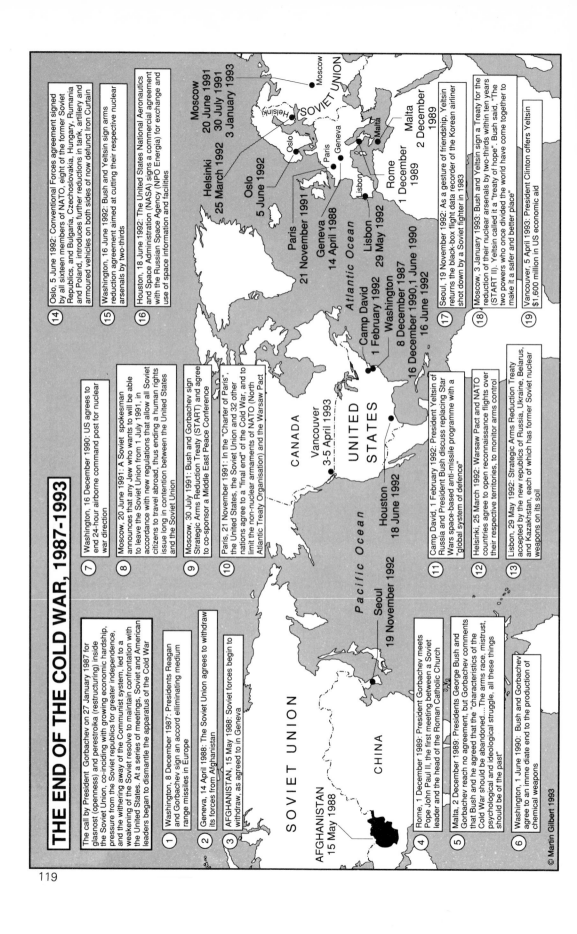

The call by President Gorbachev on 27 January 1987 for glasnost (openness) and perestroika (restructuring) inside the Soviet Union, co-inciding with growing economic hardship, pressure from the Soviet republics for greater independence, and the withering away of the Communist system, led to a weakening of the resolve of the Soviet Union to maintain confrontation with the United States. At a series of meetings, Soviet and American leaders began to dismantle the apparatus of the Cold War

(1) Washington, 8 December 1987: Presidents Reagan and Gorbachev sign an accord eliminating medium range missiles in Europe

(2) Geneva, 14 April 1988: The Soviet Union agrees to withdraw its forces from Afghanistan

(3) AFGHANISTAN, 15 May 1988: Soviet forces begin to withdraw, as agreed to in Geneva

(4) Rome, 1 December 1989: President Gorbachev meets Pope John Paul II, the first meeting between a Soviet leader and the head of the Roman Catholic Church

(5) Malta, 2 December 1989: Presidents George Bush and Gorbachev reach no agreement, but Gorbachev comments that Bush and he agreed that the "characteristics of the Cold War should be abandoned....The arms race, mistrust, psychological and ideological struggle, all these things should be of the past"

(6) Washington, 1 June 1990: Bush and Gorbachev agree to an imme diate end to the production of chemical weapons

(7) Washington, 16 December 1990: US agrees to end 24-hour airborne command post for nuclear war direction

(8) Moscow, 20 June 1991: A Soviet spokesman announces that any Jew who wants to will be able to leave the Soviet Union from 1 July 1991, in accordance with new regulations that allow all Soviet citizens to travel abroad, thus ending a human rights issue long in contention between the United States and the Soviet Union

(9) Moscow, 30 July 1991: Bush and Gorbachev sign Strategic Arms Reduction Treaty (START) and agree to co-sponsor a Middle East Peace Conference

(10) Paris, 21 November 1991: In the "Charter of Paris", the United States, the Soviet Union and 32 other nations agree to a "final end" of the Cold War, and to limit the non-nuclear armaments of NATO (North Atlantic Treaty Organisation) and the Warsaw Pact

(11) Camp David, 1 February 1992: President Yeltsin of Russia and President Bush discuss replacing Star Wars space-based anti-missile programme with a "global system of defence"

(12) Helsinki, 25 March 1992: Warsaw Pact and NATO countries agree to open reconnaissance flights over their respective territories, to monitor arms control

(13) Lisbon, 29 May 1992: Strategic Arms Reduction Treaty accepted by the new republics of Russia, Ukraine, Belarus, and Kazakhstan, each of which has former Soviet nuclear weapons on its soil

(14) Oslo, 5 June 1992: Conventional Forces agreement signed by all sixteen members of NATO, eight of the former Soviet Republics, and Bulgaria, Czechoslovakia, Hungary, Rumania and Poland, introduces further reductions in tank, artillery and armoured vehicles on both sides of now defunct Iron Curtain

(15) Washington, 16 June 1992: Bush and Yeltsin sign arms reduction agreement aimed at cutting their respective nuclear arsenals by two-thirds

(16) Houston, 18 June 1992: The United States National Aeronautics and Space Administration (NASA) signs a commercial agreement with the Russian Space Agency (NPO Energia) for exchange and use of space information and facilities

(17) Seoul, 19 November 1992: As a gesture of friendship, Yeltsin returns the black-box flight data recorder of the Korean airliner shot down by a Soviet fighter in 1983

(18) Moscow, 3 January 1993: Bush and Yeltsin sign a Treaty for the reduction of their nuclear arsenals by two-thirds within ten years (START II). Yeltsin called it a "treaty of hope". Bush said, "The two powers who once divided the world have come together to make it a safer and better place"

(19) Vancouver, 5 April 1993: President Clinton offers Yeltsin $1,600 million in US economic aid

MILITARY, ECONOMIC AND HUMANITARIAN MISSIONS, 1975-1993

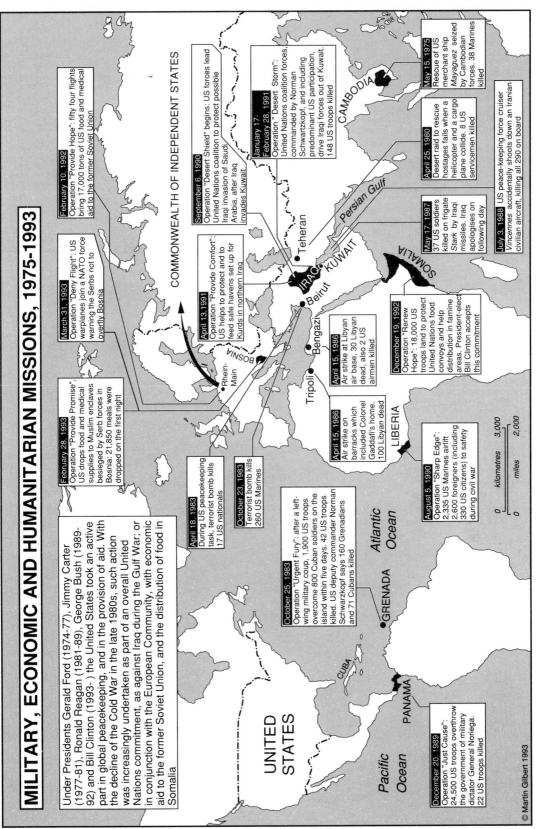

Under Presidents Gerald Ford (1974-77), Jimmy Carter (1977-81), Ronald Reagan (1981-89), George Bush (1989-92) and Bill Clinton (1993-) the United States took an active part in global peacekeeping, and in the provision of aid. With the decline of the Cold War in the late 1980s, such action was increasingly undertaken as part of an overall United Nations commitment as part of the Gulf War; or in conjunction with the European Community, with economic aid to the former Soviet Union, and the distribution of food in Somalia

COMMONWEALTH OF INDEPENDENT STATES

February 10, 1992 Operation "Provide Flight": fifty four flights bring 17,000 tons of US food and medical aid to the former Soviet Union

March 31, 1993 Operation "Deny Flight": US warplanes join a NATO force warning the Serbs not to overfly Bosnia

September 6, 1990 Operation "Desert Shield" begins: US forces lead United Nations coalition to protect possible Iraqi invasion of Saudi Arabia, after Iraq invades Kuwait

January 17- February 28, 1991 Operation "Desert Storm": United Nations coalition forces, commanded by Norman Schwartzkopf, and including predominant US participation, drive Iraqi forces out of Kuwait. 148 US troops killed

May 15, 1975 Rescue of US merchant ship *Mayaguez* seized by Cambodian forces. 38 Marines killed

April 13,1991 Operation "Provide Comfort": US helps to protect and to feed safe havens set up for Kurds in northern Iraq

February 28, 1993 Operation "Provide Promise", US drops food and medical supplies to Muslim enclaves besieged by Serb forces in Bosnia. 21,850 meals were dropped on the first night

April 25, 1980 Desert raid to rescue hostages fails when a helicopter and a cargo plane collide. 8 US servicemen killed

May 17, 1987 37 US soldiers killed on frigate *Stark* by Iraqi missiles. Iraq apologises on following day

July 3, 1988 US peace-keeping force cruiser *Vincennes* accidentally shoots down an Iranian civilian aircraft, killing all 290 on board

December 19, 1992 Operation "Renew Hope": 18,000 US troops land to protect United Nations food convoys and help distribution in famine areas. President-elect Bill Clinton accepts this commitment

April 15, 1986 Air strike at Libyan air base, 30 Libyan dead, also 2 US airmen killed

April 15, 1986 Air strike on barracks which included Colonel Gaddafi's home. 100 Libyan dead

April 18, 1983 During US peacekeeping task, terrorist bomb kills 17 US nationals

October 23, 1983 Terrorist bomb kills 260 US Marines

August 5, 1990 Operation "Sharp Edge": 2,335 US Marines airlift 2,600 foreigners (including 330 US citizens) to safety during civil war

October 25, 1983 Operation "Urgent Fury": after a left-wing military coup, 1,900 US troops overcome 800 Cuban soldiers on the island within five days. 42 US troops killed. US deputy commander Norman Schwarzkopf says 160 Grenadians and 71 Cubans killed

December 20, 1989 Operation "Just Cause": 24,500 US troops overthrow the government of military dictator General Noriega. 22 US troops killed

CAMBODIA

Teheran

Persian Gulf

IRAQ

KUWAIT

Beirut

SOMALIA

Bengazi

Tripoli

BOSNIA

Rhein-Main

LIBERIA

GRENADA

CUBA

PANAMA

UNITED STATES

Atlantic Ocean

Pacific Ocean

0   1,000   2,000   3,000 kilometres
0   2,000   miles

© Martin Gilbert 1993

MAJOR NATURAL AND ACCIDENTAL DISASTERS, 1972-1993

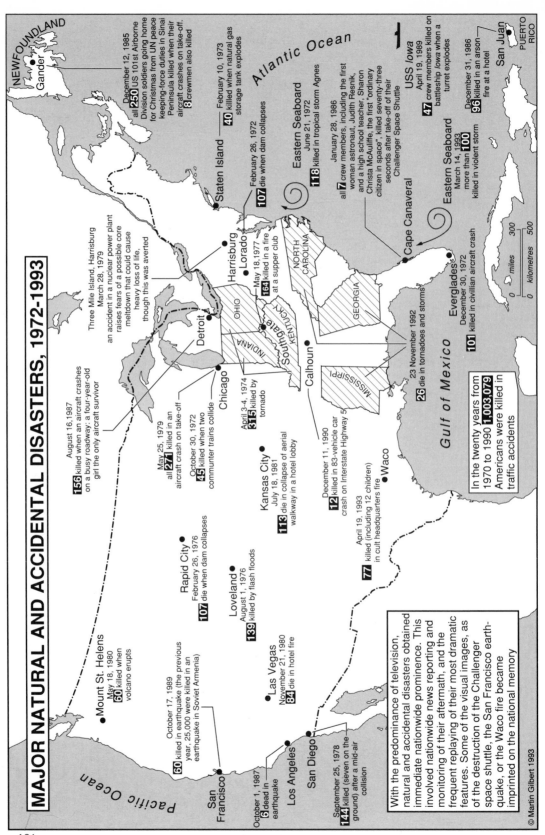

NEWFOUNDLAND
Gander ●

December 12, 1985 all **250** US 101st Airborne Division soldiers going home for Christmas from UN peacekeeping-force duties in Sinai Peninsula killed when their aircraft crashes on take-off. **8** crewmen also killed

Atlantic Ocean

Staten Island — February 10, 1973 **40** killed when natural gas storage tank explodes

February 26, 1972 **107** die when dam collapses

Eastern Seaboard June 21, 1972 **118** killed in tropical storm Agnes

January 28, 1986 all **7** crew members, including the first woman astronaut, Judith Resnik, and a high school teacher, Sharon Christa McAuliffe, the first "ordinary citizen in space", killed seventy-three seconds after take-off of their Challenger Space Shuttle

USS *Iowa* April 19, 1989 **47** crew members killed on battleship *Iowa* when a turret explodes

Cape Canaveral ●

Eastern Seaboard March 14, 1993 more than **100** killed in violent storm

December 31, 1986 **96** killed in an arson fire at a hotel

San Juan ●
PUERTO RICO

Harrisburg ●
Lorado ●

Three Mile Island, Harrisburg March 28, 1979 an accident in a nuclear power plant raises fears of a possible core meltdown that could cause heavy loss of life, though this was averted

May 18, 1977 **164** killed in a fire at a supper club

NORTH CAROLINA

GEORGIA

Detroit ●

OHIO

INDIANA

Southgate ●

KENTUCKY

Calhoun ●

MISSISSIPPI

23 November 1992 **26** die in tornadoes and storms

Everglades ●
December 30, 1972 **101** killed in civilian aircraft crash

Gulf of Mexico

August 16, 1987 **156** killed when an aircraft crashes on a busy roadway: a four-year-old girl the only aircraft survivor

May 25, 1979 all **271** killed in an aircraft crash on take-off

October 30, 1972 **45** killed when two commuter trains collide

Chicago ●

April 3-4, 1974 **315** killed by tornado

Kansas City ●
July 18, 1981 **113** die in collapse of aerial walkway in a hotel lobby

December 11, 1990 **12** killed in 83-vehicle car crash on Interstate Highway 5

April 19, 1993 **77** killed (including 12 children) in cult headquarters fire

Waco ●

0 miles 300
0 kilometres 500

Rapid City ●
February 26, 1976 **107** die when dam collapses

Loveland ●
August 1, 1976 **139** killed by flash floods

Mount St. Helens ●
May 18, 1980 **60** killed when volcano erupts

October 17, 1989 **60** killed in earthquake (the previous year, 25,000 were killed in an earthquake in Soviet Armenia)

Las Vegas ●
November 21, 1980 **84** die in hotel fire

San Francisco ●

October 1, 1987 **6** dead in earthquake

Los Angeles ●
San Diego ●

September 25, 1978 **144** killed (seven on the ground) after a mid-air collision

Pacific Ocean

In the twenty years from 1970 to 1990 **1,003,079** Americans were killed in traffic accidents

With the predominance of television, natural and accidental disasters obtained immediate nationwide prominence. This involved nationwide news reporting and monitoring of their aftermath, and the frequent replaying of their most dramatic features. Some of the visual images, as of the destruction of the Challenger space shuttle, the San Francisco earthquake, or the Waco fire became imprinted on the national memory

© Martin Gilbert 1993

121

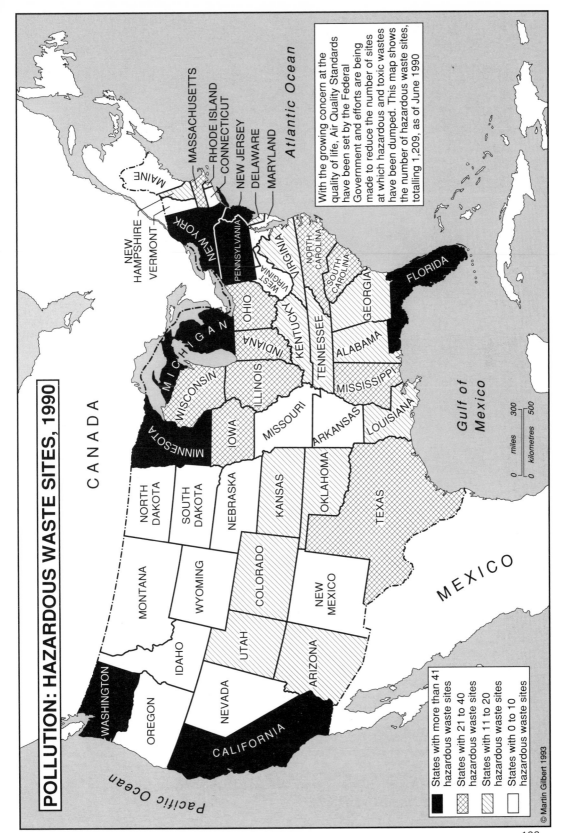

POLLUTION: HAZARDOUS WASTE SITES, 1990

With the growing concern at the quality of life, Air Quality Standards have been set by the Federal Government and efforts are being made to reduce the number of sites at which hazardous and toxic wastes have been dumped. This map shows the number of hazardous waste sites, totalling 1,209, as of June 1990.

Atlantic Ocean

CANADA

MASSACHUSETTS
RHODE ISLAND
CONNECTICUT
NEW JERSEY
DELAWARE
MARYLAND

MAINE
NEW HAMPSHIRE
VERMONT
NEW YORK
PENNSYLVANIA
WEST VIRGINIA
VIRGINIA
NORTH CAROLINA
SOUTH CAROLINA
GEORGIA
FLORIDA

OHIO
KENTUCKY
TENNESSEE
ALABAMA
MISSISSIPPI

MICHIGAN
WISCONSIN
ILLINOIS
INDIANA
IOWA
MISSOURI
ARKANSAS
LOUISIANA

MINNESOTA

NORTH DAKOTA
SOUTH DAKOTA
NEBRASKA
KANSAS
OKLAHOMA
TEXAS

MONTANA
WYOMING
COLORADO
NEW MEXICO

IDAHO
UTAH
ARIZONA

WASHINGTON
OREGON
NEVADA
CALIFORNIA

Gulf of Mexico

MEXICO

Pacific Ocean

0 miles 300
0 kilometres 500

■ States with more than 41 hazardous waste sites

▨ States with 21 to 40 hazardous waste sites

▧ States with 11 to 20 hazardous waste sites

☐ States with 0 to 10 hazardous waste sites

© Martin Gilbert 1993

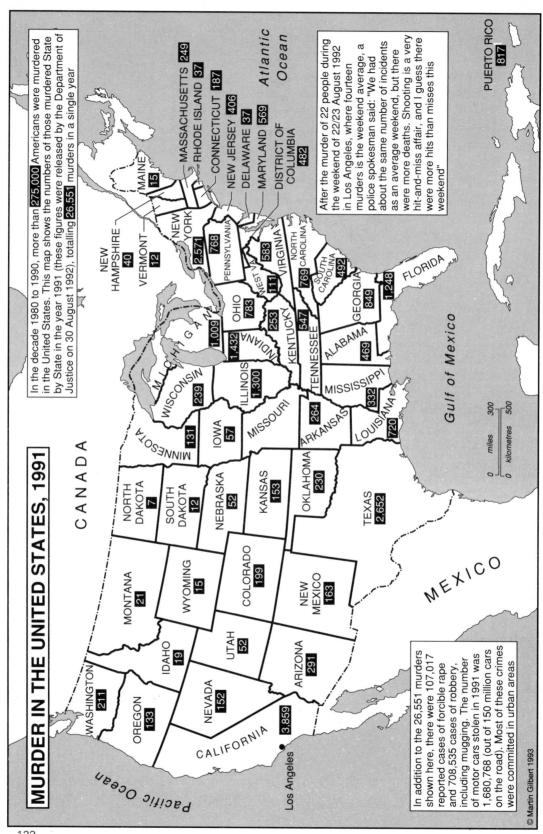

MURDER IN THE UNITED STATES, 1991

In the decade 1980 to 1990, more than 275,000 Americans were murdered in the United States. This map shows the numbers of those murdered State by State in the year 1991 (these figures were released by the Department of Justice on 30 August 1992), totalling 26,551 murders in a single year

After the murder of 22 people during the weekend of 22/23 August 1992 in Los Angeles, where fourteen murders is the weekend average, a police spokesman said: "We had about the same number of incidents as an average weekend, but there were more deaths. Shooting is a very hit-and-miss affair, and I guess there were more hits than misses this weekend"

In addition to the 26,551 murders shown here, there were 107,017 reported cases of forcible rape and 708,535 cases of robbery, including mugging. The number of motor cars stolen in 1991 was 1,680,768 (out of 150 million cars on the road). Most of these crimes were committed in urban areas

CANADA

MEXICO

Pacific Ocean

Atlantic Ocean

Gulf of Mexico

Los Angeles

WASHINGTON 211
OREGON 133
IDAHO 19
MONTANA 21
WYOMING 15
NEVADA 152
UTAH 52
COLORADO 199
CALIFORNIA 3,859
ARIZONA 291
NEW MEXICO 163
NORTH DAKOTA 7
SOUTH DAKOTA 12
NEBRASKA 52
KANSAS 153
OKLAHOMA 230
TEXAS 2,652
MINNESOTA 131
IOWA 57
MISSOURI 264
ARKANSAS 264
LOUISIANA 720
WISCONSIN 239
ILLINOIS 1,300
MICHIGAN 1,009
INDIANA 432
OHIO 783
KENTUCKY 253
TENNESSEE 547
MISSISSIPPI 332
ALABAMA 469
GEORGIA 849
FLORIDA 1,248
SOUTH CAROLINA 492
NORTH CAROLINA 769
VIRGINIA 583
WEST VA 111
PENNSYLVANIA 768
NEW YORK 2,571
MAINE 15
VERMONT 12
NEW HAMPSHIRE 40
MASSACHUSETTS 249
RHODE ISLAND 37
CONNECTICUT 187
NEW JERSEY 406
DELAWARE 37
MARYLAND 569
DISTRICT OF COLUMBIA 482

PUERTO RICO 817

0 miles 300
0 kilometres 500

DEATHS FROM AIDS, 1982 - 1992

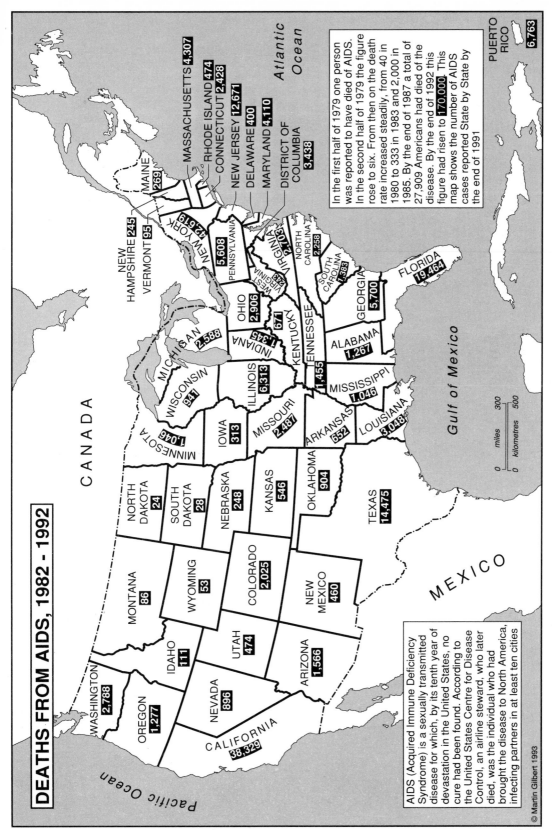

In the first half of 1979 one person was reported to have died of AIDS. In the second half of 1979 the figure rose to six. From then on the death rate increased steadily, from 40 in 1980 to 333 in 1983 and 2,000 in 1985. By the end of 1987 a total of 27,909 Americans had died of the disease. By the end of 1992 this figure had risen to 170,000. This map shows the number of AIDS cases reported State by State by the end of 1991

AIDS (Acquired Immune Deficiency Syndrome) is a sexually transmitted disease for which, by its tenth year of devastation in the United States, no cure had been found. According to the United States Centre for Disease Control, an airline steward, who later died, was the individual who had brought the disease to North America, infecting partners in at least ten cities

© Martin Gilbert 1993

124

IMMIGRATION TO THE UNITED STATES, 1991

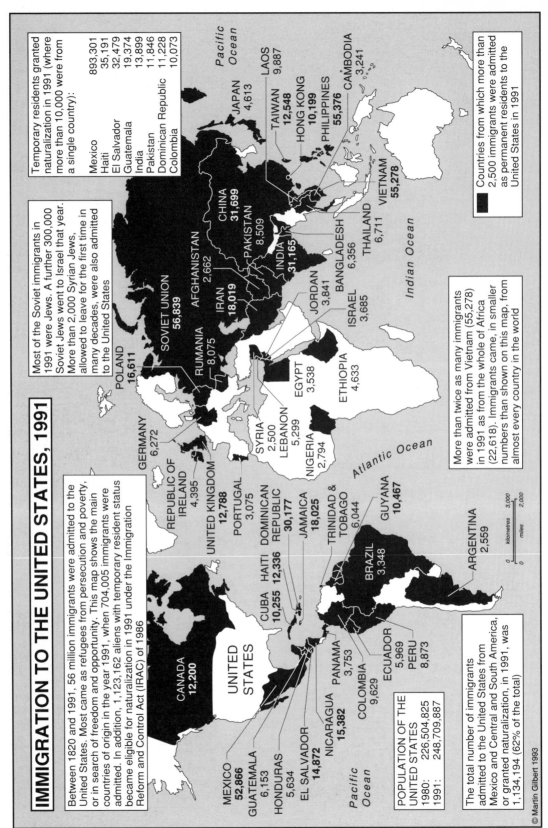

Between 1820 and 1991, 56 million immigrants were admitted to the United States. Most came as refugees from persecution and poverty, or in search of freedom and opportunity. This map shows the main countries of origin in the year 1991, when 704,005 immigrants were admitted. In addition, 1,123,162 aliens with temporary resident status became eligible for naturalization in 1991 under the Immigration Reform and Control Act (IRAC) of 1986

Most of the Soviet immigrants in 1991 were Jews. A further 300,000 Soviet Jews went to Israel that year. More than 2,000 Syrian Jews, allowed to leave for the first time in many decades, were also admitted to the United States

Temporary residents granted naturalization in 1991 (where more than 10,000 were from a single country):

Mexico	893,301
Haiti	35,191
El Salvador	32,479
Guatemala	19,374
India	13,899
Pakistan	11,846
Dominican Republic	11,228
Colombia	10,073

Countries from which more than 2,500 immigrants were admitted as permanent residents to the United States in 1991

Pacific Ocean

JAPAN 4,613
LAOS 9,887
TAIWAN 12,548
HONG KONG 10,199
PHILIPPINES 55,376
CAMBODIA 3,241
CHINA 31,699
PAKISTAN 8,509
INDIA 31,165
VIETNAM 55,278
THAILAND 6,711
BANGLADESH 6,356
AFGHANISTAN 2,662
IRAN 18,019
SOVIET UNION 56,839
RUMANIA 8,075
POLAND 16,611
GERMANY 6,272
JORDAN 3,841
ISRAEL 3,685
SYRIA 2,500
LEBANON 5,299
EGYPT 3,538
ETHIOPIA 4,633
NIGERIA 2,794
REPUBLIC OF IRELAND 4,395
UNITED KINGDOM 12,788
PORTUGAL 3,075

Indian Ocean

Atlantic Ocean

More than twice as many immigrants were admitted from Vietnam (55,278) in 1991 as from the whole of Africa (22,618). Immigrants came, in smaller numbers than shown on this map, from almost every country in the world

DOMINICAN REPUBLIC 30,177
JAMAICA 18,025
TRINIDAD & TOBAGO 6,044
GUYANA 10,467
CUBA 10,255
HAITI 12,336
BRAZIL 3,348
ARGENTINA 2,559

kilometres 3,000
miles 2,000

CANADA 12,200

UNITED STATES

MEXICO 52,866
GUATEMALA 6,153
HONDURAS 5,634
EL SALVADOR 14,872
NICARAGUA 15,382
PANAMA 3,753
COLOMBIA 9,629
ECUADOR 5,969
PERU 8,873

Pacific Ocean

POPULATION OF THE UNITED STATES
1980: 226,504,825
1991: 248,709,887

The total number of immigrants admitted to the United States from Mexico and Central and South America, or granted naturalization, in 1991, was 1,134,194 (62% of the total)

125

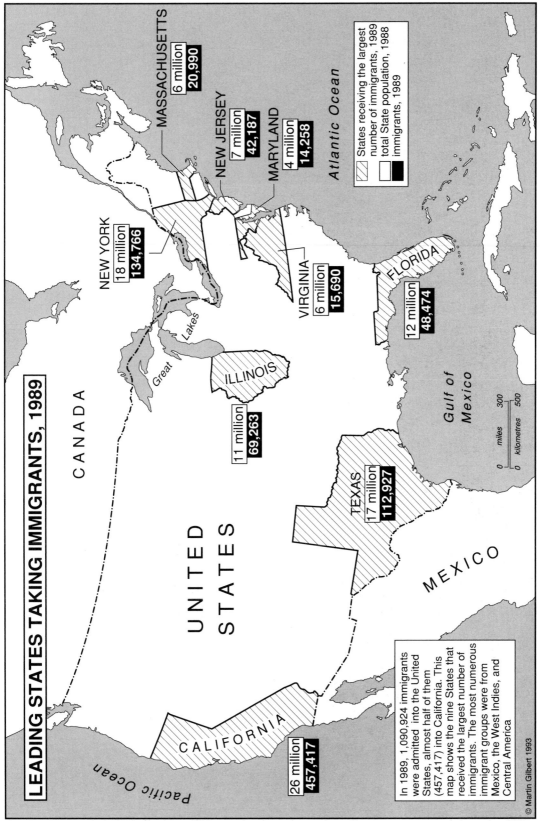

LEADING STATES TAKING IMMIGRANTS, 1989

CANADA

UNITED STATES

MEXICO

Pacific Ocean

Atlantic Ocean

Gulf of Mexico

Great Lakes

States receiving the largest number of immigrants, 1989
total State population, 1988
immigrants, 1989

CALIFORNIA
26 million
457,417

TEXAS
17 million
112,927

ILLINOIS
11 million
69,263

NEW YORK
18 million
134,766

MASSACHUSETTS
6 million
20,990

NEW JERSEY
7 million
42,187

MARYLAND
4 million
14,258

VIRGINIA
6 million
15,690

FLORIDA
12 million
48,474

0   miles   300
0   kilometres   500

In 1989, 1,090,924 immigrants were admitted into the United States, almost half of them (457,417) into California. This map shows the nine States that received the largest number of immigrants. The most numerous immigrant groups were from Mexico, the West Indies, and Central America

© Martin Gilbert 1993

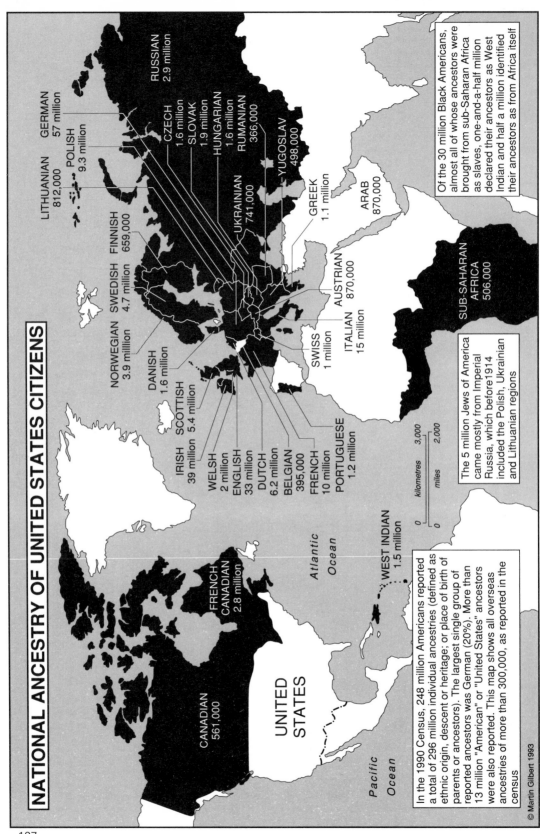

NATIONAL ANCESTRY OF UNITED STATES CITIZENS

RUSSIAN
2.9 million

GERMAN
57 million

LITHUANIAN
812,000

POLISH
9.3 million

CZECH
1.6 million

SLOVAK
1.9 million

HUNGARIAN
1.6 million

RUMANIAN
366,000

UKRAINIAN
741,000

YUGOSLAV
498,000

GREEK
1.1 million

ARAB
870,000

SWEDISH
4.7 million

FINNISH
659,000

NORWEGIAN
3.9 million

DANISH
1.6 million

SCOTTISH
5.4 million

AUSTRIAN
870,000

SUB-SAHARAN
AFRICA
506,000

SWISS
1 million

ITALIAN
15 million

IRISH
39 million

WELSH
2 million

ENGLISH
33 million

DUTCH
6.2 million

BELGIAN
395,000

FRENCH
10 million

PORTUGUESE
1.2 million

Of the 30 million Black Americans, almost all of whose ancestors were brought from sub-Saharan Africa as slaves, one-and-a-half million declared their ancestors as West Indian and half a million identified their ancestors as from Africa itself

The 5 million Jews of America came mostly from Imperial Russia, which before 1914 included the Polish, Ukrainian and Lithuanian regions

0   kilometres   3,000

0   miles   2,000

FRENCH
CANADIAN
2.8 million

CANADIAN
561,000

UNITED
STATES

WEST INDIAN
1.5 million

*Atlantic
Ocean*

*Pacific
Ocean*

In the 1990 Census, 248 million Americans reported a total of 296 million individual ancestries (defined as ethnic origin, descent or heritage; or place of birth of parents or ancestors). The largest single group of reported ancestors was German (20%). More than 13 million "American" or "United States" ancestors were also reported. This map shows all overseas ancestries of more than 300,000, as reported in the census

© Martin Gilbert 1993

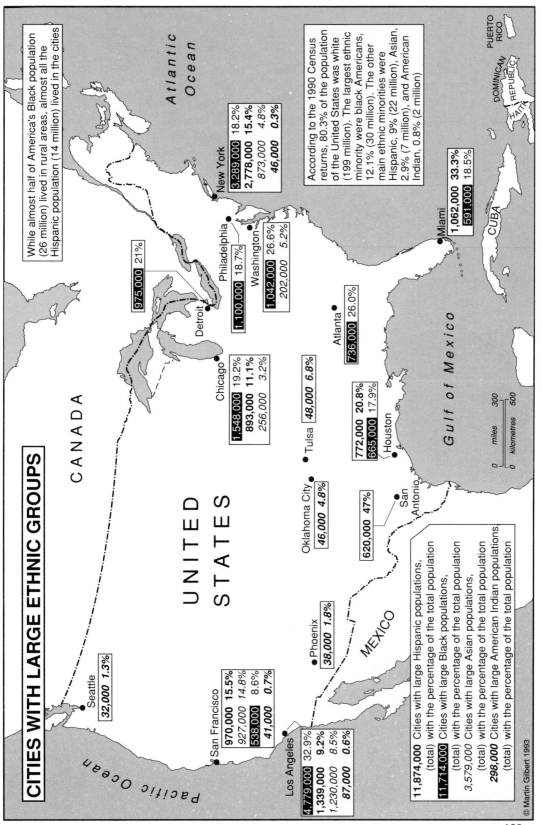

CITIES WITH LARGE ETHNIC GROUPS

CANADA

UNITED STATES

Atlantic Ocean

Pacific Ocean

MEXICO

Gulf of Mexico

CUBA

HAITI

DOMINICAN REPUBLIC

PUERTO RICO

While almost half of America's Black population (26 million) lived in rural areas, almost all the Hispanic population (14 million) lived in the cities

According to the 1990 Census returns, 80.3% of the population of the United States was white (199 million). The largest ethnic minority were black Americans, 12.1% (30 million). The other main ethnic minorities were Hispanic, 9% (22 million), Asian, 2.9% (7 million), and American Indian, 0.8% (2 million)

New York
3,289,000	18.2%
2,778,000	15.4%
873,000	*4.8%*
46,000	*0.3%*

Philadelphia
| 1,100,000 | 18.7% |

Washington
| 1,042,000 | 26.6% |
| *202,000* | *5.2%* |

Detroit | 975,000 | 21% |

Chicago
1,548,000	19.2%
893,000	11.1%
256,000	*3.2%*

Atlanta | 736,000 | 26.0% |

Tulsa | 48,000 | 6.8% |

Houston
| 772,000 | 20.8% |
| 665,000 | 17.9% |

Oklahoma City | 46,000 | 4.8% |

San Antonio | 620,000 | 47% |

Phoenix | 38,000 | 1.8% |

Miami
| 1,062,000 | 33.3% |
| 591,000 | 18.5% |

Seattle | 32,000 | 1.3% |

San Francisco
970,000	15.5%
927,000	*14.8%*
538,000	8.6%
41,000	*0.7%*

Los Angeles
4,779,000	32.9%
1,339,000	9.2%
1,230,000	*8.5%*
87,000	*0.6%*

11,874,000	Cities with large Hispanic populations,
(total)	with the percentage of the total population
11,714,000	Cities with large Black populations,
(total)	with the percentage of the total population
3,579,000	Cities with large Asian populations,
(total)	with the percentage of the total population
298,000	Cities with large American Indian populations,
(total)	with the percentage of the total population

miles 0 300 500
kilometres 0

© Martin Gilbert 1993

UNITED STATES CITIZENS RESIDENT ABROAD, 1989

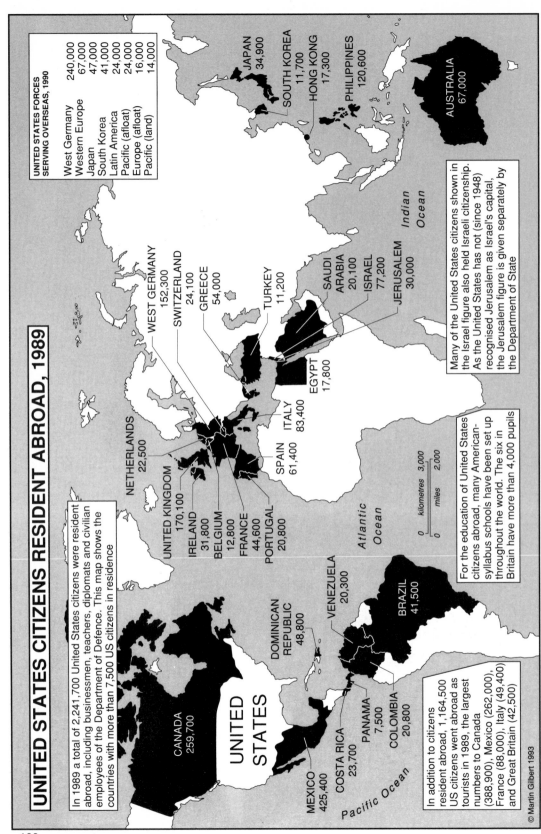

In 1989 a total of 2,241,700 United States citizens were resident abroad, including businessmen, teachers, diplomats and civilian employees of the Department of Defence. This map shows the countries with more than 7,500 US citizens in residence

UNITED STATES FORCES SERVING OVERSEAS, 1990	
West Germany	240,000
Western Europe	67,000
Japan	47,000
South Korea	41,000
Latin America	24,000
Pacific (afloat)	24,000
Europe (afloat)	16,000
Pacific (land)	14,000

JAPAN 34,900

SOUTH KOREA 11,700

HONG KONG 17,300

PHILIPPINES 120,600

AUSTRALIA 67,000

WEST GERMANY 152,300

SWITZERLAND 24,100

GREECE 54,000

TURKEY 11,200

SAUDI ARABIA 20,100

ISRAEL 77,200

JERUSALEM 30,000

EGYPT 17,800

Indian Ocean

NETHERLANDS 22,500

UNITED KINGDOM 170,100

IRELAND 31,800

BELGIUM 12,800

FRANCE 44,600

PORTUGAL 20,800

SPAIN 61,400

ITALY 83,400

Atlantic Ocean

Many of the United States citizens shown in the Israel figure also held Israeli citizenship. As the United States has not (since 1948) recognised Jerusalem as Israel's capital, the Jerusalem figure is given separately by the Department of State

For the education of United States citizens abroad, many American-syllabus schools have been set up throughout the world. The six in Britain have more than 4,000 pupils

0 — kilometres — 3,000
0 — miles — 2,000

CANADA 259,700

UNITED STATES

MEXICO 425,400

COSTA RICA 23,700

PANAMA 7,500

COLOMBIA 20,800

DOMINICAN REPUBLIC 48,800

VENEZUELA 20,300

BRAZIL 41,500

Pacific Ocean

In addition to citizens resident abroad, 1,164,500 US citizens went abroad as tourists in 1989, the largest numbers to Canada (388,900), Mexico (262,000), France (88,000), Italy (49,400), and Great Britain (42,500)

© Martin Gilbert 1993

THE VISA LOTTERY PROGRAM, 1990-1993

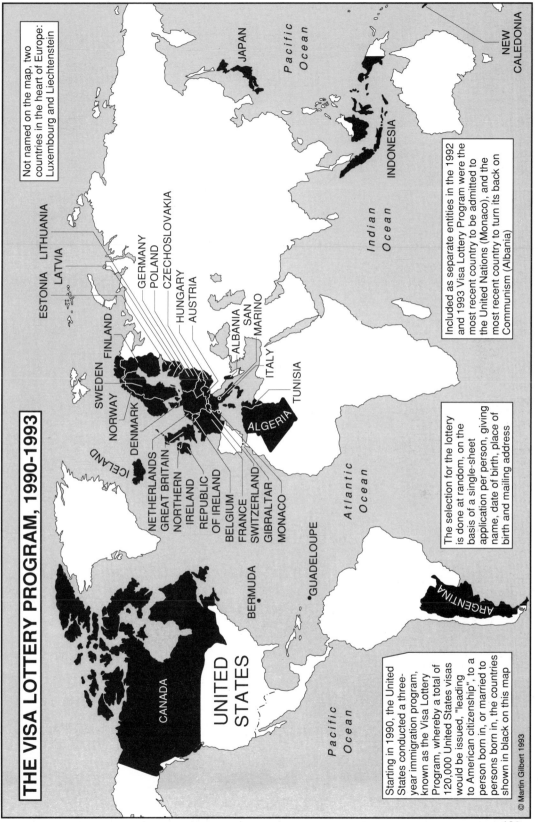

Not named on the map, two countries in the heart of Europe: Luxembourg and Liechtenstein

Included as separate entities in the 1992 and 1993 Visa Lottery Program were the most recent country to be admitted to the United Nations (Monaco), and the most recent country to turn its back on Communism (Albania)

The selection for the lottery is done at random, on the basis of a single-sheet application per person, giving name, date of birth, place of birth and mailing address

Starting in 1990, the United States conducted a three-year immigration program, known as the Visa Lottery Program, whereby a total of 120,000 United States visas would be issued, "leading to American citizenship", to a person born in, or married to persons born in, the countries shown in black on this map

JAPAN

NEW CALEDONIA

INDONESIA

Pacific Ocean

Indian Ocean

ESTONIA   LITHUANIA

LATVIA

GERMANY

POLAND

CZECHOSLOVAKIA

HUNGARY

AUSTRIA

ALBANIA

SAN MARINO

ITALY

TUNISIA

ALGERIA

SWEDEN

FINLAND

NORWAY

DENMARK

NETHERLANDS

GREAT BRITAIN

NORTHERN IRELAND

REPUBLIC OF IRELAND

BELGIUM

FRANCE

SWITZERLAND

GIBRALTAR

MONACO

ICELAND

Atlantic Ocean

GUADELOUPE

ARGENTINA

BERMUDA

CANADA

UNITED STATES

Pacific Ocean

© Martin Gilbert 1993

130

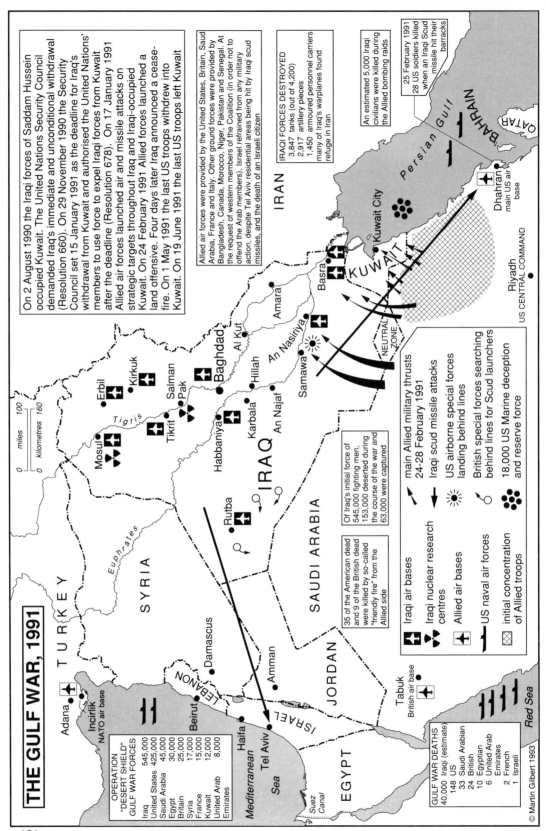

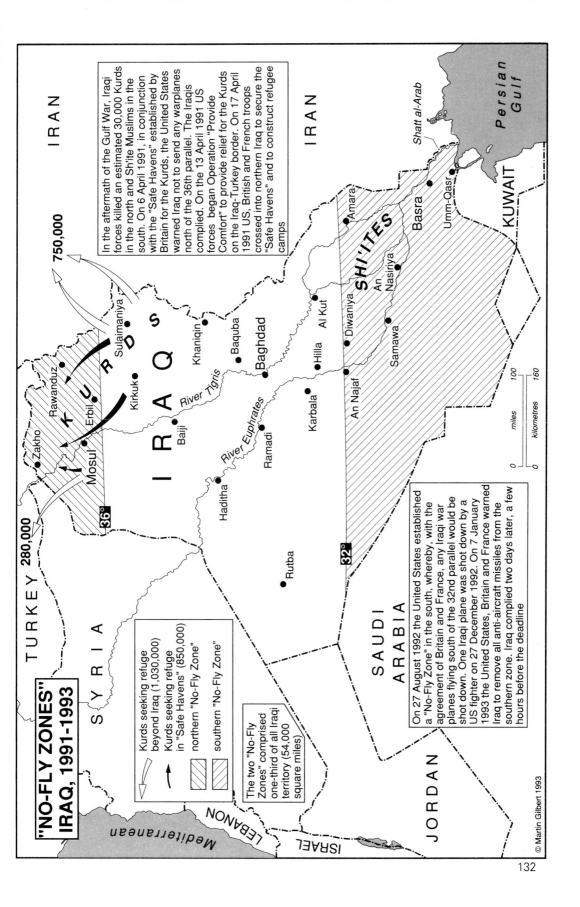

"NO-FLY ZONES" IRAQ, 1991-1993

In the aftermath of the Gulf War, Iraqi forces killed an estimated 30,000 Kurds in the north and Sh'ite Muslims in the south. On 6 April 1991, in conjunction with the "Safe Havens" established by Britain for the Kurds, the United States warned Iraq not to send any warplanes north of the 36th parallel. The Iraqis complied. On the 13 April 1991 US forces began Operation "Provide Comfort" to provide relief for the Kurds on the Iraq-Turkey border. On 17 April 1991 US, British and French troops crossed into northern Iraq to secure the "Safe Havens" and to construct refugee camps

On 27 August 1992 the United States established a "No-Fly Zone" in the south, whereby, with the agreement of Britain and France, any Iraqi war planes flying south of the 32nd parallel would be shot down. One Iraqi plane was shot down by a US fighter on 27 December 1992. On 7 January 1993 the United States, Britain and France warned Iraq to remove all anti-aircraft missiles from the southern zone. Iraq complied two days later, a few hours before the deadline

Kurds seeking refuge beyond Iraq (1,030,000)

Kurds seeking refuge in "Safe Havens" (850,000)

northern "No-Fly Zone"

southern "No-Fly Zone"

The two "No-Fly Zones" comprised one-third of all Iraqi territory (54,000 square miles)

750,000

280,000

IRAN

TURKEY

SYRIA

LEBANON

ISRAEL

JORDAN

SAUDI ARABIA

KUWAIT

Persian Gulf

Mediterranean

K U R D S

I R A Q

SHI'ITES

Zakho
Rawanduz
Sulaimaniya
Mosul
Erbil
Kirkuk
Baiji
Khaniqin
Baquba
Baghdad
Hilla
Al Kut
Karbala
Ramadi
Haditha
An Najaf
Diwaniya
An Nasiriya
Samawa
Amara
Basra
Umm-Qasr
Rutba

River Tigris
River Euphrates
Shatt al-Arab

36°
32°

0   100   miles
0   160   kilometres

© Martin Gilbert 1993

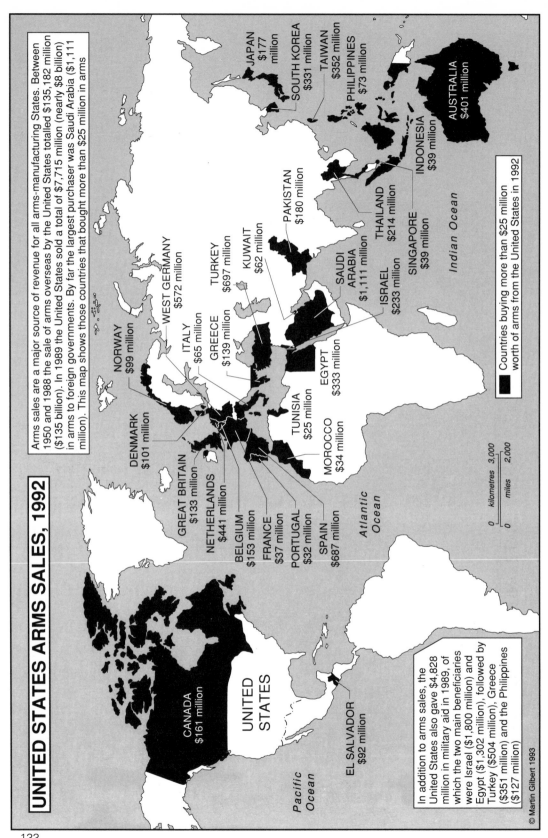

UNITED STATES ARMS SALES, 1992

Arms sales are a major source of revenue for all arms-manufacturing States. Between 1950 and 1988 the sale of arms overseas by the United States totalled $135,182 million ($135 billion). In 1989 the United States sold a total of $7,715 million (nearly $8 billion) in arms to foreign governments. By far the largest purchaser was Saudi Arabia ($1,111 million). This map shows those countries that bought more than $25 million in arms

UNITED
STATES

CANADA
$161 million

EL SALVADOR
$92 million

Pacific Ocean

Atlantic Ocean

GREAT BRITAIN
$133 million

NETHERLANDS
$441 million

BELGIUM
$153 million

FRANCE
$37 million

PORTUGAL
$32 million

SPAIN
$687 million

DENMARK
$101 million

NORWAY
$99 million

ITALY
$65 million

GREECE
$139 million

WEST GERMANY
$572 million

TURKEY
$697 million

KUWAIT
$62 million

TUNISIA
$25 million

MOROCCO
$34 million

EGYPT
$333 million

SAUDI ARABIA
$1,111 million

ISRAEL
$233 million

PAKISTAN
$180 million

JAPAN
$177 million

SOUTH KOREA
$331 million

TAIWAN
$352 million

PHILIPPINES
$73 million

THAILAND
$214 million

SINGAPORE
$39 million

INDONESIA
$39 million

AUSTRALIA
$401 million

Indian Ocean

Countries buying more than $25 million
worth of arms from the United States in 1992

In addition to arms sales, the United States also gave $4,828 million in military aid in 1989, of which the two main beneficiaries were Israel ($1,800 million) and Egypt ($1,302 million), followed by Turkey ($504 million), Greece ($351 million) and the Philippines ($127 million)

0 kilometres 3,000
0 miles 2,000

© Martin Gilbert 1993

133

MAIN RECIPIENTS OF UNITED STATES ECONOMIC AID, 1992

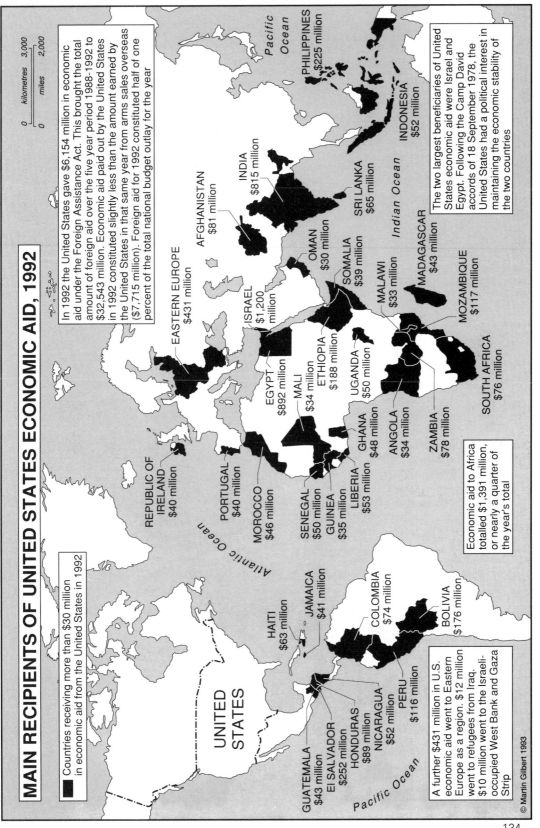

■ Countries receiving more than $30 million in economic aid from the United States in 1992

In 1992 the United States gave $6,154 million in economic aid under the Foreign Assistance Act. This brought the total amount of foreign aid over the five year period 1988-1992 to $32,543 million. Economic aid paid out by the United States in 1992 constituted slightly less than the amount earned by the United States in that same year from arms sales overseas ($7,715 million). Foreign aid for 1992 constituted half of one percent of the total national budget outlay for the year

The two largest beneficiaries of United States economic aid were Israel and Egypt. Following the Camp David accords of 18 September 1978, the United States had a political interest in maintaining the economic stability of the two countries

Economic aid to Africa totalled $1,391 million, or nearly a quarter of the year's total

A further $431 million in U.S. economic aid went to Eastern Europe as a region. $12 million went to refugees from Iraq. $10 million went to the Israeli-occupied West Bank and Gaza Strip

UNITED STATES

Pacific Ocean

Atlantic Ocean

Pacific Ocean

Indian Ocean

GUATEMALA $43 million
EL SALVADOR $252 million
HONDURAS $89 million
NICARAGUA $52 million
PERU $116 million
HAITI $63 million
JAMAICA $41 million
COLOMBIA $74 million
BOLIVIA $176 million

REPUBLIC OF IRELAND $40 million
PORTUGAL $40 million
MOROCCO $46 million
SENEGAL $50 million
GUINEA $35 million
LIBERIA $53 million
GHANA $48 million
ANGOLA $34 million
ZAMBIA $78 million
SOUTH AFRICA $76 million
MALI $34 million
EGYPT $892 million
ETHIOPIA $188 million
UGANDA $50 million
ISRAEL $1,200 million
EASTERN EUROPE $431 million
AFGHANISTAN $81 million
INDIA $815 million
OMAN $30 million
SOMALIA $39 million
MALAWI $33 million
MOZAMBIQUE $117 million
MADAGASCAR $43 million
SRI LANKA $65 million
PHILIPPINES $225 million
INDONESIA $52 million

0   kilometres   3,000
0   miles   2,000

© Martin Gilbert 1993

134

DEFENCE PREPAREDNESS ON LAND, 1991

From 1945 to 1990 the main thrust of United States defences was in the confrontation with the Soviet Union. With the collapse of Communist power from 1990, and the demise of the Warsaw Pact, defence priorities were under continuous scrutiny. This map shows the location of Air Force Tactical Fighter Wings, and of the Strategic Offensive Forces, in 1991. Further cuts in bases were made in 1992 and 1993

⊙ Air Force Tactical Fighter Wings
◪ Strategic Offensive air bases
■ Strategic Offensive naval bases
▣ Strategic Offensive missile sites

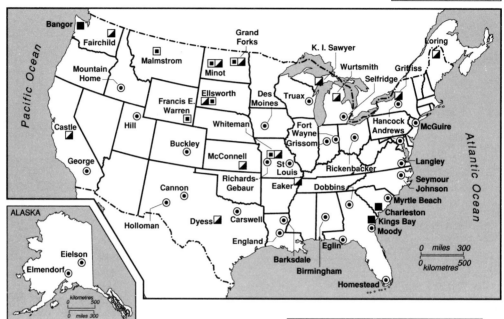

On 30 July 1991 the Department of Defence announced the shutting down of 72 United States military installations in Europe, and reduced operations at seven others

BASES TO BE CLOSED	
Germany	38
Britain	13
Italy	8
Turkey	7
Spain	5
Netherlands	1

© Martin Gilbert 1993

135

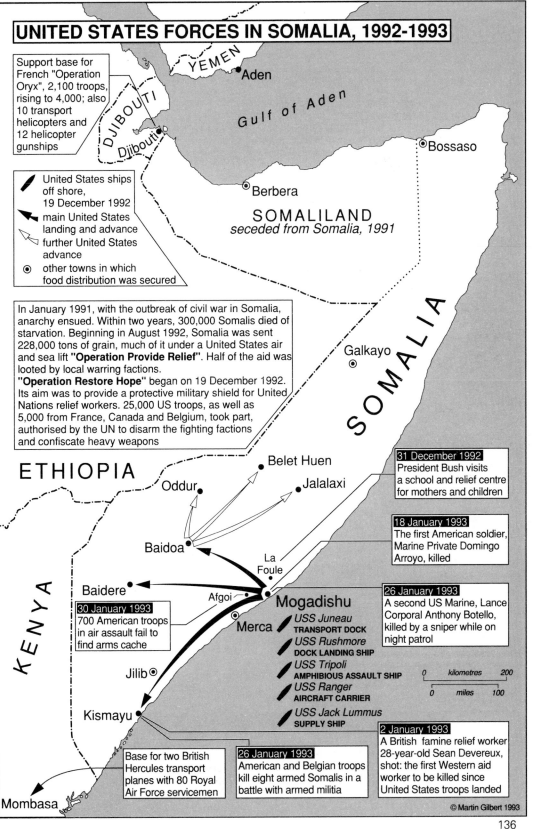

UNITED STATES FORCES IN SOMALIA, 1992-1993

Support base for French "Operation Oryx", 2,100 troops, rising to 4,000; also 10 transport helicopters and 12 helicopter gunships

United States ships off shore, 19 December 1992

main United States landing and advance

further United States advance

other towns in which food distribution was secured

In January 1991, with the outbreak of civil war in Somalia, anarchy ensued. Within two years, 300,000 Somalis died of starvation. Beginning in August 1992, Somalia was sent 228,000 tons of grain, much of it under a United States air and sea lift **"Operation Provide Relief"**. Half of the aid was looted by local warring factions.
"Operation Restore Hope" began on 19 December 1992. Its aim was to provide a protective military shield for United Nations relief workers. 25,000 US troops, as well as 5,000 from France, Canada and Belgium, took part, authorised by the UN to disarm the fighting factions and confiscate heavy weapons

YEMEN

Aden

Gulf of Aden

Bossaso

DJIBOUTI

Djibouti

Berbera

SOMALILAND
seceded from Somalia, 1991

Galkayo

SOMALIA

ETHIOPIA

Belet Huen

Oddur

Jalalaxi

Baidoa

La Foule

Baidere

Afgoi

30 January 1993
700 American troops in air assault fail to find arms cache

Mogadishu

Merca

USS *Juneau*
TRANSPORT DOCK
USS *Rushmore*
DOCK LANDING SHIP
USS *Tripoli*
AMPHIBIOUS ASSAULT SHIP
USS *Ranger*
AIRCRAFT CARRIER
USS *Jack Lummus*
SUPPLY SHIP

Jilib

Kismayu

KENYA

Mombasa

31 December 1992
President Bush visits a school and relief centre for mothers and children

18 January 1993
The first American soldier, Marine Private Domingo Arroyo, killed

26 January 1993
A second US Marine, Lance Corporal Anthony Botello, killed by a sniper while on night patrol

2 January 1993
A British famine relief worker 28-year-old Sean Devereux, shot: the first Western aid worker to be killed since United States troops landed

Base for two British Hercules transport planes with 80 Royal Air Force servicemen

26 January 1993
American and Belgian troops kill eight armed Somalis in a battle with armed militia

0   kilometres   200
0   miles   100

© Martin Gilbert 1993

136

EXPLORING THE SOLAR SYSTEM, 1962-1992

Beginning in 1962, the United States took the lead in exploring the solar system, starting with the launch of an unmanned *Mariner* spacecraft towards the planet Venus. On 3 March 1972 the unmanned, nuclear-powered spacecraft *Pioneer 10* was launched towards Jupiter: twenty years later it had travelled five billion miles from Earth

On 25 April 1990 the Hubble Space Telescope was launched, to study distant stars and galaxies, and to search for evidence of planets in other solar systems

26 January 1986
Voyager 2 passes, sends back details of planet's composition

● **URANUS**

2 March 1992
Pioneer 10 reaches five billion miles from Earth, the furthest distance travelled by any man-made object

3 December 1973
Pioneer 10 gives first close-up pictures
4 March 1979
Voyager 1 discovers rings and details of sixteen moons

3 February 1992
Ulysses flies to within 235,000 miles (and 416 million miles from Earth). Its signals take 37 minutes and 15 seconds to get back to Earth

1986
Pioneer 10 becomes the first man-made object to escape the solar system

29 March 1974
Mariner 10 takes 2,800 photographs

8 December 1992
Galileo, while bound for Jupiter (due 1995) passes within 200 miles of Earth. Its instruments detect signs of intelligent life on Earth!

● **PLUTO**

● **JUPITER**

MERCURY

SUN

● **EARTH**

NEPTUNE ●

14 December 1962
Mariner 2 passes 21,648 miles from surface
5 January 1969
Soviet space craft lands on surface and returns

● **VENUS**

MARS ●

13 June 1983
Pioneer 10 crosses the orbit of Neptune

8 November 1968
Pioneer 9 achieves sun orbit

28 November 1964
Mariner 4 trajectory passes Mars and sends 22 pictures from 6,100 miles above the planet's surface
13 November 1971
Mariner 9 in orbit 862 miles above planet's surface

● **SATURN**

November 1980
Voyager 1 sends photographs, reveals winds of 1,100 miles an hour at Equator and a total of 17 moons

RELATIVE DISTANCE BETWEEN THE PLANETS

Sun
Mercury
Venus
Earth
Mars
Jupiter
Saturn
Uranus
Neptune
Pluto

DEFENCE PREPAREDNESS IN SPACE, 1992-1993

On 31 December 1992 the United States Department of Defence awarded 6-year contracts to develop the "Brilliant Eyes" satellite. Each satellite was intended to carry sensors to monitor both space and Earth. Between 20 and 40 "Brilliant Eyes" would orbit at less than 1,000 miles above the Earth, in contrast to the 22,000-mile altitude of existing Early Warning satellites. This whole programme was cancelled by President Clinton on 13 May 1993 when he announced "the end of the Star Wars Era": a final affirmation of the end of the Cold War

In January 1992, Russian President Boris Yeltsin called for the United States and Russia to establish a Global Protection System. Following his call, talks began for the establishment of a Joint Missile Warning Centre that would receive data on missile launches

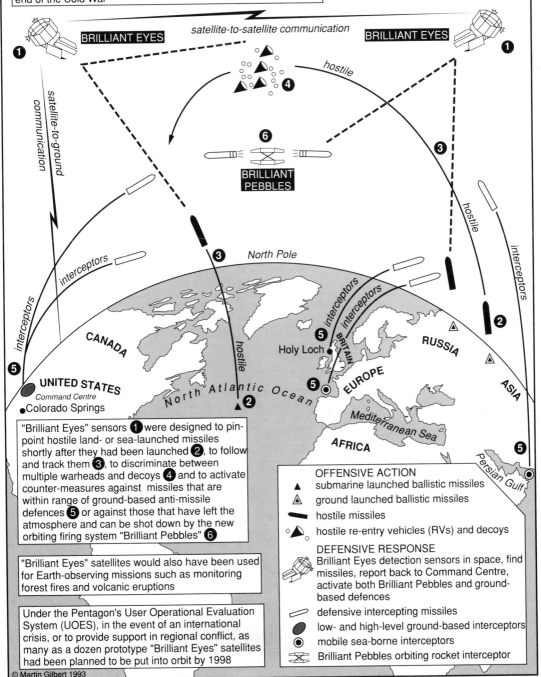

"Brilliant Eyes" sensors ❶ were designed to pinpoint hostile land- or sea-launched missiles shortly after they had been launched ❷, to follow and track them ❸, to discriminate between multiple warheads and decoys ❹ and to activate counter-measures against missiles that are within range of ground-based anti-missile defences ❺ or against those that have left the atmosphere and can be shot down by the new orbiting firing system "Brilliant Pebbles" ❻

"Brilliant Eyes" satellites would also have been used for Earth-observing missions such as monitoring forest fires and volcanic eruptions

Under the Pentagon's User Operational Evaluation System (UOES), in the event of an international crisis, or to provide support in regional conflict, as many as a dozen prototype "Brilliant Eyes" satellites had been planned to be put into orbit by 1998

OFFENSIVE ACTION
▲ submarine launched ballistic missiles
⊿ ground launched ballistic missiles
— hostile missiles
◦▲◦ hostile re-entry vehicles (RVs) and decoys

DEFENSIVE RESPONSE
Brilliant Eyes detection sensors in space, find missiles, report back to Command Centre, activate both Brilliant Pebbles and ground-based defences
▱ defensive intercepting missiles
⬮ low- and high-level ground-based interceptors
◉ mobile sea-borne interceptors
⬚ Brilliant Pebbles orbiting rocket interceptor